D1230247

Contributions to Literature.

CONTRIBUTIONS TO LITERATURE

Historical, Antiquarian, and Metrical.

MARK ANTONY LOWER

——— Ubi quid datur oti,
Illudo chartis.———
HOR. *Sat.* IV.

Essay Index Reprint Series

BOOKS FOR LIBRARIES PRESS
FREEPORT, NEW YORK

First Published 1854
Reprinted 1972

. **Library of Congress Cataloging in Publication Data**

Lower, Mark Anthony, 1813-1876.
   Contributions to literature.

   (Essay index reprint series)
   Reprint of the 1854 ed.
   1. Great Britain--History--Addresses, essays,
lectures. 2. Names, Geographical--Great Britain--
Addresses, essays, lectures. 3. Genealogy--Addresses,
essays, lectures. I. Title.
DA30.L82 1972   914.2   72-4578
ISBN 0-8369-2959-4

REV. JOHN COLLINGWOOD BRUCE, LL.D.,

F.S.A. LONDON AND NEWCASTLE), ETC. ETC. ETC.

Author of 'The Roman Wall;' 'The Bayeux Tapestry Elucidated;'
'Hadrian, the Builder of the Wall,' etc.

MY DEAR SIR,

Permit me to mark my esteem for your person
and character by dedicating to You this little Book.

The similarity of our tastes, and the interest which you
have taken in some of the topics here discussed, woul
alone justify my desiring the sanction of your name; but
I have a yet stronger motive.

You, dear Sir, have given to the world substantial evidence, that while you have devoted a portion of your time to
literature, you have not the less efficiently discharged the
important and arduous duties of the responsible position in
which you are placed, as the head of one of the largest
educational establishments in England.

You have shown how gracefully to himself, and how
advantageously to the intellectual world, one who is engaged
in the stern labours of scholastic instruction can devote his

b

few brief hours of leisure to subjects not immediately connected with his ordinary round of duties.

If I, in my similar, but humbler, sphere of action, so
dedicate a few hours snatched from periods given up by some
to mere vacuity and amusement, I have the satisfaction at
least of knowing, that no duty is thereby neglected, no
other's right infringed.

In the hope you may long enjoy health and strength,
not only to benefit those who come under your valuable
tuition and example, but also to render further services to
the cause of Retrospective Literature,

I remain,

My dear Sir,

Very faithfully yours,

MARK ANTONY LOWER.

SAINT ANNE'S HOUSE, LEWES;
   30th December, 1853.

PREFACE.

The following sheets are composed partly of articles which have already been printed ; partly of Essays which hitherto have not seen the light. The paper on Local Nomenclature appeared in nearly its present form in the New Retrospective Review, No. IV. That on the battle of Hastings is a slight extension of a Paper read before the Sussex Archæological Society, and published in their 'Collections' Vol. VI. The Memoir on the Southern Iron-Works likewise appeared in the second volume of that series. The substance of a portion of the Antiquarian Pilgrimage in Normandy was printed in the same Society's third volume, and subsequently translated into French, and published in the *Revue de Rouen*. The Essay on the South-Downs, and the observations on Genealogy, together with the minor pieces, are now first printed. Of the metrical

attempts, the one entitled ' Winchelsea's Deli-
verance ' was printed in a recent number of the
New Monthly Magazine : the others now appear
for the first time.   The Sonnet at page 163 was
published some years since in the Literary
Gazette and in some local Newspapers.

With respect to the first article of this volume,
the paper on Local Names, I would remark, that
it is a mere outline of an Essay which 1 hope at
some future time to fill up.   It is somewhat
remarkable, that amidst the multifarious subjects which at the present day occupy the pens
of the learned and the philosophical, so little
attention should hitherto have been paid to the
etymology of the proper names of places and
persons.   With the exception of my own ' English Surnames,' which has gone through severa
editions, I am not aware of any English work
worthy of the name that has been devoted to
that branch of the subject.   On the names of
Places there is no independent work, except the
small treatise of Dr. Leo, translated from the

original German by Mr. Williams. There are, it is true, many detached essays of great merit scattered through the pages of various periodical and other publications, but no one seems hitherto to have considered the subject of sufficient importance for a distinct volume. Perhaps the difficulties which surround it may have deterred abler pens than mine from attempting the task. However this may be, no one can gainsay the interest attaching to this branch of etymology. I am one of those who are presumptuous enough to think a rough and crude attempt in any species of enterprise better than none at all. All knowledge is progressive, and all efforts in a new direction will be more or less unsatisfactory. For myself I am content in this and other matters to perform the somewhat arduous and thankless task of a pioneer.

I have nothing further to remark upon these essays, except that the 'Memoir on the Iron-Works of the South-East of England' is now reproduced in consequence of the interest taken in the subject by many who are unconnected

with the local society for which it was originally
written.

I have to thank the Committee of the Sussex
Archæological Society for the loan of the wood-
cuts, made from my own drawings, which
accompany the Paper on the Iron-Works, the
Portrait of Dr. Andrew Borde, and the Views
of the Castle and Church of Bellencombre in
Normandy.

CONTENTS.

On Yew-Trees in Church-Yards.

A Lyttle Geste of a Greate Eele.

A Discourse of Genealogy.

An Antiquarian Pilgrimage in Normandy.

Miscellanea.

Contributions to Literature.

—•⁙•—

ON LOCAL NOMENCLATURE.

Nᴇxᴛ to the curiosity which nearly every one
experiences in regard to the origin of his own personal
name, that of the appellation of the locality where he
resides naturally excites inquiry; and learned clerk
and rustic wiseacre alike apply themselves to the task
of discovering an etymon for town and village, valley
and hill. This is not unfrequently accomplished with
little difficulty, since the component parts of many
names of places are but slight departures, if departures
at all, from common every-day English words. For
instance, the names of Hil-ton, Nor-ton, Heath-field,
Ling-field, Wood-ford, New-bridge, Ash-ridge, Westham, Beech-land, South-gate, and many hundred
other localities of greater or less magnitude and
importance, explain themselves to the " meanest
capacity." But it is the more recondite names that
supply the choicest food for the speculative inquirer.
The results are sometimes quite satisfactory, though
much oftener amusingly incorrect—the *ne plus ultra*
of absurdity being not rarely arrived at by men of
some pretensions to learning and judgment, as we
shall by and bye have occasion to show. But we will
first supply a few examples of rustic and traditional
etymology which occur to our recollection.

1

At Udimore, near Rye, the villagers have a legend that their forefathers, in ages long bygone, began to build themselves a church on the opposite side of the little river Ree, to that where it was eventually reared. Night after night however witnessed the dislocation of huge stones from the walls built on the preceding day, and the pious work bade fair to be interminable. Grave suspicions arose among the parishioners that they had selected an unholy, and consequently improper, site for the building, and these were eventually confirmed. Unseen hands hurled the stones to the opposite side of the stream, and an awful supernatural voice in the air uttered, in warning and reproachful tones, the words, " O'er the mere ! O'er the mere !"—thus at once indicating a more appropriate situation for the sacred edifice, and by anticipation conferring a name upon it; for the transformation of the phrase, " O'er the mere," into Udimore, was a difficulty little calculated to shake the faith of the unsophisticated Bœotians who could swallow the more wondrous and remarkable incidents of the legend. The village of Aston-Clinton, in Buckinghamshire, bears a name which few antiquarian readers will be at a loss to account for (the suffix being the appellation of its ancient lords), but here rustic etymology has also been at work, and we were not long since gravely told that it signified " a stone 'cline town," to wit, a town built upon the slope or "incline" of a hill, the ma- terial of the houses having originally been stone ! The delightful village of Hurstperpoint, not far from Brighton, has as distinct an etymology as any we happen to call to mind (—Hyrst, A.-Sax., a wood, and Pierpoint, the surname of its Anglo-Norman feudal possessors, in contradistinction to Hurst-Monceux, a parish not many miles eastward, which once belonged to another Norman family—) ; but, in spite of this obvious origin, a certain would-be etymological old gentleman used to assure his friends that local topographers were labouring under a great mistake. "*Hurst*, my dear Sir," he would say, "is a Saxon word meaning a wood; *per* is, as you will remember, a Latin preposition, signifying *by* (!) ; and *point*, the last syllable of the name, clearly refers to yonder pointed hill called Wolstonbury; hence Hurstperpoint is, as you will perceive, *the wood by the pointed hill !* " Thus did this modern village oracle,

> " Like a Cerberus pronounce
> A leash of languages at once "—

beautifully blending into one word a bit of Saxon, a fragment of Latin, and a morsel of Anglo-French !

These rustic etymologies are sometimes much more plausible, though equally erroneous. For example, the good people of another Sussex village, Alfriston, attribute its foundation to Alfred the Great ; and the known fact that that monarch had several possessions in the neighbourhood is to them " confirmation strong" of their opinion ; but alas for " Alfred's Town," a certain old book called ' Domesday ' in the space of a single line demolishes the theory : " Gilbert holds a hide in *Aluricestone* at farm from the Earl : *Aluric* did hold it as allodial land." Thus it is to an obscure freeman of the days of the Confessor named Alvric, or Ælfric, and not to the patriot-king Alfred, that the village is indebted for its designation. We may add here, *en passant*, a remark on the great utility of etymological investigations as an aid to local history. In the instance just cited we have imbedded in a single word not only the name of the Saxon proprietor who baptized the locality, but—with the

light of ' Domesday Book '—the precise period when
he flourished and settled his little colony upon it; a
period shortly antecedent to the Norman Conquest.
In the days of the Confessor the then nascent manor
brought in a rental of only twenty shillings, but at
the making of the great survey, some thirty or forty
years later, the annual value had reached the largely
augmented sum of fifty-four shillings.

Let us now turn to another class of etymologists—
the diggers up of crooked roots from the classical and
other ancient languages—the delvers after glittering
whims and fancies which crumble into dust before
the daylight of history and truth—the pigmies and
pedants of philology, who, in their *unde derivatur* of
a name, content themselves with making a pun upon
it,[1] and then gravely assigning to it a French, a
Greek, a Latin, or a Celtic origin—men who have all
the " madness " without any of the " method " of
Horne Tooke—men, we mean, who stick at nothing
short of extracting sunbeams from a cucumber, or
the cucumber itself from the name of Jeremiah King!

We are glad to find this whimsical class fast
diminishing; we wish we could pronounce it quite
extinct, but alas, whenever we are about to felicitate
ourselves upon having at length taken leave for ever
of such folly, up starts some new theory about Cold-
Harbour or Grimesdyke, which leads us mentally to
exclaim, " *Quousque tandem abutere patientia nostra ?*"

Perhaps pseudo-etymology was never so rampant as
among the topographical antiquaries of the last two
centuries. It was nothing to twist Pomfret into an
apple-garden, quasi locus *poma ferens*, in spite of the
known fact that Pontefract was the true original name

---

[1] " Conjectures étymologiques, qui ne sont que des *charades*, plus
ou moins ingénieuses."—*Salverte*, ii, 305.

of the town. Winchelsea was interpreted still more literally into *Friget mare ventus*—" Wind-chills-Sea"! But these are trifles to certain etymologies found out by a Sussex antiquary, one Mr. Elliot, who flourished somewhat less than a century ago. Here is a sample. Among the South-Down hills, a little eastward of Lewes, is a deep and romantic valley which lies at the foot of a pointed hill called Mount Caburn; the valley itself being called *Ox-settle-bottom*. "This name would appear," says our etymologist, "to be formed from the British word, *uch*, lofty, high, and *sittelth*, an arrow in Armoric English; for Mount Caburn appears to the eye of the traveller from the south or east to resemble the barb of an arrow. (!) Perhaps Caburn itself might obtain this name of *Uch-sittelth* or *Ox-settle*, originally, from the battles that had been fought on its summit," &c. Now, most unfortunately for this learning, the true name of the valley or "bottom" was never Ox-settle, but Ox-*steddle* bottom, and was derived, as everybody except Mr. Elliot knew, from a "steddle," or enclosure for oxen, which formerly stood in it. An old friend of ours lately deceased, though he could not say as did Edie to Mr. Oldbuck, " Prætorium here, prætorium there, I mind the biggin o't," well remembered the destruction of this enclosure, which the bubulci of a day only slightly anterior to Mr. Elliot's own had caused to be made!

This pseudo-etymology is by no means confined to English writers. The name of the Norican town *Virunium*, according to Suidas, was derived from ' *Vir unus.*' A wild boar, the instrument of divine vengeance, had devastated the district, when a champion, the *only man* who deserved the name, like a second Hercules, killed the monster and carried him

off upon his shoulders; and hence the town got its
name. Pliny and the Latin poets abound with similar
whimsies, which deserve to be classed with Knicker-
bocker's derivation of Manhattan (Long Island) from
the circumstance of a *man* with a *hat on* having been
seen there by the aborigines; and with the etymology
of Beauce in Rabelais. Gargantua's mare, while
swinging her tail to brush away the flies, knocked
down an immense forest, upon which Gargantua,
delighted with the exploit, remarked to the by-
standers, " Je trouve *beau ce* !" and thus *Beau ce*
became the name of the cleared ground !

Abundant derivations really not much less far-
fetched than these lie thickly scattered over most of
our county histories and other topographical works;
and we are sorry to say that notwithstanding the great
erudition of William Baxter, his *Glossarium* abounds
with derivations so extremely far-fetched that no
reasonable philologist or antiquary can travel upon
good terms with him through two consecutive pages.
Upon the whole, however, we are glad of his aid, for,
as the alchemists while in search of the *elixir vitæ*
and the philosopher's stone, though they failed of their
main object brought to light many a serviceable compound, so this author, albeit he often shoots wide of
his mark, sometimes directs us to objects which had
previously escaped our observation : besides, he generally amuses where he fails to instruct, which is more
than can always be said of more exact writers.

To turn from these vagaries of a misdirected inge-
nuity, let us now come to the more immediate purpose
of the present essay which is to show how the various
geographical and political divisions and natural features
of this country acquired their distinctive appellations
—the rules upon which our local nomenclature has

been formed. Whoever may have been the primitive
settlers upon this island, it is certain that it was in very
early times extensively occupied by tribes of Celtic
origin, and that they impressed their language upon
many of the more striking geographical features of the
land in names which remain to this day. A very large
proportion of the mountains and rivers of Britain,
not only in those nooks and corners to which these
tribes were ultimately driven by subsequent invasions,
but all over the island, bear Celtic names, which no
change of occupation or of vernacular language has
ever been able to displace. The island itself has
several times changed its names, but these features of
it retain a nomenclature as imperishable as their own
existence. With regard to political divisions, they
have usually undergone changes of name with every
fluctuation of ownership. Thus, when the Belgæ
became masters of some parts of South Britain, in an
age not long antecedent to the Roman invasion, they
gave to their colonies the designations of the districts
from which they had set out for these shores. "Mari-
tima pars," says Cæsar, "ab iis [incolitur] qui prædæ
ac belli inferendi causa, ex Belgis transierant; qui
omnes fere iis nominibus civitatum appellantur, qui-
bus orti ex civitatibus eò pervenerunt." (De Bell.
Gall. v. 10.) The feeling which prompted this is
deeply seated in human nature, and has been operative
throughout the entire history of colonisation.

On this subject an elegant French writer remarks :
"Une illusion non moins douce entraine les voyageurs
à retrouver, partout où ils abordent, la patrie dont ils
sont éloignés ; a imposer à des lieux nouveaux pour
eux les noms des lieux où s'est développée leur
enfance, ou ils ont laissé des compatriotes, des épouses,
des enfants qui soupirent après leur retour. Fidèles à

cet usage, les fondateurs de colonies laissent des monu-
ments durables de la gloire de leur nation en des lieux
dont un jour peut être doivent disparaitre toutes les
autres traces de leur presence."[2]   M. Salverte remarks
that the name of Medina, the Arabian city so famous
for the tomb of Mahomet, occurs in several places in
Spain, recalling to memory the dominion of the
Mussulmans in that country.   This may, however, be
merely accidental resemblance, for we, too, have our
English Medina as the designation of two hundreds
and a river in the Isle of Wight, where Arabians never
had influence.   He also notices the resemblance between the names of several places in the Engadine,
canton of Grisons, and those of ancient Italy, in
which Lavinium, Falisci, Ardea, and the river Albula
are almost exactly reproduced, which supports the
traditional community of origin between their ancestors, the *Rhæti,* and the Etruscans.   Again, there
were tribes of Brigantes in the north of England, in
Ireland, and in the north-east of Spain, though
Johnes thinks these had no identity of origin beyond their being all Celtic.   *Briga,* so common as a
termination on the Roman maps, as in Lacobriga,
Telabrica, Augustobriga, &c., probably means town
or community, and the name may eventually have
extended itself to the surrounding district or province.

Let us glance at the central part of the North
American Continent, and we shall find scattered over
it everywhere, in the names of its localities, such
evidence of the sources of its present population as
would serve to reveal the truth were it possible for the
annals of its unexampled colonisation to perish.   The

[2] Salverte, Essai sur les Noms d'Hommes, de Peuples, et de Lieux.
Paris, 1824.   Tom. ii, p. 247.

constant recurrence of names of places identical with those of Britain would be demonstration of the strongest possible kind. Perhaps we could not frame a better theory of the method in which local nomenclature has everywhere been formed than by an attentive study of a map of the United States. There we discover many names, particularly those of rivers, lakes, mountain-ranges, and some territorial divisions, which baffle all existing etymology, such as Ohio, Mississippi, Mohawk, Alleghany, Apalachia, Tennessee, Michigan, Massachusets. These are aboriginal names, retained partly for their own euphonious excellence, partly because it is so much easier to adopt an old name than to invent a new one. It is for these reasons, especially the latter, that our Anglo-Saxon ancestors suffered so much of the Celtic nomenclature to remain, even after they had subjugated the races who imposed it. Continuing our observations, we remark that another large section of American names are mere transcripts of those of English localities, with or without the prefix "New," such as New England, Boston, New York, Rochester, New Hampshire, Cambridge, Plymouth, Litchfield, New Hartford, &c., some of which have greatly surpassed in importance their namesakes in the mother-country. Thirdly, we find a multitude of local names derived from the names of eminent men with whom the foundation or history of the various places has been identified, as well as the *nomina obscurorum virorum* which mere property in the soil has introduced. Thus we find alongside of Pennsylvania, Georgia, Washington, and others of dignified origin, a host of Brownstons, Johnstonvilles, and Mercersburgs. Religious feeling and a respect for antiquity and genius have introduced a fourth class, such as Salem, Lebanon,

1 §

Rome, Troy, Homer, Milton, Hampden, and nearly
every name which ancient and modern history can
supply.[3] Bad taste is generally observable in the
selection of such designations, however euphonious
they may be in themselves. We very much prefer
that fifth class of American nomenclature which
describes localities by the use of familiar terms, however coarse. Sandy-hook, South-fork, *et omne hoc
genus*, are far preferable in our estimation to names of
classical origin. Even " Big-bone-lick," which has
an air of the extremest vulgarity, is justifiable on the
ground of its appropriateness. The place which bears
this name—we forget in what State it lies—was so
called on account of its geological characteristics.
A "lick," in American phraseology, is a spot to which
cattle resort to lick the saline particles of the soil, and
the one in question abounds with fossil bones of
unusual size. Now had this place been styled Tus-
culum, or Mantua, or Athens, however much might
have been gained in the alternative by the ear, nothing
would have accrued to the understanding. Euphony
is an excellent quality, but appropriateness is a better;
and to "call a spade a spade" is after all the wisest
policy.

It is for the most part upon such common-sense
rules that the local nomenclature of England has
been formed. A meaning may be said either to lie
upon, or to lurk at no great distance beneath, the
surface of most names of ancient date. Before
analysing the principal materials of our ancient
names, it may be well to classify the various lan-

---

[3] A modern writer (F. Lieber, we think) says, that, looking at a
map of the United States, you might almost fancy that all ancient
history and geography had been chopped up and put into a bag and
then shaken abroad over the face of the land !

guages which have been drawn upon, which will be found to be—

I. The Celtic dialects, with Latinizations.
II. Anglo-Saxon or Teutonic.
III. Danish or Scandinavian.
IV. French or Norman-French.
V. Modern, or existing, English.

A few words of remark upon each of these will suffice for our present purpose; and first of the Celtic. This name has been for convenience' sake attributed to the earliest settlers of Western Europe—the first great wave of population from Central Asia, which made its way by successive impulses to the remote parts of this continent, and which was ultimately driven into the nooks and corners of it, and of the adjacent islands, by the second or Teutonic wave. The remains of the Celtæ, speaking both ethnologically and philologically, either *are*, or at a comparatively recent period *were*, to be found principally in the geographical indents or insulations known as Brittany, Cornwall, Wales, Ireland, the Isle of Man, and the Highlands and Islands of Scotland. Of the language or rather languages spoken by the barbarous sun-worshipping and cromlech-building hordes bearing this name we know little except by inference and hypothesis. They had no literature; and all that we can certainly know of their intellectual character and culture comes down to us through the vague and misty channel of traditional rhapsody; while the actual *media* by which they communicated their sentiments to each other can only be inferred by a laborious collation of what remains in the obsolete or obsolescent tongues called Armorican, Cornish, Welsh, Manx, Irish, and Gaelic—tongues only com-

mitted to the custody of alphabetic writing within
the last few centuries, and corrupted and modified by
the multitudinous influences to which the vernacular
language of uncultured tribes is always necessarily
exposed from time, climate, and amalgamation with
other races. It has been very much the practice with
etymologists and topographers to ascribe to the Celtic
language those names for which no Saxon etymon
could be found, especially if they resembled some
Welsh or Gaelic word. This has necessarily led to
numerous errors. To cite a single instance, let us
take the very first word in the ' Glossarium,' ABALLABA,
which by the way Baxter wrongly identifies with
Appleby in Westmoreland, whereas its true site is
upon the Roman Wall in Cumberland :—

" ABALLABA, hodie 𝔄𝔭𝔲𝔩𝔟𝔶, quasi Britannicè dicas
Abal (vel *Gaval*) *Ab* vel *Av*; quod est Furca (vel
Sinus,) *undæ* vel *amnis*. Iberniæ Scotobrigantibus
etiam hodie *Abhal* pro *Furca* est; quò referendum et
Anglorum nostrorum 𝔊𝔞𝔟𝔩𝔢-𝔢𝔫𝔡, seu *furcalis finis* in
ædificiis. Etiam hodiernis Persis *Ab* pro *Aqua* est,
quam et Veteres nostri *Av*, *Sav*, et *Tav* appellavêre.
Eodem planè intellectu et in Cantiacis et in Regnis,
et in Damnoniis oppidula occurrunt 𝔄𝔭𝔲𝔩𝔡𝔲𝔯 et
𝔄𝔭𝔲𝔩𝔡𝔲𝔯𝔥𝔞𝔪,"[4] &c.

He afterwards goes on to inform us, that according
to the ' Notitia ' this was the station of the prefect of a
numerus or troop of Moors (*Præpositus Numeri* MAU-
RORUM *Aurelianorum*), and that it must therefore
have been one of the castella of the Brigantes alluded
to by Juvenal [in the passage—

---

[4] Baxter is quite wrong here, for the Kent and Devonshire Apple-
dores and the Sussex Appledram are obviously from the Anglo-Saxon
Appuldre, an apple-tree.

"Dirue Maurorum attegias, castella Brigantum,
    Ut locupletem aquilam tibi sexagesimus annus
    Afferat."—Sat. xiv, 196, &c.]

Now to any unprejudiced judgment, the association of a colony of Moors in Britain with so very
moresque a name as *Aballaba*, renders any appeal to
Celtic roots totally unnecessary. The Moorish troops
whom the jealousy of the Roman policy had trans-
planted to this northern region doubtless imposed
upon their settlement a word borrowed from their
vernacular tongue. And since during the prevalence
of the Roman power in this island similar bodies
of Gauls, Germans, Spaniards, Italians, and other
foreigners were also introduced here, we are not
assuming too much—though it is beside the scope of
the present essay to work out this theory—to assert
that many of the names given to localities at that
period were derived from roots wholly alien to the
aboriginal dialects of Britain. At the same time we
must admit that in a great majority of instances the
names borne by Roman stations are mere latinïza-
tions of British words, although the etymons of the
latter (in which Baxter takes so much delight) may
be altogether vague and uncertain. At the departure
of the Romans most of this nomenclature failed, but
in some instances the material part of the names is
retained to the present day, though of course in a
very corrupted orthography; thus we may trace
Regulbium in Reculver, *Dubris* in Dover, *Venta* (Bel-
garum) in Winchester, *Branodunum* in Brancaster,
Londinium in London, *Nidum* in Neath, *Mancunium*
in Manchester, *Camboricum* in Cambridge, *Uroconium*
in Wroxeter, and some others mentioned in the
'Notitia' and the 'Antonine Itinerary.' Our rivers,
too, in many instances bear the original British

names, or rather the geographical expressions and terms employed by the Celtic people. As Lhwyd properly remarks—

" As for the names of Rivers. We often find that when a country is new peopled, the new-comers take the *appellatives* of the old inhabitants for proper names. And hence it is, that our ancestors at their first coming (whenever that was) called so many rivers in England by the names of Asc, Esc, Isc, Osc, and Usc, which the English afterwards partly retained (especially in the north) and partly varied into *Ax*, whence Axley, Axholm; *Ex*, whence Exmouth, Exeter; *Ox*, whence Oxford for Ouskford; and *Ux*, as in Uxbridge. This I say proceeded from our ignorance of the language of our predecessors the Güydhelian Britains, amongst whom the word signified nothing but *water*, as it doth yet in the Highlands and in Ireland. In the same manner have the English mistaken our *Avon*, which though it signified only RIVER in general, yet serves with them for the proper name of several of their rivers." (D. E. Luidii Adversaria (in Baxter's Glossary), p. 265)[5]

Perhaps the most remarkable family of names of rivers are those which are based upon the presumed Celtic root DUR, which is closely allied to the Greek υδωρ and like it means simply water. We have the word in its primitive form in the river *Dur* in Ireland, and slightly modified in the *Dor*ia, and *Dur*ia in Cisalpine Gaul, the *Dour*o and *Der*o in Spain, the *Dor*dogne and the A*dour* in France, the Ad*der* in Scotland, the A*dare* in Ireland, and the A*dur* in Sussex, at the mouth of which the Romans placed a station, to which they gave the name of Portus

---

[5] So *ganga* signifies river, and Ganges is *the* river, par excellence.

Adurni. *Dovar*, an obsolete Irish word for water, was evidently of the same origin, and the Kentish town probably borrows its name from a similar source.

There are also several other Celtic appellatives meaning water which have become the proper names of many of our rivers. Such are *Tam* or *Tav*, *Uy*, *Cluyd*, &c. In *Tam*, whence Thames, Tamar, &c., Lhwyd thinks we have the Celtic form of the Greek ταμός in ποταμός. This root is varied into *Tav* and *Tiv*, and may be traced in the modern names of the rivers Tavy, Teivi, Dove, Dee, &c. *Uy* is the equivalent of the Gothic *Aa*, the Saxon *ea*, and the French *eau*, aqua. Hence Wye and many Welsh rivers. *Cluyd* is seen in the great Scottish river Clyde, as well as in the Clydach, Cledach, Cledog, and Clettür in Wales.

With regard to the Celtic names of mountains, Lhwyd presents us with a remarkable theory. (Gloss. pp. 268 et seq.) "The most common way of naming hills," he says, "was by metaphors from the parts of the body." His instances are principally from Wales, and from localities little known; suffice it to say, that he has found in the mountain nomenclature of that province numerous words signifying head, forehead, scull, face, eyebrow, eye, nose, mouth, neck, arm, breast, belly, hip, side, back, leg, and foot. This theory may at first sight appear more ingenious than true, but we must recollect that we still apply similar expressions to geographical features : e. g. Beachy Head, Flamborough Head, to high promontories, and Dungeness, Sheerness (A.-S. *næs*, a nose) to low projections ; while in every-day parlance we talk of an arm of the sea, the mouth of a river, and the brow, the side, and the foot of a mountain. The word *moel* or *voel*, so commonly applied to Welsh mountains destitute of wood, signifies " bald-pate."

From a misunderstanding of this root the good people of Abergavenny, in Lhwyd's time, by a droll catachresis, called a conical hill near their town "The Vale."

The principal or most usual component parts of British names, as still retained to a great extent in Wales and Cornwall, are the syllables *tin* or *din, maes caer, tre,* or *trev,* and *llan* or *lan.* Of these, the first, which was latinized in numerous instances into *dunum,* as in Muridunum, Camalodunum, is derived from an old Celtic verb, *dunadh,* signifying to shut in, or inclose. Its Anglo-Saxon representative was *tune* and *tun,* whence the modern English, Town. 2. *Maes,* or more properly *magh,* signifies field or plain, and is latinized by *magus,* as in Sitomagus, Cæsaromagus, Noviomagus. 3. *Caer,* or *Car,* as retained in Caermarthen, Caernarvon, and in many places in Ireland, Scotland, Cornwall, and Brittany, signifies an enclosed or fortified place—" any trench or bank of an old camp;" the idea was afterwards extended to mean city. 4. *Tre* or *trev* " seems to have signified anciently only a family, and to be of the same origine with the Latin *tribus.* So *pueblo,* which properly signifies a people, is a common Spanish word for a small town or village. . . . . . . *Trev* signified not a town anciently, but a house or home. . . . . Hence so many *Tre's* in Cornwall, which were for the most part but single houses, and the word subjoined to it only the name of a Briton who was once the proprietor, as Trev Erbyn, Trev Annian, Trev Vydhig. . . . . Whether the German *dorf,* called in England Thorp, Threp, and Thrup, may not put in for the same origine and signification, is left to the English-Saxon Antiquaries."—(*Glossary,* p. 272.)

There are many *Tre's* or *Trev's* in Wales, as Trevalyn, Trelydan, Trevecca; and we probably see this root in Treviri (Treves), and in A-*treb*-ates, the people about Arras.

5. *Llan* in Wales, and *lan* in Cornwall and Brittany, primarily meant an inclosure, as is satisfactorily shown by the retention of it in the Welsh *Ydlan*, a hagard; *Perlhan*, an orchard; *Güinlhan*, a vineyard; *Corlan*, a sheepfold; and *Corflan*, a churchyard. Lhwyd observes:—" This signification of it is also confirmed by the Cantabrians or Pyrenean Spaniards, who call a garden *landa*, and use also the same word for a field or any other enclosure. ꜰThe reason why we use it for a church was (as I conjecture), because before Christianity, the Druids sacrificed and buried their dead in a circle of stones, which had a Cromlech or Kist-vaen, or both, in the midst; as we find at Kerrig y Drudion in Denbighshire and elsewhere. And it is probable that from such a *Crug* of stones or a *circus* or round trench, or from both, the Teutonick nations took their *kirk*, corrupted by the southern English into *church*. *Lan* besides Wales is common in Cornwall and Basse Bretagne, but scarce used at all in Ireland and Scotland, where the old word is *Kil*, the derivation whereof I must leave to further inquiry."—(*Glossary*, p. 272.)

This prefix *Llan* or *lan*, so prevalent in Wales and Cornwall, is one of the most interesting component parts of local names in Britain. Signifying, as we have seen, "church," its suffix describes either the situation or some characteristic feature of that edifice, or records its founder or its patron-saint. E. g. Llandovery is said to be a corruption of *Llan-ym-Ddy-froed*, "the church among the waters," derived from its location near the confluence of several streams. Llan-daff is the " church on the river Taff;" Llan-asaph, " the church dedicated to St. Asaph ;" Llanhidrock, "the church of St. Hidrock;" and Launceston was anciently *Lan-Stephadon*, "St. Stephen's church."

But we have exceeded our limits upon the somewhat unsatisfactory subject of Celtic etymology, and must proceed to the other sources of our local names in the order in which we have indicated them.

II. ANGLO-SAXON OR TEUTONIC.—The majority of place-names in England are of Teutonic origin. They were *mostly* substituted for the Romano-British designations when the Germanic tribes had displaced the Celtic race, and formed what is popularly known as the Saxon heptarchy. Although this period can be ascertained with some degree of precision, there is no historical problem more difficult to solve than this: When did the Teutonic wave of population first reach these shores? and its consequent—When did it begin to be influential in modifying the languages spoken by the people of Britain? Although we are by no means inclined to favour the hyper-sceptical school who almost deny the existence of such personages as Hengist, Ella, and Cerdic, we are willing to admit that they were much less important in influence than the Saxon annalists have made them. Half conquerors, half colonists, they were by no means the first of their division of mankind who entertained designs for effecting a settlement here. We believe that long before the days of Cæsar, a considerable proportion of the inhabitants of South Britain were of Germanic blood, and that the Belgic Britons of whom he speaks, and who were much farther advanced in civilisation than the Celtæ, used a Teutonic dialect. Although there is no direct proof of this, we may infer as much from several passages of Cæsar himself, especially the one in which he tells us that the Celtæ of Gaul (the acknowledged progenitors of the earliest Britons) differed entirely from the Belgæ in language, customs, and laws. (De Bell. Gall. i, 1.) But the limits of our brief essay preclude our enlarging upon this topic, and we hasten to observe that the ' Notitia' presents us with some names of stations which *must* have been imposed by Teutonic colonists, being as unlike anything Celtic as can well be imagined. Such are *Burgovicus,* now identified with Housesteads near the Roman wall; and *Medioborgus,* which Baxter places at the mouth of the Tweed. To this military colonisation succeeded other settlements from northern Germany, so that at the decline of Roman power in Britain the south-eastern coast seems from the name which it bore—*Littus Saxonicum*—to have been principally in the hands of a Teutonic population, not (as is commonly believed) hostile to the Roman government, but under the protection of a *comes* or lieutenant of its appointment. The arrival of Hengist, Ælla, and the other reputed founders of the heptarchy, was but the following out of a stream of colonisation which had long flowed from Germany to Britain; and it was only when those bold adventurers saw the abject condition of the Celtic islanders, after the withdrawal of the Roman cohorts, that they aimed at political supremacy and introduced Germanic laws. Their language had for ages been that of a large proportion of the population, and it now became the prevailing one. The Britanno-Roman nomenclature of places was retained in a few instances, but for the most part it was utterly superseded by Anglo-Saxon designations. Wherever a Roman station of importance had existed, the termination *ceaster* (castrum, fortification) was suffixed. Thus Corinium became Ciren-ceaster; Mancunium, Man-ceaster; and Dorocina, Dor-ceaster.

For the most part, however, the name was entirely
changed, as Regnum into Cissan-ceaster (Chichester),
and Durovernum into Cantwara-burh (Canterbury).
In many cases it is only by a laborious collation of
circumstances that the Roman site can be identified
with the Roman name, so completely has the Anglo-
Saxon superseded it; for example, Anderida is now
Pevensey; Pons Ælii, Newcastle; and Ratæ, Leices-
ter. Sometimes there was an adoption of the old
name, but from ignorance of its meaning it was often
grossly corrupted. Thus Avalaria went through the
form Woollover, and is now Wooler; and Ad Pontem
is according to Baxter, the modern Paunton.

III. DANISH OR SCANDINAVIAN.—When the fierce
sea-kings of the north had formed their settlements
in Britain, and the eastern portions of the island were
occupied by a Danish race, some modification of our
local nomenclature of course occurred. It was, however, but slight, for the language used by the Northmen was a sister tongue to the Anglo-Saxon, and
the new-comers had few motives for changing names
which must for the most part have been intelligible
to them. Mr. Worsaae, however, in his recent work[6]
thinks otherwise, and labours with that special pleading
which so strongly characterises his discussions, to show
that they introduced great changes. He claims for his
countrymen the honour of having imposed all those
names which desinate in -by, -thorpe, -thwaite, -with,
-toft, -beck, -naes, -ey, -dale, -force, -fell, -tarn,-haugh;
together with many others in -holm, -garth, -land,
-end, -vig, -ho, -rigg, &c.; but a very slight acquaintance with Anglo-Saxon will convince any unprejudiced
inquirer that three-fourths at least of these termi-

'The Danes and Northmen in England.'   London, 1852.

nations belong also to that language. Some of them, however, are exclusively Scandinavian, as for instance *by*, which originally meant a single habitation, afterwards a village, or even town. This we believe is only found in those parts of the island where Danish influence prevailed—never in the purely Saxon districts. It is mostly prefixed either by an epithet, as Eastby, Westerby, Mickleby, Newby—the eastern, the western, the great, and the new villages; or by the name of a Danish proprietor, as Rollesby, Osgodby, Brandsby, Swainby, the village of Rolf, of Osgod, of Brand, and of Sweyn. *Thwaite* (O. N. *thweit*), an isolated piece of land—*tarn*, a small lake—*force*, a waterfall—with perhaps one or two others, also seem to be purely Scandinavian. Sometimes, too, places previously important were rebaptized by the Danes. Thus Streaneshalch gave way to Whitby, and Northweorthig to Deoraby, now contracted to Derby : these are matters of historical record.

IV. FRENCH. The greatest people since the extinction of the Roman name were the Normans. Of Scandinavian origin, they rose almost *per saltum* from a nation of barbarians to be the most formidable race in Europe, and within an incredibly brief space of time became masters of Northern France, of England, and of Sicily. But while they knew not how to succumb to any alien power, they readily laid down their language at the dictation of circumstances and adopted that of the races whom they subdued. They had not long taken possession of Neustria ere they repudiated their old northern dialect, and adopted the softer one of Fran ; and in like manner, on their acquisition of England they failed to introduce the newly-borrowed tongue here. Hard as the Norman scribes found it to write Anglo-Saxon local names—as witness their wretched misspellings in 'Domesday Book'—they never attempted to introduce a new nomenclature, as their predecessors in conquest had done. And for the few generations during which French most inconveniently maintained its existence as the language of the royal and legal courts, very little indeed was done in the way of imposing French names upon the seigniories which the Norman sword had acquired. In fact, it would be difficult throughout the length and breadth of the land to find fifty places bearing French names of early date. The monastery reared upon the field on which the Conquest occrrred was, it is true, designated *L'abbaie de la Bataile* (retained in the modern name Battle), and the metropolis of the newly-acquired land was ridiculously Frenchified into *Londres;* but these are exceptional instances. We have, however, Beaulieu Malpas, Beaurepaire, Beauvoir, Pontefract (*Pons-fractus*, from a ruined bridge there), Château-vert (now Shotover!), &c. &c. Of course we do not include here the Belmonts, Montpeliers, and Bellevues of modern watering-places, the best argument against the adoption of which is furnished in the vile mispronunciations which render them in vulgar mouths Bell-mount, Mount-peelier, and Belly-voo !

We must not, however, overlook the fact that after the Norman Conquest many manors and parishes received as a suffix to their Saxon names those of their acquirers. This was generally the case where two lordships in the same locality bore the same appellation, but belonged to different proprietors, as Tarring-Neville and Tarring-Peverell, Hurst-Monceux and Hurst-Pierpoint, Stoke-Gabriel and Stoke-Damerell, Newton-Morrel and Newton-Mulgrave,

Thorpe-Malzor add Thorpe-Mandeville. There are one or two curious instances in which the suffix alone is now retained; thus the original Saxon name of two Buckinghamshire manors has become obsolete, and what were formerly Isenhamsted-Cheney, and Isen-hamsted-Latimer, are now called and written Cheneys and Latimers.

V. MODERN ENGLISH. Little requires to be said under this division. Many names have been imposed since our language has taken its modern and existing form, and additions are continually being made, as new towns, hamlets, and residences spring into existence. Some of these have been formed in the ancient mode by the conjunction of the owner's name with some appellative, as Camois Court, Hill's Place, Camden Town. Sometimes places are contra-distinguished by epithets descriptive of their respective situations or extent, as East Marden, West Marden, Great Bookham, Little Bookham, Over-Compton, Nether-Compton (or by a Latin phrase, as Weston-super-Mare, Kingston-juxta-Lewes),—and sometimes by the addition of the name of the patron-saint, as Colne St. Denis, Marston St. Lawrence. Such compounds as Cherry-Hill, Oak-lands, Grove-Hall, Brick-wall, &c., explain themselves.

Lastly, when places have belonged to royal or ec-clesiastical personages, they frequently bear the name of such owners either in Latin or English, as a prefix or suffix, of which King's Langley and Lyme Regis, Aston-Abbots and Cerne Abbas, Monks' Horton, and Buckland-Monachorum, Bishop's Stortford and Ca-nons' Ashby will serve as instances.

Having thus indicated the *sources* from whence the local nomenclature of England has been derived, it

will be our object in the remainder of this essay to
examine the *materials* out of which it is composed.
We have already done this to some small extent in
reference to names of Celtic and Danish origin, and
shall not revert to those branches of the subject except perhaps for an occasional analogy. As we have
said, the great majority of our local names are of
Anglo-Saxon birth, and it is to these that we would
now direct the reader's attention.

The study of Anglo-Saxon names has been greatly
facilitated by the publication of the great body of
charters extending from the seventh to the eleventh
century, collected from various authentic sources,
and edited by Mr. Kemble, under the title of ' Codex
Diplomaticus Ævi Saxonici.' Many of these documents are in the Anglo-Saxon language, and the rest
though written in Latin retain the Saxon proper
names. These volumes would furnish matter for a
series of disquisitions of great interest; but on the
present occasion we are compelled to content ourselves
with general references and remarks immediately connected with our subject.

If we examine the name of any town or village we
shall generally find it composed of two parts—two
Anglo-Saxon words in fact. The second of these is
a *topographical expression,* implying valley, enclosure,
bridge, wood, hill, water, island, or the like. The first
is a *qualifying* word which distinguishes the particular
valley, enclosure, bridge, &c. from other like places
and objects, and is for the most part either an epithet,
a genitive form, or the personal name of its Saxon
proprietor.

Whoever gives his memory a slight fillip, or takes
a cursory glance at his county-map, will notice the
frequency with which certain terminations occur in

local names. He will also probably call to mind the old proverbial distich :—

> "In *ham*, and *ford*, and *ley*, and *ton*
> The most of English names do run ;"

and although this " wise saw " (like many other wise saws) is rather narrow and incomprehensive, it will serve well as an illustration of the staple of our local nomenclature. Let us collate it a little with our aforesaid memories and county maps, and what scores of Newhams and Oldhams, Westhams and Southams ; Oldfords and Newfords, Freshfords and Littlefords ; Hothleys and Bramleys, Horsleys and Cowleys; Nortons and Suttons, Langtons and Altons come at our invocation ! If we possess a turn for such rhyming, we have, like a committee, power to add to our *numbers*. We will try—but stay ! it has already been done for us in a well-known publication, thus :

> " *Ing*, *Hurst*, and *Wood*, *Wick*, *Sted*, and *Field*
> Full many English *place-names* yield,
> With *Thorpe* and *Bourne*, *Cote*, *Caster*, *Oke*,
> *Combe*, *Bury*, *Den*, and *Stowe*, and *Stoke ;*
> With *Ey* and *Port*, *Shaw*, *Worth*, and *Wade*,
> *Hill*, *Gate*, *Well*, *Stone*, are many made ;
> *Cliff*, *Marsh*, and *Mouth*, and *Down*, and *Sand*,
> And *Beck* and *Sea* with numbers stand." [6]

There are at least as many more terminations of

---

[6] 'English Surnames,' London, 1849, vol. i, page 58. The reader will probably recollect here the Cornish distich :—

> " By Tre, Ros, Pol, Lan, Caer, and Pen,
> You know the most of Cornishmen."

In Cornwall, local names have the topographical term as the initial instead of the final syllable, which is caused by the Celtic substantive having the precedence of its epithet as in Latin, modern French, &c., whereas the Anglo-Saxon, like modern English, places the adjective foremost. We may add, that in Corno-Celtic *tre* signifies town, *ros* a heath, *pol* a pool, *lan* a church, *cær* a castle, and *pen* a head.

less, yet still considerable, frequency, but as we wish to indicate general principles rather than to work them out to the full, we must content ourselves at present with the following illustrative table :

Termination.	Example.	Ang.-Sax. form.	Signification.	Analogies.	
HAM	Greatham, Sussex	hám	manor, house, or hamlet	heim, Germ.	96[7]
FORD	Brentford, Middlesex	ford	fordable point in a river	furt, do.	47
LEY or LY	Bletchingley, Surrey	leah	field, with some reference to neighbouring woods		70
TON	Warbleton, Sussex	tún	inclosure, village, town,	tuin, Dutch	137
ING	Malling, Kent	„	(explained below)		
HURST	Hawkhurst, Kent	hyrst	a wood which yields food for cattle	horst, Germ.	
WOOD	Goodwood, Sussex	wudu	wood (lignum)		
WICK	Warwick	wic	village, town	οικος, vicus	
STED, STEAD	Stansted, Sussex	stede	place, station, 'stead'	stat, Germ.	20
FIELD	Huddersfield, York	feld	plain open ground {	feld, Germ. { velde, Dutch	18
THORPE	Bishop's Thorpe	thorp	a collection of dwellings	dorf, Germ.	20
BOURNE	Winterbourne, Dorset	burne	a rivulet	born, Germ.	36
COTE	Woodmancote, Sussex	cote	small dwelling, cottage		
CHESTER	Silchester, Hants	ceaster	a fortified Roman station	castrum, Lat.	—
OKE, OCK	Tipnoak, Sussex	ac	an oak tree		
COMBE	Ilfracombe, Devon	cumb	a trough-like valley	cwm, Welsh	
BURY	Wednesbury, Stafford	burh, byrig	town, borough	bourg, Fr.	20
DEN	Bethersden, Kent	denu	sheltered place affording food for animals	dion, Gaelic	
STOW	Walthamstow,Essex ⎫	stów {	dwelling-place, habita-		—
STOKE	Basingstoke, Hants ⎭		tion		
EY	Pevensey, Sussex {	eá—water { ig—island {	water island or morass		
SHAW	Henshaw, Northumb.	sceaga	a small wood, or copse		—
WORTH	Mouldsworth, Chesh.	wurd, wyrd	plot of ground surround- ed by water, &c. &c., homestead	würth, Germ.	
WADE	Biggleswade, Bedford	wád	a ford—a place near one	vadum, Lat.	
HILL, HULL	Thornhill, Dorset	hyl	a hill, or elevation		
GATE	Newdigate, Surrey	gæat	a gate, or a way		30
WELL	Camberwell, Surrey	wel—wyl	a spring or its rivulet	quelle, Germ.	
STONE	Ingatestone, Essex	stan	some remarkable boun- dary or assembly-stone	stein, Germ.	
CLIFF	Rockcliffe, Cumb.	clif	a cliff	klippe, Germ.	
MARSH	Pebmarsh, Essex	mersc	a marsh	marsch, Germ.	
MOUTH	Yarmouth, Norfolk	muth	the outlet of a river		
DOWN, DON	Kilndown, Kent	dún	elevated land, down	dùn, Gaelic	
SAND	Cawsand, Devon	sand	a sand	sand, Germ.	
BECK	Troutbeck, Westmorl.	bec	a stream or rivulet	bach, Germ.	
SEA	Whittlesea, Camb.	sæ	a lake or stagnant water	see, Germ.	

[7] The figures in the last column are from the 'Rectitudines Singularum Personarum' of Dr. Leo, of Halle, who has carefully analysed the 1200 local names occurring in the first two volumes of Kemble's 'Codex Dipl.;' 96, 47, &c., are therefore to be understood as $\frac{96}{1200}$, $\frac{47}{1200}$, &c., of the names found in those volumes. See Treatise on the Local Nomenclature of the Anglo-Saxons, translated by B. Williams, Esq., F.S.A., London, 1852.

It may be remarked that most of these words also occur as place-names without any prefix.

With regard to the prefix, it is, as we have remarked, of various kinds, of which the following may be considered as the principal sources:

I. *The Teutonic Mythology.* The names of the Anglo-Saxon divinities and heroes not unfrequently occur as the initial syllable of local names; as that of *Woden* in Wódnesbeorh (Wansborough, co. Hants, and Woodnesborough, co. Kent), Wódnesbrók (Wambrook, co. Dorset)—that of *Thor* or *Thunre* in Thunresfield, and Thunresleáh (co. Hants), Thurley (co. Beds), Thurlow (co. Essex)—that of *Scyld,* a progenitor of Woden, in Scyldestreów (Shilltry?). Other names include the designations of Frea, Grime, and the fabulous Offa. We think Mr. Kemble's deductions of this kind rather far-fetched, especially where he derives Hamerton, Hammerwick, &c. from the hammer of Thor. In attributing the Hammerponds of Surrey to such a source he is clearly wrong; for they are well known to have taken their name from the fact of their waters having been employed to work the hammers of the iron-forges, which until within the last two or three generations existed there.

Connected with the Teutonic mythology, Baxter gives a curious etymology for the town of Folkestone, which is perhaps rather more ingenious than probable. He deduces it from *folces stan,* "Lemurum sive Larium lapis," the stone of the lemures or lares, fairies or " good *folks.*" For corroboration he adduces " fox-gloves," the common name of the herb digitalis, which he interprets " lemurum manicæ — folks' gloves "—

—" veteribus Britannis *Menig Eilff Uylhon,* corruptè hodie *Elhylhon,* quod idem valet : sunt enim Britannis *Eilff Uylhon,* nocturni Dæmones, sive Lemures; cum Saxonibus *Folces* dicatur Minuta plebs, et forsan etiam Manes." (p. 5.)

On a subsequent page (17) he pursues this curious theory :

" Ab Ἔρα, terra, fit et Γερα Macedonum dialecto; unde Ἔνεροι, ΕνΓεροι, et Romanis *Inferi, qui Scoto-saxonibus dicuntur Feries, nostratique vulgo corruptiùs Fairies,* Καταχθόνιοι Δαίμονες sive *Dii Manes."*

Although the Irish designate fairies as the " good people" or " good folk," we are not aware that the Anglo-Saxon *folc* is ever capable of the interpretation "*minuta* plebs," and in spite of Baxter's argument we are rather disposed to think that the Kentish town derives its name from some *stone* where the *folk* of the district in Saxon times were wont to assemble to discuss their public affairs. We know that grave consultations among our ancestors were generally carried on in the open air ; and traces of the practice are still common, especially at the election of public officials.

Connected also with the religion of our Anglo-Saxon ancestors was the respect paid to the mystic number seven. Thus in the Codex we find many such names as *Seofon-thornas,* seven thorns, *Seofon wyllas,* seven wells. Traces of this are retained in existing names, as in the town of Sevenoaks in Kent, and the Seven Sisters, a name given to that number of undulations in the Chalk Cliffs between Beachy Head and Seaford.

To this family of local names may be added the long list derived from the fairy mythology which has imprinted itself in a hundred forms not only upon streams, fields, and hills, but even upon hamlets and parishes. The names of the elves and nymphs in the poetical

traditions of our ancestors are generally monosyllabic :
see a list of some of them in Drayton's ' Nymphidia :'

> "Hop, and Mop, and Dryp so clear,
> Pip and Trip, and Skip that were
> To Mab their sovereign ever dear,
>   Her special maids of honour ;
> Fib, and Tib, and Pinck, and Pin,
> Tick and Quick, and Jil and Jin,
> Tit and Nit, and Wap and Win,
>   The train that wait upon her ;"

most of which, with numerous others, are found in
composition with Saxon words to make up a vast
variety of local names, such as Hob's Hawth, Hob-
well, Hobmoor, Dobb's Hill, Cobb's Close, Cobden
Puckwell, Puckeridge, Pinkden, Tickhill, Winslow,
Titsey, Elfenden, Elveston, Sibthorpe, Wilsham, &c.
Mr. Allies, F.S.A., in his ' Antiquities and Folk-
Lore of Worcestershire,' has collected some hundreds
of such names in that county alone.

II. *Proprietorship.* To call one's possessions by
his own name has always been a matter of ambition.
Upon this principle the numerous *villes* in Normandy
acquired their designations : Tancarville, for example,
is " villa Tancredi "—and Charleville, " villa Caroli."
Hence also the Kemp Towns and Somers' Towns of
our own times, and the Smithvilles and Jonesvilles of
America. On the colonisation of this country by the
Anglo-Saxons, when any settlement did not already
possess a name it would receive that of its proprietor.
Thus an Eadward or an Ælfric having inclosed a
piece of land would call it Eadwardes-tun, or
Ælfrices-tun, names which remain to this day in
Adferton and Alfriston. In like manner originated
Elmundwick, the habitation of Elmund, Wodeman-
cote, the cottage of Wodeman, Wimundham (now

Wyndham) the manor or residence of Wimund, and a thousand others.

Sometimes, however, the prefix implies a family proprietorship rather than a personal one. This is the case in that numerous class of local names which have *ing* in the middle. This component signifies " descendant," " offspring," and is, in fact, a patronymic form. Thus a son of Ælfred was an Ælfreding, a son of Eadmund, an Eadmunding, and their descendants at large were Ælfredingas and Eadmundingas. Hence the hám or home of the descendants of Beorm became Beorm-inga-ham, and is now by contraction Birmingham. So Chiltington was the inclosure of the sons of Cilt; and Bedingfield, the field or plain of the descendants of Beda.[8] Numerous analogous instances will suggest themselves to the reader. We may remark that those places which now terminate in *ing* often have in the charters the additional syllable ham—subsequently dropped for the sake of brevity.

III. *Natural Objects, animal, vegetable, and mineral.* Very trifling incidents have frequently given rise to names of places on the arrival of settlers in a new region. As Dr. Leo observes, the springing of a hare across their path, the appearance of a particular tree, or some peculiarity of the ground, is associated with their first impressions of the spot, which receives a name accordingly. More usually, the abundance of any particular animal or vegetable production has originated the designation ; an inclosure of ash-trees, has thus come to be called Æsces-tun, or Ashton; a

---

[8] Attention was first called to this field of etymological investigation, some years since, by my friend Thos. Wright, Esq., M.A., F.S.A., in his valuable ' History of Ludlow.'

fine bullock-pasture, Oxan-leah, or Oxley; and a
stream abounding with trout, Truht-bec or Troutbeck. The following names are derived from qua-
drupeds. From the hart and its congeners, Hertford,
Hindlip, Hartwell, Roehampton—from the boar and
sow, Eferdon (A.-S *efor*, a boar), Sowig, Swines-
head, Swinford—from the goat, Gatborough, Goatham
—from the ox, cow, or calf, Oxenden, Oxwick, Cow-
den, Cowley, Calf hanger—from the sheep, Ewecomb,
Shipley, Sheppey, Lambourne, Lambhythe, Ewell—
from the horse, Horsham, Horsley—from the dog,
Houndean,[2] Hounslow—from the hare, Harley, Ha-
renden—from the fox, Foxhow, Foxley.

Some animals now extinct amongst us, but existing
here in Saxon times, have impressed their names upon
localities; for example, the bear on Barcombe, Barley,
Barden—the wolf on Wolfridge, Wolfpit or Woolpit
—the wild cat on Catcliff, Catsfield—the beaver on
Beverley, Beverstone—the seal on Selsey. Dr. Leo
derives Apenholt and Apetun (names occurring in the
Codex) from the ape; but surely no species of *simius*
was ever indigenous to this country.

The Anglo-Saxon *deor*, as seen in Deerhurst,
Derby, &c. implies not simply deer, but all wild animals and game in general, and was so understood
among the vulgar even in Shakespeare's time.

> " Mice and rats, and such small *deer*,
>   Have been Tom's food for seven long year."
>   *King Lear.*

Birds' names enter largely into the local nomencla-
ture of England, as in Ravenshill, Cranmer, Goosford,
Cockshaw, Henshaw, Swallowcliff, Hawksborough,
Birdham, Fowlmere, Eglesham, Eaglescliff, Crowham,
Finchley, Swansbrook, Rookwood, Hernhill, Earnley

(A.-S. *erne,* an eagle), Falconbridge, Falkenham.
We must not place here Leighton-Buzzard, the suffix of
which is a vile corruption of the French name "Beau-
desert." The owl appears in Ulcombe, the cuckoo in
Cooksham (Cuceshámm in the Codex), and fowls in
general in the prefix *ful* (A.-S. fugel) as in Fulbrook,
Fulham, Fulmere.

Fishes have given name to Fishbrook, Fishbourne,
Fishwick, Fishlake, &c., but the particular species is
not often denominated: we have, however, Troutbeck,
Eelham, Pickford (for Pikeford), and Pickersgill.

From the bee come Beeford, Beebrook, &c.; and
from the leech, Leechford, Lechmere, and others.
We cannot agree with Dr. Leo in assigning the
numerous names beginning in the Charters with *Wifl*
to the weevil (*curculio granarius*) of our barns. It
is doubtless the name of an early proprietor.

The vegetable world furnishes forth another handsome quota to our local nomenclature, as

The oak　(A.-S. *ac*)　Oakley, Acton, Acworth.
　　ash　　(*aesc*)　　Ashley, Askham, Ashford.
　　beech　(*bóc*)　　Buckholt, Buckham, Bokenhall,
　　　　　　　　　　　also Coldbeech, Waterbeech,
　　　　　　　　　　　Holbeech.
　　elm　　(*elm*)　　Elmley, Elmsted, Elmsthorpe.
　　pine　　(*pin*)　　Pinehurst, Pinewell, Pinhoe.
　　thorn　(*thorn*)　Thornhurst, Thornbury, Thornton.
　　elder　(*ellen*)　Ellenford, Ellenborough.
　　lime　　(*linde*)　Linton, Lindworth, Lyndhurst.
　　birch　(*birce*)　Birchensty, Bircham, Bircholt.
　　maple (*mapledern*) Mapledurham, Maplested, May-
　　　　　　　　　　　powder.
　　apple or crab　vide p. 12, *ante.*
　　aspen　(*æps*)　　Apsley, Hapstead, Aspland.

The willow (*welig*) Willoughby, Willowshed, Willitoft.
hazel (*hæsl*) Hazelden, Haslemere, Hazelwood.
fern (*fearn*) Farnhurst, Farnley, Farnham.
moss (*meos*) Moston, Moss-side, Mosley.
reed (*hreod*) Redburne, Redford, Reedham.
rush (*risce*) Rushford, Rishbrook, Rishworth.
flax (*lin*) Linley, Lindsey, Linthwaite.
herbs (*wyrt*) Wirthorp, Wortley.
grass (*gærs*) Garston, Garstang, Garsdale.
broom (*brom*) Bromley, Bromham, Bromfield.
heath (*hæth*) Heathfield, Heathpool, Heathylee.
wheat (*hwæte*) Wheatley, Whethamsted, Wheat-
hill

From the mineral kingdom the number of names is much smaller. Thence, however, we fetch no inconsiderable list of such designations as Chalkham, Chalkhill, Sandwich, Sandham, Sandhurst, Limburne, Chiselhurst, Chiselhampton (*cisel*, gravel), Clifton, Stoneham, Stanbridge, Saltwell, Clayton, Marlow, Marldon.

IV. *Position upon Roads and Rivers.* When the Romans forsook this island, the Saxons gave to their great roads the name of 'streets,' such as Ermin Street, Watling Street, Ickenild Street, Stone Street, &c., and hence our numerous Streets, Strattons, Stratfords, &c., as well as many of our Wickhams, Wicksteds, Bridgewicks, &c., which are usually found contiguous to the Roman roads.

Far more numerous, however, are the names of places derived from rivers and streams. Among the Celtic nations whole tribes received their designations from the rivers upon which they resided, as for instance, the Tamarici, on the Tamaris in Spain, the Senones in the upper bed of the Seine in France.

2 §

So among the Saxons the kingdom of Northumbria received its name from its position relatively to the river Humber. Our Anglo-Saxon progenitors designated numbers of towns and villages from the rivers upon which they stood. Thus we have Plymouth, Plympton, and Plymstock or -stoke, upon the Plym; Tavistock and Tavy-St. Peter, upon the Tavy; Exeter, Exminster, and Exmouth upon the Exe; Stourhead, Stourbridge, Stourton, Stourport, Stourmouth upon the rivers so called. The debouchures of the Wey, the Fal, the Yare, the Wear, the Tyne, and the Dart, give names to Weymouth, Falmouth, Yarmouth, Wearmouth, Tynemouth, and Dartmouth. The Rother rises at Rotherfield. Cambridge and Weybridge stand upon the Cam and the Wey. A very obscure little river in Dorsetshire called the Piddle (A.-S. *pidl*, a thin stream) gives names to six or seven parishes in its course.

V. *Historical events, customs, social habits, &c.* Sometimes the name of a place bears reference to some event which has occurred in it, as, for example, Lichfield, the field of corses; Battlebridge, from a battle which took place there; and the like. The phrase " heathen burials," found forty-three times in the ' Codex,' and still retained in some localities, indicates the burial-place of Britons, Romans, or pre-Christian Saxons. Dr. Leo thinks that some have relation to weapons of war. Suweordleah, Swerdling, Billancomb, Billanden, &c., occur in the ' Codex.'

Ród, the rood or crucifix, is the prefix of a considerable number of places, denoting points where such objects anciently stood, as Rodborough, Rodbourne, Rodmell, Rodmersham; but this must not be confounded with the termination *royd,* or *rode* in Yorkshire, which implies a " ridding," or forest clearance, as in Ackroyd, Holroyd, &c.

The Anglo-Saxon *ceáp* implies commerce or marketing, and is retained in such names as Eastcheap, Cheapside, Chipping-Norton, Chipping-Ongar, Chippenham. Chepstow is literally "the market-place." The prefix *charl* is the Anglo-Saxon *ceorl*, churl, husbandman, and occurs in Charlton, Charlwood, Charlesworth, Charlcote—all implying the residence of serfs or bondmen. *Swán* is a herdsman, or pastoral servant; hence the analogous Swanburn, Swandean, Swanscomb, saving the right of *swan* (unaccented), which designates the aquatic fowl. There is history in such names, as well as in the ever-recurring Kingstons, Bishopstons, and Prestons (Preostes tún), which indicate the preponderance of kingly and priestly influence at the time when they were originally applied; and as the pagan Saxons have left traces of their old creed in our local nomenclature, so their Christian descendants have transmitted to us many memorials of their adherence to a purer faith in the names of which " church," "kirk," and " minster," form a part.

We have thus indicated the main sources, and examined some of the materials, of the local names of this country. To do justice to the subject would require the space of an ample volume rather than that of a brief and cursory essay ; and we know of few philological subjects that would furnish more interesting *materiel* for a full and comprehensive treatise.

ON THE BATTLE OF HASTINGS.

"At nunc horrentia Martis."

Κάρτιστοι μὲν ἔσαν, καὶ καρτίστοις ἐμάχοντο.

FEW things are more difficult to describe than the
events of the battle-field. To say nothing of that lack
of coolness which is essential to accurate observation,
an individual spectator commonly sees only a small
portion of the engagement, and is apt to overrate the
incidents occurring in the foreground of his view,
while those which take place in the distance are but
slightly noticed. Acts comparatively insignificant
thus become magnified, while those of far greater
importance are occasionally either much distorted, or
altogether overlooked. Allowances must also be made
for party prejudices, and for the flowers of rhetoric
almost inseparable from such descriptions. Now if
even contemporary accounts of modern battles are
found to differ *inter sese* in some essential particulars,
it must be a matter of great difficulty to frame an intelligible history of the sanguinary conflicts of ancient
times from the materials furnished us by partial and
often incompetent chroniclers, and written from oral
traditions at periods considerably subsequent to the
transactions themselves. It is only by a collation of
many descriptions, and a competent acquaintance with
the field whereon the battle took place, that a writer
can hope to convey a moderately accurate idea of such
a scene. Many popular accounts exist of the tremen-

dous struggle which occurred on, and gave name to, the spot now known as Battel; but they are chiefly copied one from another with little or no reference to original documents, and written in total ignorance of the geographical features of the locality.[1] In attempting to lay before the reader a few general remarks on the subject, in order to invest the event with some little additional interest, I shall adopt an opposite course, and deduce nearly or quite all my materials from authorities who lived near the time at which the battle occurred, and from personal surveys of the scene of action.[2]

On the political causes of the battle I shall say nothing : they are well known to all. And on the events which succeeded William's landing at Pevensey on the 28th of September up to the fatal day—October the 14th, 1066, I have already published some remarks.[3] The reader will therefore have the goodness to consider the Norman duke as intrenched in his temporary castellum at Hastings, and the unfortunate Harold as having erected his standard and fixed his gonfanon upon the field of Battel. Short as had been the interval between the arrival of the Saxons from the north and the morning of the battle, they had not neglected to fortify this naturally strong and well chosen position. According to the Roman de Rou, Harold "had the place well examined, and surrounded by a good fosse, leaving an entrance on each of three

---

[1] Henry of Huntingdon, also (in other respects a valuable authority, as living in times not very remote from the Conquest,) tells us that William " aciem suam construxit in *planis* Hastinges."

[2] I would here record my obligations to my friend, the Rev. John Collingwood Bruce, L.L.D., F.S.A., author of ' The Roman Wall,' &c. —with whom I lately had the pleasure of reviewing the localities of the battle—for several useful suggestions and memoranda.

[3] *Suss. Arch. Collections*, vol. II, p. 53 et seq.

sides, which were ordered to be kept well guarded." [4]
Upon the vallum his soldiery erected a barricade,
composed of their shields, and of wood from the adjoining forests, principally ash, the whole being so
joined and wattled together as to form an almost impenetrable wall. [5] We can well understand how the
army could in a few hours erect a fortification of some
strength by such means, when we remember that the
ordinary mode of constructing houses of the meaner
sort in Saxon times was by driving large stakes into
the ground, and filling up the spaces by interweaving
pliant branches of young trees, and covering the whole
with clay or mud—a style of building still retained
for out-houses in some parts of the south of England,
and known by the rather unclassical designation of
" raddle-and-dab."   Within this extempore fort were
assembled the men of London, and Kent, and Hertford, and Essex, and Surrey, and Sussex, and St.
Edmund, and Suffolk, and Norwich, and Norfolk,
and Canterbury, and Stamford, and Bedford, and
Huntingdon, and Northampton, and York, and Buck-
ingham, and Nottingham, and Lincoln, and Lindsay,
and Salisbury, and Dorset, and Bath, and Somerset,
and Gloucester, and Worcester, and Winchester, and
Hampshire, and Berkshire, and elsewhere.   This
enumeration is from Wace, who informs us that, in
addition to these, " the villains were also called to-

[4] Taylor's Chronicle of the Norman Conquest, from the Roman de
Rou, 1837, p. 143.   The Roman de Rou, a chronicle of the Dukes of
Normandy, is a Norman-French poem of the twelfth century, of great
historical interest and importance.   It was written by Master Wace,
a native of Jersey, whose Christian name is unknown.   He lived
and wrote as late as the year 1173 ; yet from incidental notices in the
work, it appears that he gathered much of his information from eye-
witnesses.

[5] Chron. Norm. Conq., p. 176.

gether from the villages, bearing such arms as they found; clubs, and great picks, iron forks, and stakes" —a mixed and motley group, animated by the fire of a generous patriotism, and fully bent upon a vigorous resistance.

The manner in which the night of the 13th of October was spent by them redounds little to their honour. On the eve of such a crisis as they knew the next day must inevitably bring, they might have been more rationally employed than in drinking and dissipation. The Saxon camp in fact rather resembled that of a victorious host, than that of one which stood upon the very brink of destruction. "All night," says our graphic chronicler, "they might be seen carousing, gambolling, and dancing, and singing; *bublie*, they cried, and *wassail*, and *laticome*, and *drinkheil*, and *drink-to-me.*"[6] Sad the contrast between that hilarious toast-drinking and the shrieks and groans which were, a few hours later, to resound from the blood-drenched hill.

Far different was the scene presented by the Norman army on the eve of the battle. The priests were everywhere busy, confessing and shriving the soldiery, and mingling with their penances and pardons exhortations to valorous deeds. All night they watched and prayed in portable chapels which had been fitted up throughout the camp.[7] Among the priests-militant so engaged, two were especially conspicuous: Odo, Bishop of Bayeux, the Conqueror's uterine brother, afterwards Earl of Kent; and Geoffrey de Mowbray, Bishop of Coutances, a name subsequently famous in

[6] Chron. Norm. Conq., p. 156.

[7] We must recollect, however, that this contrast between Saxon riot and Norman piety is drawn by a Norman pen.

English history.[8] Instead of *wassails* and *drinkheils*, misereres, and litanies, and paternosters, and holy psalms resounded on every side. In the spirit of religious zeal, the soldiers vowed, that if God would grant them the victory, they would never more taste flesh on a Saturday, the day of the week upon which the field of Hastings was to be lost or won. At break of day Bishop Odo celebrated high mass, and pronounced a solemn benediction.

The line of the Normans' march, from their camp at Hastings to the battle-field, must have lain on the south-western slope of the elevated ridge of land extending from Fairlight to Battel; that is, to the north of the village of Hollington, through what is now Crowhurst Park, to the elevated spot then called Hetheland, but now known as Telham Hill. This district, which is even at the present day encumbered with woods, must have presented many obstacles to the advance of a multitudinous army. But every possible means to facilitate their movements had been employed; and, early in the morning of the fatal 14th of October, they stood upon the heights of Telham in full view of the Saxon camp, more than a mile distant.

> " *Haud procul* hostiles cuneos nam cernit adesse,
> Et plenum telis irradiare nemus.[9]

Here the duke marshalled his followers into three columns of attack. In the first column of cavalry were the warriors of Boulogne and Ponthieu, with

---

[8] Chron. Norm. Conq., p. 157. Ordericus Vitalis, edit. Prevost, ii, p. 146.

[9] De Bello Hastingensi Carmen, 343, 344.

most of those adventurous mercenaries who so largely swelled the invading force ;[10] in the second were the auxiliaries from Bretagne, Mantes, and Poitou : the great duke himself led what might be regarded as the flower of this congeries of armies, his own proper subjects, the chivalry of Normandy. While these preparations are being made, let us take a rapid glance at the appearance presented by William's soldiery. Here we shall be chiefly assisted by that extraordinary and interesting monument, the Bayeux tapestry. The date of that work, as most are aware, is disputed, but this is not the place to enter upon the discussion; and I will simply state my belief, that it is as old as the period assigned to it by some of our best authorities, namely, the life-time of Matilda, the Conqueror's queen. Whether it is actually the workmanship of the fair needlewomen of her court is little to our present purpose. I only claim for it all the authoritativeness of a contemporary document. The tapestry represents the horsemen clad in mail which usually reaches only to the knee, though sometimes, as in the case of the duke himself, it descends to the ankle. It is usually of the ringed, but occasionally of the mascled or diamond pattern. The helmet is conical, and is remarkable for an appendage in front, called the nasal, which effectually protected the nose from injury. The feet, which rest in stirrups, are usually armed with prick-spurs. The left hand supports a kite-shaped shield, about four feet in length, sometimes plain, but often ornamented with roundles, crosses, and rudely pourtrayed wyverns : no trace of *true* heraldric bearings is found. The

[10] William "had soldiers from many lands, who came, some for land, and some for money. Great was the host, and great the enterprise." (Wace.)

offensive arms are spears, sometimes furnished with
trifurcated and other pennons, heavy swords, and
maces, or batons of command. For the modes of
warfare then prevalent, it is difficult to conceive of a
more appropriate armature than the *tout ensemble* of
a Norman cavalier, as shown in this needlework,
presents. Of the few infantry shown, some are in
mail, and others in ordinary costume, armed with
bows and arrows. The tapestry does not show war-
engines, although, according to the Carmen, there
were balistæ intermixed with the infantry. These,
however, may have been simple cross-bows.

> " Premisit pedites committere bella sagittis,
>   Et balistantes inserit in medio." [11]

During the march from Hastings, a distance of about
six miles, the Normans had not worn their armour, and
it was only when they came within view of the Saxon
camp that they proceeded to arm. The testimony of
the 'Chronicle of Battel Abbey' is tolerably conclusive on this point. It was at Hetheland, which I
take to be identical with Telham, that this prelimi-
nary was gone through. Several historians relate
an anecdote connected with it, which is worthy of
quotation:—

" Having arrived at a hill called Hethelande, situated
in the direction of Hastings, while they were helping
one another on with their armour, there was brought
forth a coat of mail for the duke to put on, and by

[11] V. 337, 338. The Carmen de Bello Hastingensi—a poem of
more than eight hundred verses, is attributed to Guy, Bishop of
Amiens from 1059 to 1075. In spite of some exaggerations, and a
violent prejudice against the Saxons, it presents internal evidence of
having been written, very early after the battle, by one who possessed exact information on the subject. Some incidents of the day
are found in no other author.

accident it was handed to him the wrong side fore-most. Those who stood by and saw this, cursed it as an unfortunate omen, but the duke's sewer (Fitz-Osborne) bade them be of good cheer, and declared that it was a token of good fortune; namely, that those things which had hitherto kept their ground were about fully to submit themselves to him. The duke, perfectly unmoved, put on the mail with a placid countenance, and uttered these memorable words : ' I know, my dearest friends, that if I had any confidence in omens, I ought on no account to go to battle to-day; but, committing myself trust-fully to my Creator in every matter, I have given no heed to omens, neither have I ever loved sorcerers.' "[12]

Wace's account of the transaction is as follows : " When he prepared to arm himself, he called first for his good hauberk, and a man brought it on his arm, and placed it before him; but in putting his head in to get it on, he inadvertently turned it the wrong way, with the back in front. He quickly changed it, but when he saw that those who stood by were sorely alarmed, he said, ' I have seen many a man who, if such a thing had happened to him, would not have borne arms, or entered the field the same

[12] " Perveniensque ad locum collis qui Hethelande dicitur, a parte Hastingarum situm, dum sese invicem armis munire contendunt, ac eidem duci lorica ad induendum porrigitur; ex improviso inversa ipsi oblata est. Quod advertentes qui aderant, dum uti infortunii præsagium execrarentur, mox memoratus ducis dapifer solita cunctos constancia compescuit, protestatus et hinc quoque prosperitatis col-latum indicium quod scilicet, ea quæ ante restabant ut proposita securiter illi cessura forent. Sed dux nihil motus, vultu placido, loricam induens, digna memoriæ concionatus dixit : " Scio karis-simi quod si sortibus crederem, bellum hodie nullatenus introirem. Sed ego me in omni negotio Creatori meo fiducialiter committens, nec sortibus credidi, nec umquam sortilegos amavi."—*Chron. Monast. de Bello*, p. 3.

day; but I never believed in omens, and I never will. I trust in God; for he does in all things his pleasure, and ordains what is to come to pass according to his will. I have never liked fortune-tellers, nor believed in diviners; but I commend myself to our Lady. Let not this mischance give you trouble. The hauberk, which was turned wrong and then set right by me, signifies that a change will arise out of the matter we are now moving. You shall see the name of Duke changed into King. Yea, a king shall I be, who hitherto have been but duke.' Then he crossed himself, and straightway took his hauberk, stooped his head, and put it on aright; and laced his helmet and girt his sword, which a varlet brought him."[13] The story is similarly told by William of Poitiers.

Then followed the duke's celebrated Vow, that if God would grant him the victory over his foe, he would found a monastery upon the field of battle as an asylum for his saints, and as a succour for the souls of those who should be there slain. William Faber, a brother of the abbey of Marmoutier, near Tours, who had joined the army for the advancement of himself and his convent, hearing the vow, obtained the duke's consent to have the establishment dedicated to his patron, St. Martin, who had the valuable recommendation of being known as the "military saint," and the tutelary of Norman soldiers.

William's arming was not completed until he had suspended from his neck a portion of the holy relics upon which Harold had so solemnly sworn that he would never oppose him in his designs upon the throne of England.[14] The bulk of these objects of

[13] Chron. Norm. Conq., p. 163.
[14] Ordericus Vitalis, ii, 146, ed. Aug. le Provost.

his veneration was also present upon the battle-field.
Three hundred amulets of gold and silver, we are
told, were enclosed in a feretory in the form of an
altar, upon which mass had been daily celebrated
from the setting out of the expedition.[15] The duke
now called for his horse, and was soon mounted upon a
noble charger, a recent present from the King of
Spain.   William's carriage on this occasion was
eulogised by one of his followers, the Viscount of
Tours : " Never," said he, "have I seen a man so
fairly armed, nor one who rode so gallantly, or bore
his arms, or became a hauberk so well; neither any
one who bore his lance so gracefully, or sat his horse
and manœuvred him so boldly.   There is no other
such knight under heaven !   A fair count he is, and
fair king he will be."[16] The Bayeux Tapestry exhibits
the duke holding his baton over his right shoulder ;
and, by representing him of the same height as the
generality of his attendants, disproves the legendary
statement of his enormous stature, a notion which
probably originated from a misconception of the
meaning of the title Willelmus Magnus, which some of
the Norman historians are fond of applying to him.

There were others too, who, from some remarkable
demeanour in preparing for the conflict, attracted the
gaze of the whole army.   Hardly less conspicuous
than the duke himself was his half-brother, the Bishop
Odo.   While most of the monks and priests withdrew
to the neighbouring heights within view, to *watch* and
pray, this valorous churchman, disdaining danger,
" drew on a hauberk over a white aube, wide in the
body, with the sleeve tight, and sat on a white horse,
so that all might recognize him.   In his hand he held

---

[15] Chronicle of Battel Abbey, page 41.
[16] Chron. Norm. Conq., p. 167.

a mace; and wherever he saw most need, he led up and stationed the knights, and often urged them on to assault and strike the enemy."[17]   There, too, was the young knight, Toustains Fitz-Rou le Blanc, bearing the sacred gonfanon which the pope had blessed and presented to William.   This had been offered, in turn, to Raol de Conches, the hereditary standard-bearer of Normandy, and to Walter Giffard, but declined, by the former on the ground of his desiring the more useful service of the sword, by the latter on account of his bald and hoary head.   " I shall be in the battle," he cried, " and you have not any man who will serve you more truly ; I will strike with my sword till it shall be dyed in your enemies' blood !"[18]

It is interesting to the southern antiquary to observe that all the great baronial houses whose estates lay in proximity to the battle-field owed their lands to the prowess of their ancestors on the field of Hastings.   Not to speak of Odo, who had, as his share of the spoil, the county of Kent—Roger de Mont-gomeri, afterwards earl of Chichester and Arundel, was there, and commanded one wing of the army ; the men of Brius were there, and at their head was doubtless William, the subsequent lord of Bramber ; William de Warenne, afterwards lord of Lewes, came too, "his helmet setting gracefully on his head ;" Robert, earl of Mortaine, the future lord of Pevensey, "never went far from the duke's side, and brought him great aid ;" Robert, earl of Eu, the counsellor of William, was there, and for his services received the rape of Hastings.   He " demeaned himself as a brave man, and those whom his blows reached were ill handled."   The names of D'Albini, De Aquila, Mon-

[17] Chron. Norm. Conq., p. 194.
[18] Ibid., pp. 168, 169.

ceux, Mowbray, and Tregoz, all afterwards eminent in the south, also receive honourable mention in the Chronicle of Wace.

At length, amidst the sound " of many trumpets, of bugles, and of horns," the Normans were drawn up in order of battle, and the duke harangued them in a set speech, which is variously reported by the different chroniclers. What he really said must have been inaudible to the great majority of his sixty thousand followers. The alleged cruelty and perfidy of the Saxons, the perjury of Harold, and the rich rewards which awaited the invaders in the event of conquest, formed excellent topics for declamation, and were no doubt seized upon. " On then! in God's name, and chastise these English for their misdeeds!" is the laconic but inspiriting peroration put into his mouth by one of the chroniclers.

They now proceeded to march from Telham Hill, and to cross the valley which separates that elevation from the one upon which Harold's army was encamped, the graceful and gradually-rising spot upon which "the Abbey of the Battel" now rears its time-stained turrets. A finer site for a camp cannot be conceived; almost in its whole circumference bounded by low, and, in those days, marshy ground, it was difficult of access to the attacking army, and proportionably easy of defence; and had the Saxons adhered to their original purpose of remaining within their lines, the result of the battle would probably have been favourable to the defenders.

Within the barricaded embankment, in view of the approaching army, stood Harold attended by his brothers, Girth and Leofwine, and the chief men of his realm, while above his head waved the gonfanon, a noble standard sparkling with gold and precious stones, which he little dreamed was so soon to be stricken down, and sent as a thank-offering and a trophy of his enemy's triumph to the successor of the apostles, in return for the blessed banner of William, which was now waving at a distance in the morning breeze. This flag is particularly mentioned by the chroniclers. William of Poitiers notices it as " the memorable standard of Harold, having the figure of an armed man woven of the purest gold;" and William of Malmesbury says that " it was of the shape of a fighting man wrought with costly art of gold and precious stones." Packed in a very contracted space stood the army of Harold, which appears to have been in point of numbers nearly or quite equal to the duke's. The Saxon regular troops wore short and close hauberks, and hemlets that hung over their garments.[19] Their arms were swords, bills, lances, and clubs; but their favourite weapon was the battle-axe which they had borrowed from the Norwegians. It was commonly employed with both hands, and had a heavy blade a foot in length.[20] Of their shields, some were kite-shaped, like the Normans'; others, particularly those of the nobles, round and very convex.[21] The peasants, who had been hastily collected during Harold's hurried march, wore their ordinary costume, chiefly of leather, and were furnished with the rude but easily available weapons already mentioned.

The Saxons were all on foot. The Carmen contemptuously says of them:—

> " Nescia gens belli, solamina spernit equorum,
> Viribus et fidens hæret humo pedibus."[22]

[19] Chron. Norm. Conq. The Bayeux Tapestry makes little or no distinction between the dress of the Saxons and that of the Normans.

[20] Chron. Norm. Conq., p. 200.

[21] Bayeux Tapestry.　　　[22] V. 369, 370.

and again tells us, that on their arrival on the field of battle :—

"Omnes descendunt, et equos post terga relinquunt ;" [23]

while Wace assures us that they were ignorant of jousting and of bearing arms on horseback—a statement which might be deemed incredible did it not rest upon such excellent authority.

At length, according to Wace (to whose ample account of the battle every writer on the subject must be largely indebted), "the English stood ready to their post, the Normans still moving on; and when they drew near, the English were to be seen stirring to and fro; men going and coming; troops ranging themselves in order; some with their colour rising, others turning pale; some making ready their arms, others raising their shields; the brave man rousing himself to the fight, the coward trembling at the approaching danger."[24] Now was the struggle about to begin—a struggle fraught with tremendous consequences; and many an islander trembled, and many a transmarine heart beat high, at the recollection of an old prophecy attributed to Merlin,[25] "that a Norman people in iron coats should lay low the pride of the English," "Then," to quote the monk of Battel, it "was manfully fought with arms."[26]

But first, there comes upon the stage of this eventful drama, a character to whom the old historians, Guy, Benoit, Gaimar, and Wace, allude with peculiar

[23] V. 377. Yet a popular picture, by A. Cooper, R.A., represents Harold (receiving the arrow in his eye) on horseback.

[24] Chron. Norm. Conq., p. 186.

[25] "Juxta Merlini vaticinium, gente Normannica in tunicis ferreis Anglorum audacter dejiciente supercilium, armis viriliter decertatum est."—Chron. de Bello, p. 4.

[26] Ibid.

3

gusto. Among the Norman knights was one who, from his prowess and agility, had acquired, according to the usage of the times, the sobriquet of Taillefer or "cut iron." He is usually designated a jouglere or a minstrel; but whatever his accomplishments might have led others to call him,[27] it is evident from what follows, that he was also a personage of equestrian rank, a noble or a knight. He asked and obtained the duke's permission to strike the first blow,[28] but previously, he commenced in lofty strain the composition known as the Cantilena Rolandi, and which Wace describes as the song of "Karlemaine, and of Rollant, of Oliver, and the vassals who died in Renchevals."[29] He then began a series of exploits, which Gaimar graphically enumerates:—[30]

> "Un des Franceis donc se hasta,
> Devant les altres chevalcha.
> Taillefer ert cil apelez,
> Joglere estait, hardi asez.
> Armes aveit e bon e cheval:
> Si ert hardiz e noble vassal.
> Devant les altres cil se mist;
> Devant Engleis merveilles fist.
> Sa lance prist par le tuet,
> Com si co fust un bastunet:
> Encontrement; halt le geta,
> E par le fer recevé l'a.
> Trais fez issi geta sa lance;

[27] The Carmen styles him "Incisor ferri," "mimus," "histrio."

[28] Chron. Norm. Conq., p. 190.

[29] The song has not been recovered. It appears very probable that it was *improvised* for the occasion. Had it been a composition previously committed to writing, I think Gaimar and others would have given us at least the substance of it.

[30] Maister Geffrei Gaimar's History of the English is a very long Norman-French poem, which appears to have been written about the middle of the twelfth century: It has recently been edited by Thomas Wright, Esq., M.A., F.S.A.

La quarte feiz, mult pres s'avance,
Entre les Engleis la lanca,
Par mi le cors un en naffra.
Puis traist s'espee, arere vint
Geta s'espeé, k'il tint,
Encontremont, puis la receit.
L'un dit al altre, ki co veit,
Ke co estait enchantement
Ke cil fesait, devant la gent," &c.

Lines 5272, *et seq.*

Which Andrews renders—

" Forth from the French, with gallant haste,
The juggler Taillefer then pressed,
Armed and on a fiery horse,
And placed him 'fore the Norman force,
Where wonders in the English sight
He played with all a master's sleight;
First, to incite them to advance,
High in the air he hurled his lance,
And caught it by the point—and then
As nimbly threw it up again.
This daring feat he thrice did shew,
Then launched his weapon 'midst the foe,
A luckless wight of whom it struck,
So skilfully his aim he took;
Then drawing forth the sword he wore,
Thrice drew and caught it as before,
With an address so magical,
It seemed enchantment to them all."

Gaimar goes on to inform us that when Taillefer " had
three times thrown the sword, his horse rushed at the
English at full gallop, with his mouth wide open,
insomuch that some of them thought they should be
eaten up, *the horse gaped so;* the minstrel had taught
him the trick.[31] Taillefer next raising his sword

---

[31] The horse seems to have been worthy of his master. There is,
however, no reason for supposing that this 'bon cheval' actually bit
the English, as some modern writers appear to think he did.

strikes at an Englishman, whose hand flies off at the
blow :

> " Quant treis faiz out geté l'espee,
> Le cheval, od gule baiee,
> Vers les Engleis vint a esleisé ;
> Si i ad alquanz kí quident estre mangé,
> Pur le cheval ki issi baiout,
> Le jugleor apris li out.
> Del espee fiert un Engleis ;
> Le poing li fait voler maneis."

Thus began the battle of Hastings—"that battle
whereof," to employ the words of Wace, "the fame
is yet mighty ! Loud and far resounded the bray of
the horns, and the shocks of the lances, the mighty
strokes of clubs, and the quick clashing of swords."[32]
The Norman war-cry, " Dieu aide " was answered by
the Saxon-English " Out, out ! " " Holy Cross ! "
" God Almighty ! " [33] Taillefer was still conspicuous
in the mêlée. The first victim of his prowess was an
English standard-bearer ; then fell a second ; in the
third attempt, amidst a clashing of swords upon helmets
and a shower of Norman arrows, he himself fell. [34]

The close order in which Harold's army was drawn

---

[32] Chron. Norm. Conq., p. 191.

[33] Spelt by Wace, " Ut !" " Olicrosse !" " Godemitè !

> " Olicrosse est en engleis
> Ke Saint Croix est en franceis ;
> E Godemité altretant
> Com en frenceiz Dex tot poissant."

> " Normans escrient, Dex aie ;
> La gent englesche, Ut s'escrie."

[34] Henry of Huntingdon. His fate is not mentioned by other historians.

up is noticed by several of our authorities. The
Carmen says :—

> " Anglorum stat fixa solo densissima turba,
>   Tela dat et telis, et gladios gladiis ;"[35]

and Huntingdon compares it to a castle, impenetrable
to the Normans—"quasi castellum impenetrabile
Normannis." "Each side," says Wace, "defies the
other, yet neither knoweth what the other saith ; and
the Normans say that the English *bark* (as in more
modern times they tell us they whistle with ' la langue
des oiseaux,' and for the same reason)—because they
understand not their speech;" and thus the war of
bitter words and still bitterer wounds went on. For
some hours, apparently, little progress towards a de-
cision of the conflict was made. The men of Harold
stood well together, as their wont in battle was, and
woe to the hardy Norman who ventured to enter their
redoubts; for a single blow of a Saxon war-hatchet
would break his lance and cut through his coat of
mail.[36] What force therefore could not do was at
length effected by stratagem. To quote the words
of the monk of Battel : " By a preconcerted scheme
the duke feigned a retreat with his army, and Eustace,
the valiant count of Boulogne, nimbly following the
rear of the English who were scattered in the pursuit,
rushed upon them with his powerful troops." [37] It
was during this retreat and pursuit that there occurred an incident of a frightful character, which is particularly described by Wace. "In the plain," says
he, "was a fosse . . . The English charged and drove
the Normans before them, till they made them fall

[35] Carmen, v. 415, 416.
[36] Guill. Pictav., p. 201, quoted by Thierry.
[37] Chron. of Battel Abbey, p. 6.

back upon this fosse, overthrowing into it horses and men. Many were to be seen falling therein, rolling one over the other, with their faces to the earth, and unable to rise. Many of the English also, whom the Normans drew down along with them, died there. At no time in the day's battle did so many Normans die, as perished in that fosse. So those said who saw the dead."[38] The account given in the 'Chronicon de Bello' is similar. "There lay," says our monk, "between the hostile armies a certain dreadful precipice, caused either by a natural chasm of the earth or by some convulsion of the elements. It was of considerable extent, and being overgrown with bushes or brambles was not very easily seen; and great numbers of men—principally Normans in pursuit of the English—were suffocated in it. For, ignorant of the danger, as they were running in a disorderly manner, they fell into the chasm, and were fearfully dashed to pieces and slain. And the pit, from this deplorable accident," he adds, "is still called *Malfosse*."[39] According to William of Malmesbury the slaughter was so great, "that it made the hollow level with the plain with the heap of carcases." According to Ordericus Vitalis, Eugenulph or Engerran de Aquila, whose descendants afterwards gave to their barony of Pevensey the name of the "Honour of the Eagle," was

[38] Chron. Norm. Conq., p. 193.

[39] "Siquidem et inter hostiles gladios miserabile quoddam, in proximo spatiose protentum, ex naturali telluris hiatu vel forsan ex procellarum concavatione, præcipitium vaste patens, licet uti in vastitate dumis vel tribulis obsitum, oculis minus prævideretur, innumeros, et maxime Normannorum Anglos persequentium, suffocavit. Nam dum inscii cum impetu dissilirent ibidem in præceps acti flebiliter contriti necabantur. Quod quidem baratrum, sortito ex accidenti vocabulo, Malfosse hodieque nuncupatur."—Chron. de Bello, p. 5.

among the number of those who thus ingloriously fell.
The scene is graphically described in the Bayeux
Tapestry, and the accompanying legend is : HIC CECI-
DERUNT SIMUL ANGLI ET FRANCI IN PRELIO. Upon an
elevated bank some Saxon soldiers are shown hurling down darts upon the Normans as they struggle
and plunge in the fosse. This exactly agrees with
Malmesbury's statement—" By frequently making a
stand, they slaughtered their pursuers in heaps ; for,
getting possession of an eminence, they drove down
the Normans, when roused with indignation and
anxiously striving to gain the higher ground, into the
valley beneath, where, easily hurling their javelins and
rolling down stones on them as they stood below, they
destroyed them to a man." [40]

There is no place near Battel which can, with a due
regard to the proprieties of language, be called a
" dreadful precipice" (*miserabile præcipitium vaste
patens*), though, by comparing Malmesbury with the
monk of Battel, I think I have succeeded in identifying the locality of this " bad ditch." From all the
probabilities of the case it would seem that the flight
and pursuit must have lain in a north-westerly direction, through that part of the district now known as
Mountjoy. Assuming this, the eminence alluded to
by Malmesbury must have been the ridge rising from
Mount Street to Caldbeck Hill, and the *Malfosse*,
some part of the stream which, flowing at its foot,
runs in the direction of Watlington, and becomes a
tributary of the Rother. This rivulet still occasionally overflows its banks, and the primitive condition of
the adjacent levels was doubtless that of a morass, overgrown with flags, reeds, and similar bog vegetables.
Thanks, however, to good drainage, the " bad ditch "

[40] Edit. Giles, p. 277.

no longer remains. The name was corrupted, previously to 1279, to Manfosse, and a piece of land called Wincestrecroft, in Manfosse, was ceded to the abbey of Battel in that year. Now Wincestrecroft is still well known, and lies in the direction specified, west by north of the present town of Battel.[41]

To return to our narrative. A cry now ran through the Norman host that the duke had fallen in the disaster at Malfosse, and the varlets,[42] who had been set to guard the harness, seeing the sad loss of life in the fosse, began to quit their post and to fly from the impending danger. But William having been apprised of the report, and seeing numbers running away, hastened to stop them. Brandishing a spear with his right hand in a menacing manner, and at the same time removing his helmet with his left, he cried out,

[41] See more on this subject in the notes to my translation of the Chron. Monast. de Bello, pp. 6, 7, in which I was assisted by the exact local knowledge of Mr. Vidler, an old inhabitant of the parish, and author of a little work called 'Battel and its Abbey.' Since the preceding paragraphs were written, I have learned the existence of an opinion that this "deplorable accident" must have occurred "on the precipitous slope and dell behind Beauport, where Sir Charles Lambe, not long ago, found many bones in the lower swampy ground." But a diligent examination of the various accounts of the battle convinces me that the statement I have given is the correct one; and that William's pretended retreat could not have been to so great a distance from Harold's camp as Beauport, which is three miles from the spot. Besides, the name *Malfosse*, which was retained in 1176, and (in the slightly corrupted form of *Manfosse*) in 1279, is clearly identified with the accident, by its contiguity to Winchester-croft, a place well-known, and lying, as I have stated, west by north of the town. "Adam, son of Adam Picot, Deed of release to Reginald Abbot of Battel of nine acres of land and wood in *Manfosse*, called Wincestrecroft, in exchange for twelve acres of land and wood near the Birechette. Dated Battel, Eve of St. Michael, 1279. Seal fine and perfect."—*Thorpe's Cat. Battel Abbey Charters*, p. 50.

[42] The servants, attendants, grooms, or "gillies" of the Norman knights.

"Look! I am alive, and with God's help I will yet conquer." [43]   On this they returned to their charge. Bishop Odo at the same time galloped towards the varlets, and said to them: "Stand fast! stand fast! be quiet, and move not! Fear nothing; for, please God, we shall conquer yet!"[44]

> "Estez, estez,
> Seiez en paiz, ne vos movez;
> N'aiez poor de nule rien,
> Kar se Dex plaist, nos viencron bien!"

This scene is depicted in the Bayeux Tapestry, and the inscription accompanying it is: HIC ODO EPISCOPUS TENENS BACULUM CONFORTAT PUEROS : "Here Bishop Odo, holding his baton, exhorts or encourages the varlets."

Thus reanimated, these men stood to their post; while Odo (who throughout the battle showed himself —though not exactly in the clerical sense of the term —a good "episcopus") returned at a hand gallop to the barricades, holding aloft his mace, and urging on the knights, wherever he saw most need, to assault and strike the enemy.[45]

And so continued the main battle. "From nine in the morning, when the conflict began, till three o'clock came," says Wace, "the battle was up and down, this way and that, and no one knew who would conquer and win the land." In one of the fluctuations in favour of Harold, William's chances appeared so desperate, that even Eustace of Boulogne, who else-where conducted himself so courageously, seriously

---

[43] Orderic. Vit. ii, 148. This incident is also represented in the Tapestry.

[44] Chron. Norm. Conq., p. 194.

[45] Chron. Norm. Conq., p. 194.

3 §

advised him to escape from the field, since the battle
was lost beyond recovery.

" Morz est por veir, sens faille,
Sil ne se part de la bataille ;
Nul recovrer n'a mais ès suens."[46]

Harold's personal bravery throughout was unimpeachable. Not content with the functions of a
general in exhorting his followers, he was assiduous,
we are told, in every soldier-like duty; often would
he strike the enemy when coming to close quarters,
so that none came within his reach with impunity ;
for in an instant he brought down at one blow both
horse and rider.[47] On his part, William was equally
intrepid, everywhere ready to encourage his chevaliers
by his voice, his presence, and his example. " He
lost," says Malmesbury, " three choice horses[48] that
were pierced under him that day." Yet he does not
appear to have suffered the loss from his person of a
single drop of blood.

The discharge of archery, though incessant, took
but little effect: the wooden shields of the Saxons
were so many targets, which received, but were not
penetrated by, the Norman arrows. At length the
archers, at the suggestion, it is said, of William himself, shot into the air in such a manner that the arrows
should fall upon the faces of the enemy.[49] Many
were immediately blinded, and received frightful

[46] Benoit de Ste. Maure, L'estoire des Dux., in Chron. Ang. Norm.,
vol. i.

[47] W. of Malmesbury.

[48] Wace says but *two.*

[49] "Docuit etiam dux Willielmus viros sagittarios ut non in hostem
directe, sed in aëra sursum sagittas emitterent, cuneum hostilem
sagittis cæcarent: quod Anglis magno fuit detrimento."—Henry of
Huntingdon, in Mon. Hist. Brit. 763.

wounds in their faces. "Then it was," says Wace, "that an arrow that had been thus shot upwards, struck Harold above his right eye, and put it out. In his agony he drew the arrow, and threw it away, breaking it with his hands, and the pain to his head was so great that he leaned upon his shield. So the English," he adds, "were wont to say, and still say to the French, that the arrow was well shot, which was so sent up against their king; and that the archer won them great glory who thus put out Harold's eye."[50]

According to the Roman de Rou, the Normans now feigned a retreat: but I think it will be found that the incident is misplaced, and that it belongs to that earlier part of the day's proceedings which is connected with the disaster at Malfosse; we can hardly imagine that such a stratagem would be resorted to a second time. It would appear that the conflict sometimes degenerated into mere skirmishes and personal encounters; and the historians, particularly Wace, give us some very interesting episodes of this kind, which, from internal evidence, would seem to have been furnished to him by eye-witnesses. Some of these may be quoted:—

"The Normans were playing their part well, when an English knight came rushing up, having in his company a hundred men, furnished with various arms. He wielded a northern hatchet, with the blade a full foot long; and was well armed after his manner, being tall, bold, and of noble carriage. In the front of the battle, where the Normans thronged most, he came bounding on swifter than the stag, many Normans falling before him and his company. He rushed

---

[50] Chron. Norm. Conq., p. 198.

straight upon a Norman who was armed and riding on
a war-horse, and tried with his hatchet of steel to
cleave his helmet; but the blow miscarried, and the
sharp blade glanced down through the horse's neck
down to the ground, so that both horse and master
fell together to the earth. I know not whether the
Englishmen stuck another blow; but the Normans
who saw the stroke were astonished, and about to
abandon the assault, when Rogier de Montgomeri
came galloping up with his lance set, and heeding not
the long handled axe, which the Englishman wielded
aloft, struck him down, and left him stretched upon
the ground. Then Rogier cried out, ' Frenchmen,
strike! the day is ours!' And again a fierce mêlée
was to be seen with many a blow of lance and sword;
the English still defending themselves, killing the
horses and cleaving the shields.

"There was a French soldier of noble mien, who
sat his horse gallantly. He spied two Englishmen,
who were also carrying themselves boldly. They
were both men of great worth, and had become companions in arms and fought together, the one protect-
ing the other. They bore two long and broad bills,
and did great mischief to the Normans, killing both
horses and men. The French soldier looked at them
and their bills, and was sore alarmed, for he was
afraid of losing his good horse, the best he had; and
would willingly have turned to some other quarter,
if it would not have looked like cowardice. He soon,
however, recovered his courage, and spurring his horse
gave him the bridle and galloped swiftly forward.
Fearing the two bills, he raised his shield by the
' enarmes,' and struck one of the Englishmen with his
lance on the breast, so that the iron passed out at his
back. At the moment that he fell, the lance broke, and

the Frenchman seized the mace that hung at his right side, and struck the other Englishman a blow that completely fractured his skull."

" On the other side was an Englishman who much annoyed the French, continually assaulting them with a keen-edged hatchet. He had a helmet made of wood, which he fastened down to his coat, and laced round his neck, so that no blows could reach his head. The ravage he was making was seen by a gallant Norman knight, who rode a horse that neither fire nor water could stop in its course when its lord urged it on. The knight spurred, and his horse carried him on well till he charged the Englishman, striking him over the helmet, so that it fell down over his eyes; and as he stretched out his hand to raise it and uncover his face, the Norman cut off his right hand, so that his hatchet fell to the ground. Another Norman sprang forward, and eagerly seized the prize with both his hands, but he kept it little space, and paid dearly for it; for as he stooped to pick up the hatchet, an Englishman, with his long-handled axe, struck him over the back, breaking all his bones, so that his entrails and lungs gushed forth. The knight of the good horse meantime returned without injury; but on his way he met another Englishman, and bore him down under his horse, wounding him grievously, and trampling him altogether under foot."[51]

The fair hands that wrought the embroidered history of the Conquest have introduced several such encounters, without giving us the names of the cham-

---

[51] Chron. Norm. Conq., p. 209, *et seq.* The reader will understand that the citations from Wace in this essay are from the excellent translation, by Edgar Taylor, Esq., F.S.A., of so much of the *Roman* as relates to the Norman Conquest; except in the few instances where the original Norman-French is quoted.

pions concerned. They have also strewed not only
the main portion of the design, but its borders, with
the "scuta virûm, galeasque, et fortia corpora" of
the slain. In a spirit the opposite of that of most of
his brother chroniclers, the monk of Battel thus expatiates on the scene: "A fearful spectacle! The
fields were covered with dead bodies, and on every
hand nothing was to be seen but the red hue of blood.
The dales all around sent forth a gory stream, which
increased at a distance to the size of a river. . . . .
Oh! how vast a flood of human gore was poured out
in that place where these unfortunates fell and were
slain! What dashing to pieces of arms; what clashing of strokes; what shrieks of dying men; what
grief, what sighs, were heard! How many groans;
how many bitter notes of direst calamity then sounded
forth, who can rightly calculate? What a wretched
exhibition of human misery was there to call forth
astonishment! In the very contemplation of it our
pen fails us." [52]

The time when Harold received the arrow-wound
may be regarded as the moment from which the tide
of battle turned in favour of the Normans. His
patriotic warriors fought on still, but the struggle had
become with them one of fierce despair rather than of
courageous and confident hope. Now it was that
twenty of the Norman knights bound themselves to
each other by a solemn vow that they would 'break
the Saxon's ranks and bear off his standard, or perish
in the attempt. In this hazardous enterprise many
fell, but the rest, hacking a path with their swords,
made themselves masters of the prize. [53]   With this

[52] Chron. of Battel Abbey.

[53] Henr. Hunt. in Mon. Hist. Brit., p. 763.   "Signum regium,
quod vocatur Standard."

ensign of his regal authority fell Harold himself. "An armed man," says Wace, "came in the throng of the battle and struck him on the ventaille of the helmet, and beat him to the ground; and as he sought to recover himself, a knight beat him down again, striking him on the thick of the thigh, down to the bone."[54] The men who struck the fatal blows were never known, and probably they themselves fell in the desperate mêlée. The princes Girth and Leofwine were killed in the same fatal onset. This is shown by several authorities, although the Bayeux Tapestry places their death at a much earlier stage of the battle.

Respecting the precise spot where Harold and his standard fell, there is no doubt. William had vowed to build his monastery upon the site of the conflict, and that he built it upon the identical place where the crowning-point of his victory happened, is stated by several authorities, and the Chronicle of Battel Abbey, written upon the spot, furnishes conclusive proof of it. When William of Marmoutier and his brethren, some time after the battle, engaged in the work of rearing the abbey, not liking the place on account of its lack of water, they proceeded to build on a more eligible site on the western side of the hill, at a place called *Herst;* [55] but the Conqueror hearing of what they had done waxed wroth, "and commanded them with all haste to lay the foundation of the temple on the very place where he had achieved the victory over his enemy." The brethren suggested the inconvenience which would arise from the dryness of the site, when William gave utterance to the memorable promise that, if God would spare his life, he would so amply endow the establishment, that wine

[54] Chron. Norm. Conq., p. 252.
[55] I cannot identify this locality.

should be more abundant there than water in any
other great Abbey.   The chronicler goes on to inform
us that, "in accordance with the king's decrêe, they
wisely erected the high altar upon the precise spot
where the ensign of Harold, which they call the
Standard, was observed to fall."[56]

The place is still pointed out.   The noble Abbey-
Church had been destroyed at the Reformation, and
all traces of its parts and arrangements had been wellnigh obliterated; shrubs and parterres covered the
ground once drenched with the blood of patriots, and
long hallowed by the offices of religion; but the finger
of tradition faithfully pointed to a spot which art, and
nature, and time had combined to conceal.   Sir
Godfrey Webster, in the year 1817, anxious to test
the truth of the popular belief on the subject, caused
excavations to be made in the northern part of the
abbey grounds, and there, in the very place indicated,
discovered the most satisfactory evidence that could
be required.   Sunk below the general level of the
ground, and filled up with earth and rubbish, he dis-
closed what was originally the undercroft or subterra-

[56] "Igitur cum inter hæc regis animus sollicitus de fabricæ provectu
quæreret, ab isdem fratribus ei suggestum est quod locus ille ubi
ecclesiam fieri decreverat uti in colle situs, arenti gleba, siccus, et
aquarum foret indigus, atque ob hoc oportere tanto operi aptiorem
locum in proximo, si placitum haberetur, delegari.   Quod cum rex
percepisset, indignatus refugit, ociusque jussit in eodem loco quo
hoste prostrato sibi cesserat triumphus basilicæ fundamentum jacere.
Cumque obniti non præsumentes, aquarum penuria causarentur,
verbum ad hæc memoriale magnificus rex protulisse fertur: '*Ego*,'
inquit, '*si Deo annuente vita comes fuerit, eidem loco ita prospiciam
ut magis ei vini abundet copia, quam aquarum in alia præstanti
abbatia!*'"—Chronicon de Bello, p. 7.

"Secundum regis statutum altare majus in eodem loco quo regis
Haraldi signum, quod Standard vocant, corruisse visum est, provide
statuunt."—Ibid. p. 8.

neous chapel beneath the east end of the church, with the foundations of the massive columns by which the vaulting of its roof had been upheld, and two flights of steps which had led upwards to the north and south aisles of the church. In the easternmost recess of this crypt are considerable remains of an altar, and this must be regarded as the representative of the exact *locus in quo,* which hangs in the air a few feet above, where upon the floor of the choir once stood the high altar itself.

But to conclude the narrative of this eventful day. The fighting continued some time after Harold was known to have fallen, even when the sun had set upon the awful scene. Amidst the gloom of that October evening, either rampant with victory or mad with revenge, they still fought on—only distinguishing foes from friends by their language—until the thickening darkness and the exhaustion of their strength compelled them to desist. Never was discomfiture more complete, or triumph more decided. The majority of those Saxons who escaped from the field, made their way to London; but many others betook themselves to the neighbouring woods, some to bind up their wounds and bewail the sad issue of the day, others to lay themselves down and die.

> "Solum devictis nox et fuga profuit Anglis,
> Densi per latebras et tegimen nemoris."
> *Carmen,* 559–60.

The battle was over; the courageous Harold— more deserving of our pity for his misfortunes than of admiration for any kingly right or regal qualification that he possessed—was dead; a greater and wiser, if not a better, monarch had virtually, though not actually by holy chrism and solemn benediction ascended the throne. William had conquered and won the land! An old, and decayed, and corrupt dynasty had ceased to be; a greater and nobler people had come to improve and elevate our race; a battle was won—a conquest gained—for which we have infinite cause to be thankful.

"Then," says Master Wace, "William returned thanks to God, and in his pride ordered his gonfanon to be brought and set up on high, where the English standard had stood, and that was the signal of his having conquered." What follows is not a little revolting to those unaccustomed to the horrors of war: "He ordered his tent to be raised on the spot among the dead, *and had his meat brought thither, and his supper prepared there.*"[57] His barons pressed round him to offer their congratulations and to extol his deeds. Never had there been such a knight, they said, since Rollant and Oliver. "And the duke stood among them, of noble mien and stature, and rendered thanks to the Kĭng of glory, through whom he had the victory; and thanked the knights around him, mourning frequently for the dead. And he ate and drank among the dead, and made his bed that night upon the field."[58]

The sabbath morning that dawned upon the scene brought few of the calm, and bright, and holy concomitants, proper to the season. Nought was there to tell of "peace upon earth and goodwill to men;" but instead of it, the sad and sickening fruits of pride, ambition, and the primal curse. Even the iron-hearted Conqueror is said to have wept at the spectacle. Then calling to his presence a clerk who, previously to the departure of the armament from

[57] Chron. Norm. Conq., p. 256.
[58] Ibid. p. 258.

St. Valery, had written down the names of the chief men of the army, he caused him to read the roll, to ascertain who had fallen and who had survived;[59] and Bishop Odo, truer now to his sacred functions, " sang mass for the souls that were departed." The document alluded to, if preserved, was the true Roll of Battel Abbey, but it has not come down to our times, and the various lists which we possess are of subsequent date, and more or less apocryphal in their character.[60]

William's next duty, before setting out for his castellum at Hastings, was to see to the interment of the dead. If we may trust the author of the Carmen, he was in this matter guilty of a great and inexcusable breach of humanity, of which even his enemies do not accuse him. " He traversed the field, and selecting the dead bodies of his friends, buried them in the bowels of the earth ;[61] but left the corses of the English strewed upon the ground to be devoured by worms, and *wolves*, and birds, and dogs."

> " Lustravit campum, tollens et cæsa suorum
> Corpora dux, terræ condidit in gremio ;
> Vermibus atque lupis, avibus canibusque voranda,
> Deserit Anglorum corpora strata solo."
> V. 569–572.

Ordericus, however, says that William gave the

[59] Chron. de Normandie, quoted by Thierry. John Foxe, Act. and Mon.

[60] See a paper by the Rev. Joseph Hunter, F.S.A., on this interesting subject, in Suss. Arch. Coll. vol. vi.

[61] During the recent excavations for the railway from Hastings to Tunbridge Wells, which passes within a few hundred yards eastward of Battel Abbey, it was rather confidently expected that some traces of the battle, such as arms or human bones, would be brought to light ; but this expectation was not realized, and this proves, I think, the correctness of my opinion, that the battle and the retreat took place in the opposite, or westerly and north-westerly direction.

Saxons permission to bury their dead.[62]   And Wace
informs us that the noble ladies of the land came also,
some to seek their husbands, and others their fathers,
sons, or brothers. They bore the bodies to the villages,
and interred them at the churches ; and the clerks
and priests of the country were ready, and, at the
request of their friends, took the bodies that were
found, and prepared graves and laid them therein.[63]
The body of Harold was found frightfully gashed with
wounds and not easily to be identified among the mass
of his followers.   The story of his mistress, Edith
Swanhals, having been called in for this purpose,
rests upon slender authority, and appears quite improbable.   According to the Carmen, the duke had the
lacerated corse wrapped in purple linen, and carried
to his marine camp[64] at Hastings.

> Heraldi corpus collegit dilaceratum,
> Collectum texit sindone purpurea,
> Detulit et secum repetens sua castra marina.
>
> Vv. 573-4-5.

There by his command it was buried upon the cliff,
beneath a stone insolently inscribed with the words :
" By the orders of the Duke, you rest here, King
Harold, as the guardian of the shore and the sea."

> " PER MANDATA DUCIS, REX HIC HERALDE, QUIESCIS,
> UT CUSTOS MANEAS LITORIS ET PELAGI." [64]

Pictavensis also says, that he was buried by the sea-
shore, and Ordericus agrees with the Carmen in
asserting that the duke peremptorily denied the
request of the Countess Ghitha for the remains of

[62] Ord. Vit. ii, 153.
[63] Chron. Norm. Conq. p. 258.
[64] Vv. 591, 592.

her son. " I have lost," was the sorrowing mother's
plea, " three of my sons in this war; will you deny
a bereaved widow's heart the consolation of possessing
the bones of *one* of them ? Give me but those beloved
remains, and I will pay you for them weight by weight
in pure gold."[65] The duke, with characteristic stern-
ness, replied, that he despised such traffic as that, and
that he considered it unjust that one should receive
burial at the hands of a mother, whose cupidity had
caused so many mothers' sons to lie unburied.[66]
William of Malmesbury, however, tells the story in a
manner more creditable to William's humanity. " He
sent the body of Harold to his mother, who begged
it, unransomed, though she proffered large sums by
her messengers. She buried it at Waltham, a church
which he had built at his own expense in honour of
the Holy Cross." It is added by some minor authorities that Ghitha's request was seconded by two
monks, Osgod and Ailric, who had been despatched
by the abbot of Waltham for that purpose. The
popular belief, encouraged for their own purposes by
the fraternity at Waltham, was, that Harold had
found honourable sepulture among them; though it
may deserve a place among historic doubts whether
his real grave is not upon the cliffs of the Sussex
shore.

[65] Carmen, v. 577, &c.

> " Heraldi mater, nimio constricta dolore,
>   Misit adusque Ducem, postulat et precibus,
>   Orbatæ miseræ natis tribus et viduatæ,
>   Pro tribus unius reddat ut ossa sibi;
>   Si placet, aut corpus puro præponderet auro.
>   Sed Dux iratus prorsus utrumque negat."

[66] Ordericus Vit. iii, 152.

The number of the slain is variously stated. The *Carmen*, with admirable latitude of expression, says, that William killed "two thousands, besides innumerable other thousands!" Ordericus tells us, from the information of eye-witnesses, that the Normans lost 15,000 men. "How great think you," asks the monk of Battle, "must have been the slaughter of the conquered, when that of the conquerors is reported, upon the lowest computation, to have exceeded ten thousand?" All things considered, we should probably not greatly err in fixing 30,000 as the number who perished on this memorable field.

I have extended these remarks far beyond my original intention, though I trust that the nature of the subject and its historical and local importance will form a sufficient justification for the length of my essay—which I will now conclude with a few remarks upon the localities which history and tradition have identified with the battle.

1. I have shown the Hetheland of the Battel Chronicle and Telham Hill to be one and the same spot. Tradition says as much, but corrupts the name to *Tellman* Hill, because there the conqueror *counted* his troops!

2. There has been much conjecture as to the original name of the place now called Battel. It has been stated to be *Epiton, Sothope, Senlac, St. Mary, Heathfield*, &c. I believe that no town or even village existed here in Saxon times. It was probably a down covered with heath and furze—a wild, rough common, without houses and almost without trees. The Saxon chronicler had no better mode of indicating the locality of

the hostile meeting than by saying that it occurred
AT THE HOARY APPLE TREE (*æt thære háran apuldran*)[67]
—probably from some venerable tree of that species
growing near at hand.[68]

3. The portion of the town of Battel which lies
eastward of the church is called the Lake, and sometimes *Sanguelac*, i. e. the "lake of blood." Tradition
says, that the Conqueror gave the place this name
because of the vast sea of gore there spilt; and the
Battel chronicler's account of the conflict would
almost warrant the name.[69] Even but a few years
since, the springs of chalybeate water hereabouts—
the sources of the little river Asten—were believed to
have received their redness from the blood of the
slaughtered Saxons. Drayton, with his usual grace,
embodies the beautiful idea in his Polyolbion :

> "Asten once distained with native English blood ;
> Whose soil yet, when but wet with any little rain,
> *Doth blush*, as put in mind of those there sadly slain."

Most unfortunately, however, for tradition and poetry,
the true original name of the spot referred to was not

[67] Sax. Chron. in Mon. Hist. Brit. But the phrase has been translated in a totally different sense.

[68] In Saxon and early Norman times it was very usual to mark
places by some particular tree. See the Codex Dipl. Sax. Æv.
passim. An instance may be cited in this immediate neighbourhood. According to the 'Battel Chronicle,' when William Faber
commenced the founding of the Abbey, he began to build (as
already stated) on a site to the westward of the spot where the battle
had taken place, and where the abbey was eventually erected. "The
place is to this day called Herst ; *and a certain thorn-tree growing
there is a memorial of this circumstance*," p. 10. The *hoar apple-tree*
was a common land-mark in the Saxon period. Mr. Hamper, in his
elaborate paper on Hoar-stones, in Archæologia, vol. xxv, cites no
fewer than fourteen instances in different counties.

[69] Vide, p. 62, *supra*.

Sanguelac, but Santlache, and it is so spelt in all the earlier monastic documents.

4. One of the boroughs or subdivisions of the hundred of Battel is called *Mountjoy*. Now Boyer defines *Mont-joie* as " a heap of stones made by an army as a monument of victory," and this may be the origin of the name. In this district, and on the line by which the Saxons must have retreated, is another spot, known as *Call-back-hill;* and this, tradition—ever fond of playing with words—has made the place where the duke " called back" his pursuing troops. Here again legendary history must yield to etymological criticism, for the true name is *Cald-bec*, i.e., " the cold spring;" and such a spring is yet seen bursting from a cavernous recess on the spot.

5. To the westward of the town of Battel, on the London road, is a large tree, called the *Watch-Oak*, which is supposed to have derived its epithet from some watch set either the night before or the night after the battle ; but the tradition is very vague. One other place may be noticed : this is *Standard-hill*, in the adjacent parish of Ninfield, where somebody's standard, William's or Harold's, was set up. So says tradition ; but there seems nothing to support such a notion. Harold's standard was first pitched at Battel, and there it remained until it was supplanted by the oriflamme of the Conqueror; and there, as we have already seen, subsequently arose that majestic edifice " the Abbey of the Battle"—an expiatory offering for the slaughter which had taken place.

> " KING WILLIAM bithought hym alsoe of that
> Folke that was forlorne,
> And slayn also thoruz hym
> In the bataile biforne.

And ther as the bataile was
   An Abbey he lete rere
Of Seint Martin fo the soules
   That ther slayen were
And the monkes wel ynoug
   Feffèd without fayle,
That is callèd in Englonde
   Abbey of Bataile."

So sings Robert of Gloucester; but upon the history of this celebrated monastery, which in after-times its monks delighted to style *the token and pledge of the royal crown,* I cannot now enter, although that history is by no means either an unimportant or an uninstructive one.

4

THE LORD DACRE—HIS MOURNFUL END.

A TRUE HISTORY.

The Argument.

" THERE was executed at Saint Thomas Waterings three gentlemen
—John Mantel, John Frowde, and George Roidon. They died for a
murther committed in Sussex in companie of Thomas Fines, Lord
Dacre of the South : the truth whereof was thus. The said Lord
Dacre, through the lewd persuasion of some of them, as hath beene
reported, meaning to hunt in the parke of Nicholas Pelham, esquire,
of Laughton, in the same countie of Sussex, being accompanied with
the said Mantel, Frowde, and Roidon, John Cheinie and Thomas
Isleie, gentlemen, Richard Middleton and John Goldwell, yeomen,
passed from his house of Hurstmonceux the last of Aprill, in the
night season, toward the same parke, where they intended so to hunt ;
and coming unto a place called Pikehaie in the parish of Hellingleigh,
they found one John Busbrig, James Busbrig, and Richard Sumner
standing togither ; and as it fell out, through quarelling, there in-
sued a fraie betwixt the said Lord Dacre and his companie on the
one partie, and the said John and James Busbrig and Richard
Sumner on the other, insomuch that the said John Busbrig received
such hurt that he died thereof the second of Maie next insuing.
Whereupon as well the said Lord Dacre as those that were with him,
and diverse other likewise that were appointed to go another waie to
meet them at the said parke, were indicted of murther ; and the seaven
and twentith of June the Lord Dacre himselfe was arreigned before the
Lord Audleie of Walden, then Lord Chancellor, sitting that daie as
high steward of England, with other peeres of the realme about him,
who then and there condemned the said Lord Dacre to die for that
transgression. And afterward, the nine and twentith of June, being
Saint Peter's daie, at eleven of the clocke in the forenoone, the shirriffs
of London accordinglie as they were appointed, were readie at the
Tower to have received the said prisoner, and him to have led to
execution on the Tower Hill ; but as the prisoner should come forth
of the Tower, one Heire, a gentleman of the Lord Chancellor's house,
came, and in the king's name commanded to staie the execution till

two of the clocke in the afternoone, which caused manie to thinke
that the king would have granted his pardon. But neverthelesse, at
three of the clocke in the same afternoone, he was brought forth of
the Tower and delivered to the shirriffs, who led him on foot betwixt
them unto Tiburne, where he died. His bodi was buried in the
church of Saint Sepulchers.

"He was not past foure and twentie yeeres of age when he came
through this great mishap to his end, for whome manie sore lamented,
and likewise for the other three gentlemen, Mantel, Frowde, and
Roidon. But for the said yoong lord being a right towardlie gentleman, and such a one as manie had conceived great hope of better
proofe, no small mone and lamentation was made ; the more indeed
for that it was thought he was induced to attempt such follie, which
occasioned his death, by some light heads that were then about him."
—*Holinshed's Chronicle.*

"His great estate, which the greedy courtiers gaped after, caused
them to hasten his destruction."—*Camden.*

"It is said that the murder could not have been charged upon
him if he had pleaded Not guilty, for he was not in the fray ; but
some courtiers, who gaped after his estate, persuaded him to plead
Guilty, and submit himself to the king's mercy, which they took care
he should not have—and so he lost his life, honour, and estate at
once."—*Magna Britannia.*

The practice of deer-stealing, which prevailed in the early and
middle parts of the sixteenth century, seems to have been regarded
by the criminals themselves more in the light of a frolic than as a
serious offence. They looked upon deer as *feræ naturæ,* and therefore as common property, much as the vulgar poacher views hares
and pheasants in our own days. The story of Shakspeare's deer-
stealing in Sir Thomas Lucy's park, be it true or false, shows that
the offence was not in his youthful days an uncommon one. Stowe,
in his 'Annals,' under the year 1526, says, "In the month of May
was proclamation made against all unlawful games . . . : in all
places, tables, dice, cards, and bowls were taken and brent ; and
when young men were restrained of these games and pastimes, some
fell to drinking, some to ferretting of other men's conies, and *stealing
of deer* in parkes, and other unthriftness."

A few more words of explanation are necessary. The scene of the
tragedy was not Laughton Place, the *seat* of Sir Nicholas Pelham,
but Hellingly, where he possessed a deer-park, and where some of
his descendants subsequently resided. The spot is situated within
four miles of Herstmonceux, the ruined but still magnificent seat of
the Lords Dacre. Pikehay, the exact spot where Busbrig fell, is a
field near Hellingly Church, and still bears the same name. A friend

who knew the place more than half a century ago, tells me that it had the evil reputation of being haunted by a ghost.

It is but fair to the memory of Sir Nicholas Pelham to remark that he was anything but the churlish person that poor Lord Dacre's bad advisers are made to represent him. In fact he was a man of generous and patriotic spirit, and a gallant defender of his native shores against the French. In the year 1545 he succeeded in repulsing from the Sussex coast a hostile armament which had been prepared for its annoyance. He lies buried at St. Michael's, in Lewes, and his epitaph informs posterity that

> "What time the French sought to have sackt Seafoord,
> This *Pel*ham did *repel* 'em back aboord."

I have only further to add that *Amberstone* is the name given to an ancient boundary-stone near Hellingly Park. As '*Amber*' is a word often found connected with Druidical remains, it is assumed that the stone referred to in the ballad may have been held sacred by our Celtic ancestors.[1]

I.

As late I journeyed—on my way,
  Hard by the Druids' Amber-stone,
An ancient man, with locks of grey,
  Sat silent weeping all alone.

' Why run the tears adown thy face ?
  What art thou, aged man ?' I said.
  ' Thy tottering limbs and hoary head
Should have some meeter resting-place.'

Then slowly rose that ancient man,
  And, with his sleeve of homely frieze,
  When nature's flood had brought him ease,
Brush'd off his tears and thus began :—

---

[1] Much valuable information respecting 'Herstmonceux Castle and its Lords' will be found in a recent publication by my friend, the Rev. Edm. Venables, M.A.

' Thou art a stranger, Sir, I trow,
   To all this saddened country side,
   Or news, that goes so far and wide,
Of our good Lord thou sure must know.

' The good Lord Dacre dies this morn
   (God rest his soul !) at Tyburn's tree.
   Alas that I should live to see
His fair young head exposed to scorn !

' Tis scantly two short months ago,
   That noble Dacre of the South
   (Ne'er Heaven saw a fairer youth)
Made gallant sport at Hérstmonceux.

' To celebrate his infant's birth,
   Brave hospitality was then
   Shewn ladies, knights, and gentlemen ;
The castle rang with noise of mirth.

' Then thither came from west and east,
   With many a guest of high degree,
   Squires, yeomen, husbandmen to see,
And glad them at that joyful feast.

' Cheney of ancient line was there,
   Roydon, and Froude, and Mantel free,
   Isley and all of this countrie,
To honour young Lord Dacre's heir.

‘ And feats of chivalry were done,
　　At tilt and eke at high tournay,
　　And balls and masks and pageants gay,
Such as in kingly courts are known.

‘ For three long days Herstmónceux's towers
　　Reëchoed far the minstrel's strain ;
　　And park and forest rang again
From morning's dawn till midnight hours.

‘ 'Twas the third night when all were glad,
　　'Midst song, and quip, and merrie cheer,
　　(As thou, alas ! too soon must hear)
These joys a mournful ending had.

‘ The guests were gathered in the hall,
　　My lord and lady on the dais,
　　And seated in their proper place,
Were friends and neighbours great and small.

‘ “ My friends, I pledge you from my heart,
　　In loving-cup of Malmsey bright ;
　　Let us be merrie all, this night,
Since 'tis to-morrow we must part.

‘ “ I thank you for the honour done
　　By your most gentle courtesie,
　　In coming hither thus to me ;
Of neighbours I miss only one.

' " Pelham hath not vouchsafed to fill
    A station at our Christening feast ;
    He might have given, at the least,
Some token of a friend's good-will."

' " Well said !" quoth many a hearty friend ;
    " My Lord, we give you health and joy !
    God bless, fair ladye, your sweet boy !
And let not Pelham you offend."

' " He 's but a churl !" Froude muttered low ;
    Wine-heated Roydon spake outright :—
    " We 'll be revenged on him this night,
We 'll teach him courtesy ere we go.

' " He hath good bucks within his park,
    The night is fair, the moon is clear ;
    There 's nought like hunting fallow-deer,
Whether by daylight or by dark."

' In evil moment Dacre lent
    To this bad counsel willing mind ;
    He vowed he 'd not be left behind,
And for his deer-hounds straightway sent.'

The old man ceased—his quivering tongue
    Refused its office, and, at last,
    (Relief of anguish) tears fell fast,
And on his beard like dewdrops hung.

II.

'High sailed the moon the crisp air through
   Above the old Hern-wood;[2]
The trees o' the chesnut avenue
   Like gaunt retainers stood.

'As o'er the drawbridge took their way
   That too light-hearted crowd,
Lord Dacre, Mantel, Isley gay,
   Mad Roydon, wanton Froude.

'And high-born Cheney leading on
   Of yeomen half a score,
With crossbow, pike-staff, spear, and gun;
   While buck-hounds ran before.

'"Now heigh for Pelham's fattest deer,
   My merrie men with speed!
All for their owner's surly cheere
   Their flanks this night shall bleed!"

'Softly along Marsh-lane they stretch,
   And Magham Downe pass by,
And presently a compass fetch
   To th' park of Hellinglighe.

'Into two bands they now divide,
   The better sport to find;
One ranges o'er the park so wide,
   Lord Dacre's stays behind.

---

[2] The ancient heronry still exists in Herstmonceux Park, as well as the lichen-clad trunks of the chesnut avenue, coeval with the castle itself.

' Roydon and Froude urge on the hounds
   Mid covert, bush, and brake;
Lord Dacre stands without the bounds,
   The flying game to take.

' Two hours these wild youths hunted so,
   Then rounded to Pikehay,
With yeomen and with dogs, when, lo,
   There happed a fereful fray.

' For Pelham's parker heard the rout,
   (John Busbrig, yeoman good,)
And straightway fetched his keepers out,
   And Roydon's band withstood.

' Foul words and biting taunts ensue,
   And wounds on either side,
Till, with a flood of crimson hue,
   Pikehay's fair lea is dyed.

' The young Lord Dacre, far away
   The noise and tumult heard,
And rushed to where John Busbrig lay,
   Stretched out by Roydon's sword.

' "Enough! we all this night shall rue,
   By heaven!" Lord Dacre said.
They gat them back to Herstmonceux;
   The parker soon was dead.'

4 §

Once more his grief forbade to speak ;
   Groaned deep that ancient man ;
And coursing o'er his pallid cheek,
   (Like torrents down some mountain bleak,)
      The tears of anguish ran.

III.

'Five days are past, a tempest lowers ;
   The lightnings fly ; the maddened breeze
   Great waving arms of ancient trees
Dashes against Herstmónceux's towers.

'Torrents assail its moated walls ;
   Each turret fair and chimney-stack
   With rattling thunder seems to crack,
And bode destruction to its halls.

'Meet emblem of the storm that tears
   The young Lord Dacre's aching breast,
   A stranger both to peace and rest,
Since Busbrig's moans assailed his ears.

' 'Twas sad to mark within the hall,
   Erewhile so gay, so changéd now,
   A heavy cloud o'ercast the brow
Of fond retainers great and small.

'And sadder far—most sad of all—
   To see that beauteous ladye mild
   All grief-struck (great Bergany's child [3])
For dread what should her Lord befal.

[3] The lady of the unfortunate Lord Dacre was a daughter of the Earl of Abergavenny, or Bergany.

' But now the faithful warder hears
  Sounds that proceed not from the storm,
  And flashes, not of lightning's form,
Sees glittering from a hundred spears.

' What this should mean, his heart misdoubts;
  No errand, sure, of love and peace
  Brings men abroad on days like this
All armed—and then, " A Foe !" he shouts.

' High mounts the drawbridge—with a clank
  Descends the barred portcullis strong,
  That startles all the sheriff's throng
In order ranged upon the bank.

' A moment more—a bitter cry
  In Baron's hall and Ladye's bower,
  That, echoing wildly from each tower,
More than the thunder rends the sky.

' Out spake the shrieve—" An entrance free,
  In th' king's high name I charge you all,
  Or you shall answer, great and small,
Scorn of his crown and dignitie."

' All needless this—for, at a sign
  From Dacre given, the bridge descends;
  " Forbear !" he cries, " my trusty friends,
Resist them not—Heaven's will be mine !"

' They entered—but no tongue hath power
    To tell the grief !   That Ladye fair
    With shrieks right awsome pıerced the air ;
    And all his faithful followers hung
    About their Lord, so fair, so young—
Who by the shrieve that selfsame hour
Was borne away to London's Tower.

' Some secret foȩs, who seek his lands,
    Have counselled him to own the guilt
    Of blood that was by others spilt,
And yield him to king Henry's hands.
But mercy dwells not near *his* throne ;
    The vengeance of his blood-stained sword,
    This morning have my much-loved lord,
And Mantel, Froude, and Roydon known.

' Have pity on an old man's moan,
    Now blessed Jesu, Saviour mild,
And let him quick to rest begone !—
And wote thou, courteous stranger, well,
Why with such grief this tale I tell ;
    Lord Dacre was my foster-child ;
    John Busbrig was MY ELDEST SON !'

No more he wept : when all was spoken,
    The torrent of his tears was dried ;
    The hoary Druid-stone beside,
    He gently laid him down and died,
His prayer was heard—his heart was broken !

HISTORICAL AND ARCHÆOLOGICAL MEMOIR

ON THE

IRON-WORKS

OF THE SOUTH-EAST OF ENGLAND.

(PARTICULARLY OF SUSSEX).

BEFORE entering on the history of this manufacture, now extinct in this part of England, it may be as well to premise that the strata which produced the iron ore lie in the central portion of the Wealden formation, in the vast beds of sandstone constituting what is provincially called the Forest Ridge, and known among geologists as the Hastings Sand. These beds extend from Hastings, inland, in a direction nearly west, and form a ridge of elevated land, the course of which will be easily indicated by naming Ashburnham, Heathfield, Crowborough, Ashdown Forest, Worth, Tilgate Forest, and St. Leonard's Forest, as prominent points, the loftiest being Crowborough, which attains an elevation of 804 feet above the level of the ocean. This formation, which stretches on one hand to within a few miles of the chalk ridge known as the South Downs, and, on the other, to within a similar distance of the chalk hills of Kent and Surrey, was, in the earliest periods of historical record, one vast forest, designated Coit Andred, Andred's-Wald, or the Forest of Anderida. In the still more remote periods, the investigation of which belongs to geological science, it was first overflowed by the waters of an immense river, then submerged by those of a profound ocean, and, lastly, elevated by successive deposits to its existing form. It was in the first of these periods that the ferruginous matter, which was afterwards to become so useful for the purposes of mankind, had its origin. In a private letter with which I was favoured by my friend, the late Dr. Mantell, that distinguished geologist, remarks:

"It is a very interesting fact that all our principal iron-works obtained their metal from the ferruginous clays and sands of the Wealden; in other words, *from iron produced by vegetable and animal decomposition* in the bed and delta of a mighty river, which flowed through countries inhabited by the Iguanodon and other colossal reptiles." [1]

Another able geologist, P. J. Martin, Esq., whose opinion will also be received with great respect, observes:

"It appears to me that the ore in the Forest Ridge was the clay iron-stone of the 'Wealden beds.' At the western extremity of the district it is thought that the ferruginous sands of the 'Lower Greensand' were used; but in the clay country of the Weald I have found sufficient evidence of the exclusive use of a comparatively recent concretion—a kind of 'bog-iron,' frequently turned up by the plough, and called *iron rag*. It is composed of clay, gravel, and perhaps about 25 or 30 per cent. of oxide of iron, and is a

---

[1] Dr. Mantell adds: "The great coal-field of Hanover is in the Wealden formation. What a pity that the forests of the Iguanodon country which furnished the materials of those carboniferous strata drifted so far north! Had it not been so, we should have had abundance of coal in our Wealds, and Sussex might have furnished rivals to Manchester and Birmingham."

superficial and fragmentary formation—a recent 'pudding-stone.'"

To all who are acquainted with Sussex history, there is no fact more familiar than the former existence, to a great extent, of the manufacture of iron within its limits. Of the history of the trade, however, little has hitherto been known, or, if known, certainly never presented to public notice. Its origin was still further shrouded in mystery, and whether it should be assigned to the fifth, the tenth, or the fifteenth century was a matter of total uncertainty; and so it might have remained for years to come, but for the archæological acumen of the Rector of Maresfield. To the Rev. Edward Turner we are indebted for the discovery of the highly interesting fact, that it dates as far back as the period of the Roman dominion in Britain.

A most agreeable and important illustration of the now familiar truth that archæology is the best handmaid of history is furnished by Mr. Turner's researches. The maid, indeed, has in this case, been more trustworthy than her mistress; for History has transmitted us no record to show that the Romans were acquainted with the ferruginous riches of the wealds, and it was left for the inductions of Archæology to supply the omission. In the year 1844 Mr. Turner observed, upon a heap of *cinders*,[2] laid ready for use by the side of the London road, a small fragment of

---

[2] The *scoriæ* of the disused furnaces are called *cinders*, and are much employed for the repair of turnpike and other roads. That they have long borne this somewhat improper name appears not only from documents of ancient date, but from the designations of many localities in the iron district, as Cinderford, Cinderhill, Cindersgill, &c.

pottery, which on examination proved to be Roman. His curiosity having being excited by so unusual a circumstance, Mr. Turner ascertained, on inquiry, that the cinders had been dug upon Old Land Farm, in his own parish of Maresfield, and immediately contiguous to Buxted. He at once visited the spot, and found that the workmen engaged in the digging were exposing to view the undoubted remains of a Roman settlement.

The place in question is the site of one of the innumerable fields of iron scoriæ marking the localities of the extinct furnaces and forges of the Weald. The bed was originally of great extent, no less than six or seven acres of it (varying in depth from two to ten feet) having been already removed for the useful purpose referred to in the note. A few days previously to Mr. Turner's visit, the labourers had opened, in the middle of this field, a kind of grave, about twelve feet in depth, at the bottom of which lay a considerable quantity of broken Roman pottery, evidently the remains of a regular funeral deposit. The superincumbent stratification was as follows: the ground had been excavated, first, through about one foot of earth, then through a layer of cinders, two feet in thickness, and, lastly, through about eight or nine feet of earth. The cavity had been filled up entirely with cinders.

The digging had been carried on many months previously to Mr. Turner's investigations. About two years before, the foundations of a building, measuring according to the statement of the workmen about 30 feet by 12 were uncovered. They were very rudely constructed of stone, and lay about six feet beneath the surface. A human skeleton, in a very perfect state, was discovered at the same time, but it crumbled to dust on exposure to the air.

Mr. Barratt, the surveyor, by whom the workmen are employed, informs me that he has seen several skeletons exhumed from the cinder-bed, in which the bodies had been interred as in ordinary soil. If these were Roman interments—which can scarcely be questioned—we are led to suppose that they were made long subsequently to the original deposit of scoriæ, since a *recently-formed* cinder-bed would have been a very unlikely spot to be selected for the burial of the dead. The fair inference from these considerations is, that the iron-works at this place were carried on by the Romans during a long series of years.

So extremely numerous are the remains of Roman pottery on the spot, that scarcely a barrow-load of cinders is driven out that does not contain several fragments of it. Hardly any of the vessels have been found entire,—a circumstance not to be wondered at, when we consider their fragile nature and the great weight of the superincumbent cinders.

At the Sussex Archæological Society's annual meeting, held at Lewes in August 1848, I had the pleasure of exhibiting a collection of the various articles discovered during the progress of the digging; it is hardly necessary to add that many others had been overlooked, while many more had been thrown away as useless by the labourers, or sold for a trifle to casual passers-by, previously to the examination of the spot by competent observers. The objects most worthy of attention which have been rescued from destruction are—

1. Coins, in second brass, of Nero, Vespasian, and Tetricus, and a fragment, much oxidized, of one of Dioclesian. Some have undergone the action of fire,

and cannot be identified. The Vespasian is of the most common occurrence.[3]

2. A brass fibula. Portions of other fibulæ, and of armillæ, were noticed by Mr. Turner.

3. Fragments of coarse fictile vessels, principally domestic. The pottery of this kind is in great quantities, and of great variety as regards shape, colour, and fineness. Several fragments of the vessels known as *mortaria* have the potters' names boldly stamped upon them, particularly IVCVN (for Jucundus?) and EVAI.

4. Fragments of fine red or Samian ware, both figured and plain. Several of these likewise bear potters' marks or stamps, particularly OF. (officinâ) MIRAVI, and IVAN or IVANI.

Fig. 1.

Fig. 1 is a beautiful shallow cup, 3¾ inches in dia-

[3] The coins which I have inspected are as follows:

Nero (A.D. 54-68), two.

Vespasian (69-79), about eight or ten.

Tetricus (circ. 274), one.

Dioclesian (284-286), one or two.

Of those which cannot be appropriated, some may belong to the intervening emperors. Until recently, the labourers have regarded these valuable relics as "old halfpence;" and, according to their own unsophisticated statement, "*chucked*" them away, "*because the letters on 'em was pretty near rubbed out !*"

meter, and adorned upon the rim with the peculiar ornament of such frequent occurrence on Roman ware, and generally believed to represent the ivy-leaf.

Figures 2 and 3 are also fragments of Samian. The man on Fig. 3 appears to be in the act of throwing the *discus*, a well-known Roman game.

Fig. 2.   Fig. 3.

I have caused these objects to be engraved, less from the idea that they exhibit any peculiarity, than for the purpose of proving that their workmanship is unquestionably Roman.

5. Fragments of glass.

6. Pieces of sheet-lead full of nail-holes, some of which had fragments of wood adhering to them. Much broken brick was also found.

7. An implement of mixed metal, very hard; probably a *stylus*.

Length, $5\frac{1}{4}$ inches.

In the absence of further evidence, I am unwilling to speculate largely upon the date of the commencement of these iron-works; but from the preponderance of the coins of Vespasian, we may hazard a conjecture that it took place during the reign of that emperor, or his successor, Titus, at a time when Agricola, then governor of Britain, was successfully introducing the arts of civilization into this island. That the works were still carried forward in Dioclesian's time is clear, from the coin of that monarch.

It is worthy of remark, that the Romans would appear, so far at least as the evidence of the discovery under notice goes, to have been but imperfectly acquainted with the art of smelting ores.[4] The scoriæ at Maresfield retain a far greater proportion of the metal than the cinders of other beds in the neighbourhood, and are, on that account, much more valuable for the purpose of road-making.

Since the discoveries at Maresfield, I have been furnished with further proofs of the fact that the Romans availed themselves of the iron of Sussex. From the information of Robert Mercer, Esq., of Sedlescombe, it appears that many Roman coins have been found in a cinder-bed in that parish, on the land of Richard Smith, Esq. They have generally been greatly corroded, and some have evidently been burnt, as at Maresfield. All knowledge of the fact that iron-works had ever existed on the spot was lost until the discovery of the cinder-bed. Roman coins have also been met with upon the site of iron-works on the property of Hercules Sharpe, Esq., at Westfield, in

[4] The greatest iron-works carried on by the Romans in this country were in Gloucestershire. So extensive were these works, and so imperfect the smelting, that in the sixteenth and following centuries the iron-masters, instead of digging for ore, resorted to the beds of scoriæ for their principal supply of the metal.—*Encycl. Britan. in voc. " Iron."*

the same neighbourhood. I am also assured that fragments of pottery, apparently Roman, were found, some years since, in a cinder-bed in the parish of Chiddingly.

In October, 1853, a first-brass coin of Faustina was found in a cinder-bank at Poundsley, in the parish of Framfield.

It is not improbable that the iron of Sussex was wrought in times even anterior to the conquest of this island by the Romans. Previously to the advent of Cæsar, the inhabitants of Britain must have made a considerable advance in the arts of civilization. To have subjugated the horse, and to have made such proficiency in many of the details of military science as the conqueror of Gaul found to his cost that they possessed, may well assert for them a degree of refinement quite at variance with the too generally received opinion, that they were mere savages and barbarians. If the use of iron be taken as the point at which pure barbarism ends and civilization begins, the ancient Britons had certainly passed that point, as the formidable scythes attached to the axles of their chariots sufficiently prove, to say nothing of the chariots themselves, which obviously were not made without the use of iron tools. Cæsar mentions that the currency of the people consisted partly of *iron rings*, adjusted to a certain weight (*utuntur aut ære aut annulis ferreis, ad certum pondus examinatis, pro nummo*), and, as he states, in the same breath, that their brass was imported (*ære utuntur importato*), it may reasonably be inferred that their iron was of home manufacture. And assuming that such was the case, the iron of our wealds could hardly have escaped notice.

However great the error of Cæsar in asserting that Britain produced but little iron (*nascitur ibi in maritimis* [*regionibus*] FERRUM ; *sed ejus exigua est copia*[5]), his allusion is useful as proving his knowledge of the fact that the island was not destitute of this invaluable mineral. And how he became acquainted with that fact, except from the information of the Britons themselves, it would be difficult to determine. It may be further remarked that the " maritime regions" referred to by him were, in all probability, the wealds of Kent and Sussex.

The extent of the knowledge of the Romans with regard to the mineral productions of Britain in those after times when their power was well established here, is a subject worthy of a fuller investigation than has hitherto been made. Tacitus tells us that Britain produces " gold, silver, and other metals;" Pliny alludes to the smelting of iron in this province; and Solinus not only mentions the British iron, but specifies the agricultural and other implements fabricated from it in his time. The researches of modern geology and archæology have confirmed these statements.

Sir H. T. de la Beche has found *gold* in the quartz formation of Gogofau, near Lampeter, in the vicinity of a traditional Roman settlement. Enormous mounds of broken and pounded quartz remain to attest the labour expended in the acquisition of the precious metal.[6] *Silver* is still found in Devonshire and Cornwall; and it was probably there that the silver mentioned by Tacitus was procured. The *tin* of Cornwall (the *album plumbum* of Cæsar and Pliny) was known before the very name of Rome existed. Pigs of *lead*, stamped with Roman inscriptions, have frequently been found in Derbyshire and elsewhere.

[5] De Bell. Gall. lib. v, cap. 12.

[6] Vide 'Thoughts on Ancient Metallurgy,' &c., by John Phillips, Esq., F.R.S., G.S. Yorkshire Philos. Soc., March, 1848.

Four such pigs of British lead were found at Pul-
borough, in Sussex, in 1824.   Our *copper*, too, was
well known to the Romans, and, as I believe, to the
primitive Celtic race who preceded them.   A due ad-
mixture of this metal with tin forms the imperishable
bronze of which the instruments called " celts " are
composed.

With regard to the seven or eight centuries which
succeeded the departure of the Romans from Britain,
history and archæology seem alike silent on the subject
of the iron of the South.   It can scarcely be doubted,
however, that the Romanized Britons retained this most
useful art of smelting and working iron, and that the
Anglo-Saxons, after them, continued it *upon the old
sites*.   Further examinations of our cinder-beds may
hereafter bring to light Romano-British and Saxon
remains, and prove for those peoples what Maresfield
has proved for the Romans.   In the meantime we are
perhaps justified in assuming that when so valuable
and necessary a manufacture had been once introduced,
it would be retained so long as the three essentials for
its perpetuation, the ore, the fuel, and the flux, continued in sufficient abundance of supply ; in other
words, that the iron-trade of the South was carried on
uninterruptedly from Roman times till its extinction,
in consequence of the failure of fuel, almost within
our own recollection.

It is proper, however, to observe, that the trade, if
in existence here at the date of Domesday Book, was
very unimportant, since that invaluable record makes
no mention of iron under the county of Sussex,
though it does under those of Somerset, Hereford,
Gloucester, Cheshire, and Lincoln.

Perhaps the earliest actual *record* of the iron-trade
in the South is contained in the murage-grant made

by Henry III to the town of Lewes.[7]   This grant,
which is dated 1266, empowers the inhabitants to raise
tolls for the repair of the town walls after the battle.[8]
Every cart laden with iron from the neighbouring
Weald, for sale, paid one penny toll, and every horse-
load of iron, half that sum.   From that period we
have data, however slight, for the history of the manufacture.

In 1290 a payment was made for the iron work of
the monument of Henry III in Westminster Abbey,
to Master Henry of Lewes.[9]   Some years previously,
the name of a Master Henry of Lewes, probably the
same person, appears in connexion with iron work for
the king's chamber.[10]

In 7th Edward I, iron appears to have been smelted
on St. Leonard's Forest, and the works were afterwards carried on by the Crown.   In 1300, according
to Stowe,[11] the ferrones, or ironmongers of London
made complaint to Elia Russell, mayor of London,
that the smiths of the wealds (*fabri de waldis*) brought
in irons for wheels, which were much shorter than
they ought, according to custom, to be, to the great

A letter, written between the years 1233-1244 to Ralph, Bishop
of Chichester, by his steward, Simon de Senliz, appears to militate
against the existence of the iron-trade, at least in the western part
of Sussex, at that period.   It relates to an order from the bishop to
one H. de Kynard for the purchase of iron ("x marcas de minuto
ferro, si inveniri potest, sive autem, v marcas de grosso, et v marcas
de minuto ferro"), to be procured in the neighbourhood of Gloucester, and thence conveyed to the *domus hospitis* at Winchester ; an
order which would scarcely have been necessary, if the iron-works
which in the next century we find within a few miles of Chichester,
had then been in operation.   The letter is among the *Tower MSS.*,
No. 677.

[8] Blaauw's Barons' War.   Horsfield's Lewes.

[9] Househ. Exp. Rot. Mis. 56, 17.

[10] Devon's Issues of Excheq.   [11] Survey of Lond.

scandal and loss of the whole trade of ironmongers ; and required a remedy, which was accordingly granted. From some incidental notices occurring about this period, it appears that the iron manufactured near the Sussex coast was conveyed to London by water—a proof of the impassable state of the roads in those days.

In the 13th year of Edward II, Peter de Walsham, sheriff of Surrey and Sussex, by virtue of a precept from the king's exchequer, made a provision of horse-shoes, and nails of different sorts (*providencias de ferris equorum et clavis pro eisdem, diversimode fabrice*), for the expedition against the Scots. The number furnished on the occasion was 3000 horse-shoes and 29,000 nails, and the expense of their purchase, from various places within the sheriff's jurisdiction, and their delivery in London, by the hands of John de Norton, clerk, was £14. 13*s.* 10*d.*[12]

The Nonæ return for the parish of Lynch in Western Sussex proves the existence of the iron trade there in 1342. It also affords an early instance of metals being subject to tithes : " Item, decima ferri ecclesiæ prædictæ valet per annum decem solidi." The rector likewise received ten shillings for the tithe of iron ore.[13]

A curious specimen of the iron manufacture of the fourteenth century, and, as far as my own observation extends, the oldest existing article produced by our foundries, occurs in Burwash church. It is a cast-iron slab, with an ornamental cross, and an inscription in relief. In the opinion of several eminent antiquaries, it may be regarded as unique for the style and period.

[12] Wardrobe Account, Edward II. Carlton Ride MSS.
[13] Dallaway's Rape of Chichester, p. 300.

The inscription is much injured by long exposure to the attrition of human feet. The letters are Longobardic, and the legend appears, on a careful examination, to be :—

ORATE P. ANNEMA JHONE COLINE (or COLINS.)
"Pray for the soul of Joan Collins."

Of the identity of the individual thus commemorated I have been unable to glean any particulars. In all probability she was a member of the ancient Sussex family of Collins, subsequently seated at Socknersh, in the adjacent parish of Brightling, where, in common with many of the neighbouring gentry, they carried on the manufacture of iron, at a place still known as Socknersh Furnace.

The manufacture probably continued to increase during the fifteenth century, though that supposition is based more upon the flourishing state in which we find the trade in the early part of the sixteenth, than upon documentary evidence or archæological remains. A few relics of the latter portion of this period are, however, to be met with. Among these should probably be included a singular object, preserved at the archiepiscopal palace of Mayfield, to which my attention has kindly been drawn by Albert Way, Esq., who conjectures it to be a mustard-mill. It is about $9\frac{1}{2}$ inches square, with a hemispherical basin, at the bottom of which is a circular hole, an inch in diameter. It has four projections, like handles, by which it was probably worked.[14] To this date also

[14] The well-known objects preserved at Mayfield palace as genuine relics of St. Dunstan, seem to refer as much to the iron-trade, so famous of old in these parts, as to the alleged proficiency of the saint in the craft of a blacksmith. They consist (besides an old-

belong a few of the andirons and chimney-backs
which remain to attest the taste and skill of our local
founders. The accompanying cut represents one of a
pair of andirons from Eastbourne, now in my possession. From the form of the shield, upon which the
sacred monogram i𝔥𝔰 appears, it probably belongs to

the reign of Edward IV. Another specimen of the
same type was formerly preserved at Netherfield Toll

fashioned sword) of an anvil, a pair of tongs, and a hammer.
The anvil and tongs are of no
great antiquity, but the hammer,
with its solid iron handle, looks
like a genuine relic of medieval
times. The massive hand-rail of
the great stone staircase is another interesting specimen of the
local manufacture. I may add
that it was probably here, upon
the archiepiscopal manor, that
the iron copings of Rochester

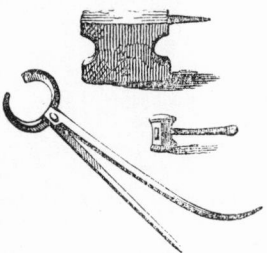

bridge, presented to that city early in the sixteenth century by the
primate Warham, were manufactured.

farmhouse, in the parish of Battel. At Michelham
Priory are a pair of andirons of extremely interesting
character, which are believed to have formerly occupied
the curious antique chimney-piece in the apartment

traditionally known as the "Prior's Chamber." They
terminate in a human head, and the fashion of the
head-dress fixes their date not later than the reign of
Henry VII. The series of Sussex andirons ranges
from the end of the fifteenth century to that of the
seventeenth, or later, and during the whole of that
period a regular decadence in the style of their devices
is strikingly observable. In many of the old farm-
houses, where, either from motives of economy, or
from a predilection for old manners, the good wife,
like the one celebrated by Horace,—

> " Sacrum *vetustis* exstruat *lignis* focum,
>   Lassi sub adventum viri,"

these venerable and picturesque articles of furniture

retain the post they have occupied for centuries. And could the uncouth heads, with which they are frequently decorated, open their mouths to reveal the forgotten past, how many a tale could they unfold of the scenes of homely felicity and of domestic wretchedness, which have transpired around them ! [15] The chimney-backs are not generally of so ancient a date as the andirons, though one or two specimens may probably be referred to the fifteenth century. Others of a later style have some *details* belonging to this period, proving that the founders preserved the models which had been employed by their predecessors. Thus a "back" at Buxted (belonging to Mr. T. Wickens), which bears the badge and initials of Queen Eliza-beth, is decorated with a band composed of grapes and vine-leaves, in a running pattern, belonging to a considerably earlier date ; and I have met with simi-lar instances elsewhere.

The sacred monogram iȟș occurs on the shield, which is almost uniformly introduced into the design of the andirons, up to the time of the Reformation, when it is generally superseded by a coat of arms, or some other device. Overleaf is one of a pair belonging to Mr. Wickens, of Buxted : it was probably cast in the early part of the sixteenth century. At the Sergisson's Arms public-house, Hayward's Heath, is a very large pair, ornamented in a rather singular manner. The shield, which occupies the ordinary position at the insertion of the legs, bears the arms

---

[15] I employ the word Andiron as a term generally known. The Promptorium Parvulorum has "Awnderne, Awndyryn, Awndyrn." Vide *Way's Prompt. Parv.* Camd. Soc. *in voc.* The etymology is uncertain. In Sussex, the word more generally employed is either *Brand-dogs,* or *Brand-irons,* the latter from the Anglo-Saxon "*Brand-isen,*" or "Brandiren ;" an interesting example of the local retention of an ancient word which has grown out of general use.

of France, a favourite device on our iron-works; and above it, on another shield attached to the pillar or stem of the andiron, is the legend F holy on.   The

letters R.F. above, and the G.B.C. below, may be the initials of the founder, and of the person for whom they were made, with, perhaps, that of his place of residence. With respect to the meaning of the legend, there is much scope for conjecture : perhaps it should be read *"Jesus Holy One."* If this be a correct interpretation, it affords another instance of the vulgar misapprehension of the meaning of the Greek IHΣ, the very ancient contraction of 'Ιησοῦς, corrupted during the middle ages to I.H.S. or ihs, and interpreted to signify " Jesus, hominum Salvator." Sometimes the Σ was taken to be a c, and the ihc was read "Jesus, hominum Consolator." These misapprehensions originated with the clergy, who were, in those days, generally unac-

quainted with Greek; but the vulgar, who were equally
unlearned in Latin, had *their* reading also, and made
I.H.S. stand for " Jesus Holy Saviour," which is still
retained as its meaning by the illiterate in Sussex.
When the monogram took the form of ihc, the
last letter might be easily mistaken for an o, and
in this way, I am disposed to believe, the founder
made it the initial of " one," and thus developed a
new theory upon this *diu vexata quæstio* by producing
the " Jesus Holy One," upon this andiron. I must
add, however, a suggestion made since the original
publication of this memoir, namely, that the legend is
simply *I holp* or *help on,* alluding to the usefulness of
an andiron.

To return to the history of the manufacture. There
is little doubt that ordnance was made in this county
in the fifteenth century. It is believed that some of
the old banded guns of wrought iron preserved in the
Tower of London, and elsewhere, and dating so far
back as the reign of Henry VI, were of Sussex manufacture. In the tenth volume of the ' Archæologia,'[16]
is an engraving, from a drawing by James Lambert,
jun., of a mortar, formerly at Eridge Green, in the
parish of Frant, and the account given of it is as
follows :

" It has always been understood that this mortar
was the first that was made in England. . . . . [It]
now lies at Eridge Green, and has served for many
years for the amusement of the people on a holiday
or fair-day, when they collect money to buy gun-
powder to throw the shell to a hill about a mile
distant. The weight of the shell sinks it so deep into
the earth, that it costs no little pains to dig it out

[16] Page 472 (June, 1790).

after each discharge, which is repeated as long as the money lasts. The chamber of the gun is cast-iron, the other part, as is evident, wrought."

From the engraving, the chamber appears to have been polygonal, and the tube to have consisted of many small bars or rods, bound together by nine hoops. This was the original method of constructing these tremendous engines of war.[17]   A French writer, St. Remy, says, " Qu'elles ne consistoient qu'en de fortes tables de fer qu'on disposoit à peu près cylindriquement, les serront avec de cercles de fer."[18] There can be no reasonable doubt that the Eridge gun was of Sussex manufacture; and it is equally probable that many, if not most, of the pieces employed by our armies in the continental wars of the fourteenth and fifteenth centuries were the productions of the southern iron-works.

These hooped guns were at length superseded by cannons cast in an entire piece, and bored, as at the present day. The invention of gun-founding is ascribed to the French, who appear to have used cast pieces many years before the introduction of the art into this country. The first iron cannons cast in England were manufactured at Buxted, in Sussex, by Ralph Hoge or Hogge, in 1543 (35 Henry VIII).[19] This founder employed, as his assistant, Peter Baude, a Frenchman, whom he had probably brought over to teach him the improved method; and Peter Van

[17] For a very able and interesting account of ancient ordnance, see a paper by C. D. Archibald, Esq., F.R.A.S., &c., in Archæologia, vol. xxviii, p. 373. Our historians generally assert that cannon were first employed at the battle of Crecy, in 1346: but Mr. Archibald adduces strong reasons for the belief that they had been previously used by Edward III in his expedition against the Scots in 1327.

[18] Artillerie, 1, viii, quoted in Archæologia, vol. xxviii, p. 380.

[19] Holinshed, ii, 960.—" Bucksteed."

Collet, a Flemish gunsmith, about the same time, " devised and cast mortar pieces from 11 to 19 inches bore ; for the use whereof they caused to be made bombs, or certain hollow shot, of cast iron, to be stuffed with fireworks, &c.   And after the king's return from Bullen, the said Peter Bawde, by himself, in 1 Edward VI, made ordnance of cast iron, of divers sorts, as *fawconets, fawcons, minions, sakers,* and other pieces."   It seems that Baude's connection with Hogge was of no long continuance ; for we find that " John Johnson, covenant servant to the said P. Bawd, succeeded and exceeded his master in this his art of casting ordnance, making them cleaner and to better perfection.   And his son, Thomas Johnson, a special workman, in and before the year 1595, made 42 cast pieces of great ordnance of iron, for the Earl of Cumberland, weighing 6000 lbs., or three tons a-piece." [20]   Whether Sussex was the scene of these operations, however, does not appear.

The family of Hogge resided at a place near Buxted Church, called, from their rebus or " name-device,"

still existing over the front door, the *Hog-house,* and now the property of Colonel Harcourt.   They were connected with the business of gun-founding for at least three generations.   About the 16th of Elizabeth (1574), *Bryan Hogg* held the office of Clerk

[20] Hayley's MSS., British Museum.

of the Deliveries, with a fee of £18. 5s. per annum; and his successor was *George Hogg*.[21]

The name of Hogge or Hoggé seems to have been confounded with that of Huggett; and there is a place on the confines of Buxted and Mayfield, called Huggett's Furnace, where, according to tradition, the first iron ordnance was cast. The traditionary distich that

> "𝕸aster 𝕳uggett and his man John,
> They did cast the first Can-non,"

is firmly believed in the locality.[22]

But to return : Peter Baude, the associate of Ralph Hogge, did not limit his exertions to iron pieces. Some fine specimens of brass or " gun-metal " ordnance from his hand are still extant. One John Owen, it seems, had, at a somewhat earlier date (1521, Stowe —1535, Camden), made great brass ordnance, as cannons and culverines.[23] Whether this man did not succeed, or whether he died previously to 1543, is not mentioned, but at that date Baude was busily engaged in the fabrication of brass guns, two of which still remain in the Tower of London collection. One of these is an elegant octagonal piece, adorned with the royal arms, the fleur-de-lis, and the king's initial " H," surmounted by a crown, with the date 1543, and the

[21] Strype's Stowe's London, vol. i, p. 107.

[22] As an instance of the tenacity with which families sometimes adhere to a particular vocation, it may be mentioned that many persons of the name of Huggett still carry on the trade of blacksmiths in East Sussex.

[23] "There are now at Woolwich several guns lately recovered from the wreck of the 'Mary Rose,' which was sunk at Spithead in 1545; and among them two large brass cannons, the one a 68, the other a 24 pounder, which, in beauty of design and workmanship, are equal to anything that could be produced in the present day."—Archæologia (ut supra).

initial of the founder's name, "B," over the touch-hole.[24] The other is a very fine specimen of the " triple chamber piece," which was unfortunately broken into several pieces, and otherwise mutilated, by the fire of 1841.   It is 6½ feet in length, and has three bores, 2⅛ inches in diameter.   Its upper surface is ornamented with the Tudor badge of the rose and crown, the latter supported by Cupids; and with the kind of arabesque device prevalent at this period. Beneath the badge is the legend—

> HENRICVS OCTAVVS
> DEI GRACIA ANGLIE ET
> FRANCIE REX FIDEI
> DEFENSOR DNS HIBERIE.

near the muzzle—

> POVR DEFENDRE;

and at the opposite end—

> PETRVS . BAVDE . GALLVS . OPERIS . ARTIFEX.

Among the Battel Abbey Deeds[25] is a document called 'Westalle's Book of Pannyngrydge, A° regni Regis Hen. VIII, xxxviij" (1546).   It is the account-book of some iron-master, and exhibits his expenditure in carrying on an extensive trade during the year indicated.   Among the items are payments made to the wood-cutters for "coards" of wood, at 3d. per coard.   The "collears," or charcoal-burners, were paid in wood, and money for coals, at the rate of 22d. per load.   There are also charges for the carriage of coals out of Pannyngrydge, Olyver's Wood, and Asyldey, at 4d. and 6d. a load ; and for the "moyne digged out of Pannyngrydge."   "Moyne"

---

[24] Hewitt's History of the Tower, 12mo, 1841.

[25] Formerly in the possession of the Webster family, now in that of Sir Thomas Phillipps, of Middle Hill ; a most valuable collection of Sussex MSS., bound in 97 folio volumes.

was, of course, the iron ore, still called "iron-mine," and giving name to many spots, as "Mine-pit Field," "Mine-pit Shaw," &c. The price of digging was 7*d.* per load; and many payments to "Black Jack," and others, occur in these accounts. Several sums are paid to Warnet, the founder, and to Anthony, the "filler." One entry shows the locality where these operations were carried on :

"For carying of lodes of sand from Pannyngrydge unto my forge at *Robertsbridge,* at xvjd. the lode."

There are further sums paid to Mr. Chanceller for the farm of his woods at Pannyngrydge, and to the parson of *Penherst* for the farm of the *phurner* (furnace) pond there, and for tithe. Also for the hewing and felling of timber, "for drawing of timbre to the saw-stage," &c. The accounts close with an entry of v*s.* v*d.* paid "for a wrytte and a warrant for Jackson, the carpenter."[26]

The manufacture of heavy ordnance gave a great impulse to the iron trade. Many foreigners were brought over to carry on the works. This perhaps may account for the number of Frenchmen and Germans whose names appear in our parish registers about the middle of the sixteenth century. New works were established, and ultimately almost every landed proprietor in the districts where the ore was found became an iron-master. Among the persons engaged in the trade at this period, was Richard Woodman, one of the ten Protestant martyrs burnt at Lewes in 1557. He was a native of Buxted, where he probably learned the business. At the time of his apprehension, at the beginning of Queen Mary's reign, he resided at Warbleton, and carried on an extensive

[26] Vide Thorpe's Descriptive Catalogue of the Muniments of Battel Abbey, 8vo, London, 1835.

trade. In one of his examinations before the Bishop of Winchester, he says, " Let me go home, I pray you, to my wife and children, to see them kept, and other poore folke that I would set aworke, by the helpe of God. I have set aworke *a hundreth persons*, ere this, all the yeare together." [27] Several Sussex families, enriched by the iron manufacture, assumed the rank of gentry about this time.

This rapid growth of the trade in the wealds of Sussex and Kent was viewed with disfavour by many. Archbishop Parker, writing to Queen Elizabeth in 1570, says : " Sir Richard Sackville intends, as I was credibly informed, in this wood [Longbeech Wood, in Westwell, Kent] to erect up certain iron mills, *which plague*, if it shall come into the country, I fear it will breed much grudge and desolation." [28]

It is curious to find about this time the ancestors of many of the existing representatives of what is called the " landed interest" busily employed in the iron trade —and to trace their augmentation of wealth by this means. In the days of Elizabeth, the Ashburnhams, the Pelhams, the Montagues, the Nevilles, the Sidneys, the Sackvilles, the Dacres, the Stanleys, the Finches, the Gages, and even the Percys and the Howards, did not disdain such lucre, but pursued it to the destruction of old ancestral oak and beech, and with all the apparent ardour of Birmingham and Wolverhampton men of these times. We may add after these, the Culpepers, the Dykes, the Darrels, the Apsleys, the Coverts, the Morleys, the Shirleys, the Burrells, the Greshams, the Bullens (kinsmen of royalty), the Gratwickes, the Bakers, and the Fullers. Concerning the last-mentioned there is a foolish tradition that the first of the name and family in Sussex gained his wealth by

[27] John Foxe, Acts and Mon., Ed. 1570, p. 2192.
[28] Strype's Life of Archbishop Parker, p. 315.

hawking nails about the county on the backs of donkeys! This is absurd; but at the same time it is generally understood that the family were greatly enriched by the manufacture—a fact which is indeed frankly avowed in their singular motto: " *Carbone et forcipibus*."

About 1572 much ordnance was exported, in consequence of the Lord Admiral having granted a license for that purpose to Sir Thomas Leighton, who had made use of one Garret Smith to obtain it of the admiral, and who was, in return for his intervention, to enjoy the deputyship, with a fourth part of the profits ;[29] " but the merchants of London, knowing how this might furnish the enemies' ships to obstruct their trade, and bring other great damages upon the queen and her subjects, petitioned her, in a great body, to withdraw this license." The petition was not presented ("whether it were shuffled off by some about the queen") ; however, they petitioned again, and in Sept. 1572, a proclamation strictly restrained all transport of iron and brass ordnance, and forbade the owners of all iron-works, furnaces, or forges, to make any kind of ordnance larger than a minion.

The following year a declaration was made to the council, of the great consumption of oaken wood in Sussex, Surrey, and Kent by the iron mills and furnaces.[30]

In the State Paper Office, Jan. 1574 (No. 15), there is a petition from Ralphe Hogge, "manufacturer of guns and shot for the Ordnance office," to the council, complaining of the infringement of the patent granted by the queen, for the sole exportation of ordnance ; whereupon a return was procured on February 15th following (No. 18), giving a list of the owners of

[29] Strype's Stowe, vol. ii, p. 293.
[30] State Paper Office, 1573 (No. 96).

iron-works in the three counties. The chief men were summoned before the council, and from the others bonds were taken, under a penalty of £2000 not to found or sell ordnance without license from the queen.

In defiance of these measures, however, the surreptitious exportation of Sussex cannon went on for some years longer. In 1587, the Earl of Warwick, master of the ordnance, despatched " a gentleman of his, one Mr. Blincoe," into Sussex, to summon all the gunfounders of the county up to London, to understand his pleasure respecting their further continuance of the manufacture. " Henry Nevel, and the rest of that occupation," obeyed the summons, and the matter was referred to the arrangement of Mr. Hockenal, the deputy-master of the ordnance, and Mr. Blincoe. The result was, that a fixed quantity of cannon should be cast annually, for the necessary provision of our own navigation; a certain proportion being allowed to each founder. It was also stipulated that no ordnance should be sold except in the city, and not even there but to such merchants " as my lord or his deputy should name." [31]

The bonds into which the iron-masters entered on this occasion seem to have been little regarded by them; for on August 8th, 1589, Thomas Lord Buckhurst wrote a letter to the justices of Lewes Rape, complaining of their neglect. " Their lordshypps doe see the little regard the owners of furnaces and the makers of these peeces have of their bondes, and how yt importeth the state that the enemy of her majesty should not be furnished oute of the lande with ordnance to annoye us." The lord-treasurer goes on to direct the magistrates to enforce the provisions of the master of the ordnance. Another letter, from the same officer to the justices of the three eastern

[31] Strype's Stowe, vol. i, p. 108.

rapes, dated 6th October, 1590, directs them as to
"straighter restraint of making shott and ordnance,"
and to take bonds of £1000 each of every furnace-
owner and farmer; and also to forward their bonds,
and a list of their names, to him with all convenient
speed.[32]

To return to the *archæology* of our subject: the
eastern division of Sussex still abounds with specimens of the workmanship of the sixteenth century,
particularly andirons and chimney-backs. Some of
these are decorated with fanciful devices, and others
with armorial bearings. The royal arms and badges
are of the most usual occurrence. At Riverhall, in
the parish of Wadhurst, is one of the former class.
It probably belongs to the early part of this century.
Besides the royal arms—France and England quar-
terly, with supporters—and the Tudor badge of the

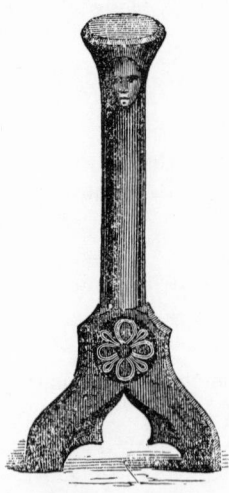

rose and crown four times
repeated, it exhibits a crowned shield, charged with the
initials E. H., probably those
of the original proprietor, and
ten human figures, with mon-
key or doglike heads (perhaps
intended for "*mummers*"),
and two swords. The back is
of large dimensions, and the
figures which make up its
fanciful device were evidently
impressed separately in the
sand from the same models.
According to tradition, this
curious article was cast at a
furnace on the estate. I may
also mention two other "backs"

Andiron at Old Land
Farm, Maresfield.

[32] These letters are printed in full in Horsfield's Lewes, i, 192.

of this century. The first, much mutilated, has the royal arms, supported by a dragon and a greyhound, with the initials E. R., probably for Edward VI. The side ornaments are a dragon's head, the *rose-en-soleil* and the double rose. The orthography of the royal motto, DV ET MOVN DR—, and of that of the garter, HONY SOYT QVE MAL Y PAVNC, bespeak it the work of an unlettered artisan, and the inscription beneath the shield exhibits the name of the founder, 𝕴𝖓 𝕾𝖚𝖘𝖘𝖊𝖝—𝕭𝖞 𝕵𝖔𝖍𝖓 𝕳𝖆𝖜𝖘 (or Hawo—, perhaps intended for Haworth, but incomplete for want of room). Another " back " has the badge and supporters of Queen Elizabeth, and the legend—

> "THOMAS VNSTEAD, ISFILD, AND DINIS
> HIS WIF, ANO DOMINO, 1582."

A third specimen, in the possession of Captain Richardson, of Sutton Hurst, has the badge and supporters of Queen Elizabeth, and the legend:
"THIS . IS . FOR . IAMES . HIDE . AND . JON HIS . MIF . 1582."

A very singular type of chimney-back is found in some old houses in Surrey, and there is a specimen in the Sussex Archæological Society's Museum at Lewes. It is of the ordinary shape, and has the common ornaments of the period, and this inscription:

```
HER : LIETH : ANE : EORST
R : DAVGHTER : AND :
HEYR : TO : THOMAS
GAYNSEORD : ESQVIER
DECEASED : XVIII : OE
IANVARI : 1591 : LEAVING
BEHIND : HER : II SONES
AND : V : DAVGHTERS.
```

In Crowhurst Church, Surrey, an iron slab bearing this inscription with some accessories, covers the remains of the lady whose memory it records. It is evidently cast from the same mould as the "backs;" but the reason for thus publishing the lady's heirship to the ancient line of Gaynsford on the hearths of strangers is not easily to be adduced.

Many of the andirons of this period have the arms of the families for whom they were cast embossed upon their shields. The accompanying example, from a sketch by Mr. C. Howard Ellis, is in the possession of Mr. Marchant, of Hurstperpoint. It was brought from Slaugham Place, the seat of the Coverts, but

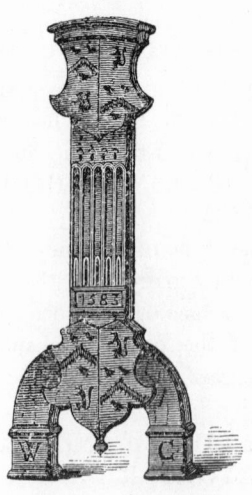

bears the arms of the Kentish family of Cromer. It will be observed that this specimen has nothing of the "Gothic" or medieval character of the earlier examples. The founders uniformly imitated the architectural details of their respective eras.

The left-hand andiron next shown, from a sketch

by Mr. William Figg, is at Rowfant, in the parish of
Worth. The date is 1591. The arms are those of
the family of Ashburnham, and the ornament upon
the pillar is a rude attempt at their punning crest—
an ash-tree springing from a ducal coronet. This is
doubtless a production of the Ashburnham furnace.
The other is a mutilated andiron at the Crow and
Gate public-house, near Crowborough, and is ornamented with emblems of the smith or farrier's occupation displayed upon the shield.

The great extent which the manufacture had now
reached threatened an evil which had to be warded off
by legislative enactments—I mean the annihilation of
timber in the Weald. Up to a certain period the
destruction of trees and underwood had been beneficial in clearing the land for agricultural purposes; [33]

[33] In illustration of this remark it may be mentioned, that in
30 Edward III, one Robert de Dole died possessed, *inter alia*, of
sixty acres of land at Billingshurst, which was declared to be worth
only 10s. per annum, or 2d. per acre, because the land was barren
and lay in the Weald ("et jacet in *Wealdâ*"), and was of no value
to sow, on account of the quantity of wood ("propter magnitudinem
bosci").—*Inq. post Mort.*

but so early as the reign of Henry VIII (1543), it became necessary to enact—that no wood shall be converted into pasture—that in cutting coppice-woods at twenty-four years' growth, or under, there shall be left standing and unfelled, for every acre, twelve *standils* or *storers* of oak, or in default of so many, then of elm, ash, asp, or beech—and that if the coppice be under fourteen years' growth, it shall be inclosed from cattle for six years; " provided always, &c., that this act do not extend or be prejudicial to any of the lords or owners of the woods, underwoods, or woodlands growing or being within any of the towns, parishes, or places commonly called or known to be *within the Wilds* of the counties of Kent, Surrey, and Sussex, other than to the *common woods* growing and being within any of the said Wilds," &c.[34]

A series of enactments of similar character succeeded. The act 1 Elizabeth, cap. 15, provides that no person shall convert into coal or other fuel for the making of iron, " any timber-trees of oak, beech, or ash of the breadth of one foot square at the stub," within fourteen miles of the sea, or the rivers Thames, Severn, &c., or any other navigable river. The county of Sussex, the *weild* of Kent, and the parishes of Charlewood, Newdigate, and Leigh, in the weild of Surrey, were however excepted from the operation of this act.

The act of 23 Elizabeth, cap. 5 (1581), declares that " by reason of the late erection of sundry iron-mills in divers places," near London, and " not far distant from the Downs and sea-coasts of Sussex," decay of timber hath ensued; and forbids, therefore, the converting " to coal or other fewel, for the making of iron-metal in any iron-mill, furnace, or hammer,"

[34] Statutes of the Realm, 35 Hen. VIII, cap. 17. This act was passed for seven years, but made perpetual by 13 Eliz. c. 25.

any wood within twenty-two miles of London, or within four miles of the foot of the hills called the Downs, betwixt Arundel and Pemsey, or within four miles of the towns of Winchelsey and Rye, or within two miles of the town of Pemsey, or within three miles of the town of Hastings, under a penalty of forty shillings for every load of wood so employed. " Provided always, that this act shall not extend to any woods growing or to grow in the weilds of Surrey, Sussex, and Kent," if eighteen miles from London, and eight from the Thames. It also forbids the erection of any new iron-works within twenty-two miles of London, or four miles of the Downs, or of the towns of Pemsey, Winchelsey, Hastings, and Rye, upon pain of £10. The woods of Christopher Darrell, gentleman, at Newdigate, in Surrey, are exempted from the force of this enactment, on the ground of their having been preserved and coppiced for the especial use of his iron-works in those parts. The act 27 Elizabeth, cap. 19 (1585), rehearses, " Whereas by the over great negligence or number of iron-works which have been and yet are in the weilds of Sussex, Surrey, and Kent, it is thought that the great plenty of timber which hath grown in those parts hath been greatly decayed and spoiled, and will in short time be utterly consumed and wasted, if some convenient remedy be not timely provided," and therefore forbids the erection of any manner of iron-mill, furnace, *finary*, or *blomary*,[35] for the making or working of any

---

[35] For the meaning of these expressions see, Ray's account of the manufacture, in a subsequent page. I may add, here, that the phrase *bloma ferri* occurs several times in Domesday Book. "Bloma," a Saxon word, is defined by Bosworth as "metal, a mass, lump." "Isenes-bloma, *massa ferri*, bloom of iron."—(First Report of Record Commiss., p. 416.)

manner of iron or iron-metal," except upon ancient sites.

The highways of Sussex were, at that time, as well as at a much more recent date, proverbially bad, wherefore the act above cited enjoins upon all persons carrying charcoal, *mines,* and iron, between October and May, "for every six loads of coals or mine, or for every ton of iron, to carry one usual cart-load of cinder, gravel, stone, sand, or chalk, meet for the repairing or amending of the said highways."

In spite of the enactments for the preservation of wood, the waste still continued. John Norden, in his 'Surveyor's Dialogue,' [36] after referring to the statute of 35 Henry VIII, says, "but mee thinks this statute is deluded and the meaning abused ; for I have seene in many places at the fals, where indeed they leave the number of standils and more; but in stead they cut downe *them that were preserved before,* and at the next fall them that were left to answer the statute, and yong left againe in their steads; so that there can be no increase of timber-trees." "But," he adds, "some countries are yet well stored, and for the abundance of timber and wood were excepted in the statute, as the welds of Kent, Sussex, and Surry, which were all anciently comprehended under the name of *Holmesdale,* . . . and yet he that well observes it, and hath known the welds of Sussex, Surry, and Kent, the grand nursery of those kind of trees, especially oake and beech, shal find such an alteration within lesse then 30 yeres, as may well strike a feare, lest few yeeres more, as pestilent as the former, will leave fewe good trees standing in those welds. Such a heate issueth out of the many forges and furnaces for the making of iron, and out of the glasse kilnes, as hath

[36] London, 1607, p. 213.

devoured many famous woods within the welds; as about *Burningfold, Lopwood Greene* (Loxwood), the *Minns, Kirdford, Petworth* parkes, *Ebernowe, Wassals, Rusper, Balcombe, Dallington,* the *Dyker,* and some forests, and other places infinite.

'Tantum ævi longinqua valet mutare vetustas.'

"The force of time and men's inclination make greater changes in mightie things. But the croppe of this commodious fruit, which nature itself doth sowe, being thus reaped and cut downe by the sickle of time, hath been in some plentiful places, in regard of the superfluous abundance, rather held a hurtfull weed than a profitable fruit, and therefore the wasting of it held providence, to the end that corne, a more profitable increase, might be brought in, in stead of it. . . . But it is to be feared that posterities will find want, where now they think is too much."

To this the Baylie, one of the interlocutors of the dialogue, replies:

"It is no mervaile if Sussex and other places you speak off be deprived of this benefit; for I have heard, there are or lately were in Sussex *neere* 140 *hammers and furnaces for iron,*[37] and in it and Surry adjoining three or four glasse-houses; [38] the hammers

[37] It is a somewhat singular coincidence that the number of corn-mills in Sussex, at the time of the Domesday survey (finished in 1086), was 148; and that of iron-mills, about five centuries later, 140. A great proportion of the latter probably occupied the sites of the former, which the introduction of windmills had caused to be deserted.

[38] The dearth of information regarding the glass manufacture in the south is much to be regretted. The Rev. E. Turner conjectures that one of the "glasse-houses" was at Maresfield, near the site of the Roman iron-works. The scoriæ found there differ considerably in character from those of the ordinary iron-works, having a more vitreous appearance. This however may result from some peculiarity in the flux.

and furnaces spend, each of them in every 24 houres, two, three, or foure loades of charcoale, which in a yeere amounteth to an infinit quantitie, as you can better account by your arethmetique-then I."

The surveyor rejoins: "That which you say is true; but they worke not all the yeere, for many of them lacke water in the summer to blowe their bellows. And to say truth, the consuming of much of these in the weld is no such great prejudice to the weale publike, as is the overthrow of wood and timber in places where there is no great quantitie, for I have observed that the clensing of many of these weld grounds hath redounded rather to the benefit then to the hurt of the country; for where woods did grow in superfluous abundance there was lacke of pasture for kine, and arable land for corne, without which a country, or country farme, cannot stand, or be releeved but by neighbour helpes, as the Downes have their wood from the weld. Beside, *people bred amongst woods are naturally more stubborne and uncivil, then in the champion countries !*" [39]

The quietness of our beautiful Weald at the present day offers a striking contrast to the ceaseless activity and bustle which characterised it in its *Iron Age,* the days of the Tudors and Stuarts. Camden, speaking of Sussex, says : "Full of iron mines it is in sundry places, where, for the making and founding thereof, there be furnaces on every side, and a huge deal of wood is yearly burnt; to which purpose divers brooks in many places are brought to run in one channel, and sundry meadows turned into pools and waters, that they might be of power sufficient to drive hammer-mills, which beating upon the iron, resound all

[39] Vide "Certificate concerning Sussex Justices," Suss. Arch. Coll. II, 60.

over the places adjoining." A later edition of the
Britannia (edit. 1722) gives a more graphic account :
" A great deal of meadow ground is turned into ponds
and pools for the driving of mills by the flashes, which,
beating with hammers upon the iron, fill the neighbourhood round about, night and day, with continual
noise."

" Yet," adds our great antiquary, " the iron here
wrought is not in every place of like goodness; but
generally more brittle than the Spanish iron ; whether
it be by nature, or tincture and temper thereof. How-
beit commodious enough to iron-maisters, who cast
much great ordnance thereof, and other things to their
no small gain. Now whether it be as gainful and
profitable to the commonwealth may be doubted ; but
the age ensuing will be better able to tell you."

That *some* of the iron wrought here was of the first
quality there can be no doubt. The Ashburnham
iron, particularly, excelled in the quality of toughness,
and I have been assured by smiths who have used it,
that it was in nowise inferior to the Swedish metal,
generally accounted the best in the world. Camden's
remark respecting the superior texture of Spanish iron
is scarcely reconcilable with the statement of Fuller :
" It is almost incredible how many great guns are
made of the iron in this county. Count Gondomer
[the Spanish ambassador] well knew their goodness,
when of King James he so often begged the boon to
transport them."[40]

Although the English monarch very properly declined the solicitation of Gondomer, one of his subjects, Sir Anthony Sherley, is known to have presented
the King of Spain with a hundred pieces of cannon.
" How he came by them," says Captain Alexander

[40] Fuller's Worthies, Sussex, iii, 241, edit. 1840.

Hepburn, "I know not; but this is true by God in heaven." [41]   There is, however, little mystery as to the source whence this artillery was derived; for Sir Anthony's father, Sir Thomas Sherley of Wiston, was an extensive manufacturer of Sussex iron.

This brings us to the seventeenth century, a period in which the Sussex iron trade reached its greatest extent.   The number of mills and furnaces had increased yearly, in spite of the statutes limiting their extension, and the waste of timber was again brought before the notice of government.   In 1636, Charles I granted a commission to Sir David Cuningham, Bart., Christopher Lewknor, Esq., and others, for its better preservation.   "Whereas several offences have been heretofore and still are done and committed by . . . maisters, owners, and occupiers of iron-works, forges, furnaces, or hammers, for melting and making of iron, by felling, cutting, and converting of timmer trees (*sic*) and woods into coals for the melting and making of the said iron, &c. . . . and by felling the said trees and underwood at unseasonable parts of year, whereby the bark thereof hath been lost; and by ingrossing of iron and iron works, &c., and thereby inhancing the prices of iron, &c., contrary to our laws and proclamations made for the preservation of timber and woods."   It appears that there were several suits touching these offences pending in the court of Star Chamber, and the duty imposed on the commissioners was, "to treat and compound with" the offenders, and to levy, for the king's use, such sums as they should see fit.   The commission was dated at Canbury, 19th August, 1636.[42]   On the 14th of October following, an office, "to be for ever con-

[41] Shirley's 'Three Brothers.'   Roxburghe Club.
[42] Rymer, xx, 68.

tinued," was erected for the better management of the iron trade, and the king appointed " John Cupper and Grimbald Pauncefoote, gentlemen, surveyors of all iron-works, and of all woods to be used and employed thereat, and for the surveying and marking of iron with divers stamps or marks distinguishing the several kinds." On the 29th July, 1637, by an order in council these regulations were put in force, and very stringent methods were adopted for the rectification of the evils complained of.[43]

The founders of this century did not limit their operations to iron. I am not aware that bronze cannon continued to be made, but the casting of brass was extensively carried on. Bell-founding was successfully practised. The churchwardens' accounts at Eastbourne show that a new peal for their church was cast at Chiddingly. The following extracts are interesting :

DISBURSEMENTS, A.D. 1651.

	£.	s.	d.
" Item, to the bell-ffounder, John Lulham, for castinge the bells by composition	7	0	0
" Item, to John Lulham, for addition of belmettall, and for six daies labour about the bells, besides the remaininge mettall after the castinge . . .	2	5	0
" Item for carrying the bells and belmettall to Chittingly, and from Chittingly, June the 5th and July the 8th	1	10	0
"Item, to Mr. ffrench [of Chiddingly] and the fforger, for the treble clapper	0	8	0
" Item, to J. L. for his dyet and horsemeate, 3 daies .	0	3	0"

There are many other entries relating to expenses about the bells.

" Item, to Richard Miller, of Chittingly, for two *brasse pots*, weighing 36 li. at 5*d.* the pound . . . 15*s.*" [44]

---

[43] Rymer, xx, 161. Both the foregoing instruments were revoked by a proclamation, "given at York" in 1639. Rymer, xx, 340.

[44] Ex orig. olim penes Lt.-Col. J. H. Willard.

The third bell at Chiddingly bears the inscription
—" ROBERT TAPSELL MADE ME," and the name of
this person appears in the parish register as a resident
there.

In the register of Berwick is this entry : " Nov.,
1690. The little bell was new cast at Alfriston."

At Ripe, there is a tradition that some of the bells
of that church were cast on the waste close to the
churchyard. Those of Hailsham Church were founded
at a spot near the town still called Bell-Bank.

Many of the culinary articles called *skillets* were
also manufactured between the years 1625 and 1670.
Some of them bear the name of Rummins.   Tradition states that a family of this name, natives of
Lamberhurst, travelled about the country with these
articles, which they cast at the various foundries of
the district, as occasion required.[45]

Steel was also manufactured in several places; particularly at Warbleton, where there is a place still called
the Steel-Forge Land, and at Robertsbridge. In 1609,
John Hawes held the site of the abbey of Robertsbridge with the buildings, &c., " lying between two
fresh-water rivers, abutting at the great stone bridge
at the Forge Pond," and including various buildings
for the steel-makers, among which were eight steel
forges; "also one great gate-house, called the West
Gate, built of lime and stone, and used in part as a
dove-house, and in part for the steel-makers; also a
great gate called the East Gate, employed as a store-
house for iron, with a house attached to it for James
Lamye, the hammer-man."

Drayton in his ' Polyolbion,' published in the
year 1612, makes the Sussex woods complain of the
injury done them by the iron works, in the following

[45] Ex inf. Rev. E. Turner.

passage, which may be regarded as one of the finest
in that noble, though singular and laborious, topographical poem :—

> "These forests, as I say, the daughters of the Weald,
> (That in their heavy breasts had long their griefs concealed,)
> Foreseeing their decay each hour so fast come on,
> Under the axe's stroke, fetch'd many a grievous groan,
> When as the anvil's weight, and hammer's dreadful sound,
> Even rent the hollow woods and shook the queachy ground ;
> So that the trembling nymphs oppress'd through ghastly fear,
> Ran madding to the Downs with loose dishevell'd hair.
> The Sylvans that about the neighbouring woods did dwell,
> Both in the tufty frith and in the mossy fell,
> Forsook their gloomy bowers, and wander'd far abroad,
> Expell'd their quiet seats and place of their abode,
> When labouring carts they saw to hold their daily trade,
> Where they in summer wont to sport them in the shade.
> Could we, say they, suppose, that any would *us* cherish,
> Which suffer (every day) the holiest things to perish ?
> Or to our daily want to minister supply ?
> These Iron Times breed none, that mind posterity.
> 'Tis but in vain to tell what we before have been,
> Or changes of the world that we in time have seen ;
> When, not devising how to spend our wealth with waste,
> We to the savage swine let fall our larding mast.
> But now, alas ! ourselves we have not to sustain,
> Nor can our tops suffice to shield our roots from rain ;
> Jove's oak, the warlike ash, vein'd elm, the softer beech,
> Short hazel, maple plain, light asp, the bending wych,
> Tough holly, and smooth birch, must altogether burn,
> What should the builder serve, supplies the forger's turn ;
> When under public good base private gain takes hold,
> And we, poor woful woods, to ruin lastly sold."
>
> *Polyolbion*, Song xvii.

The relics of the iron trade during this century are
very abundant, particularly andirons, of almost every
imaginable pattern. The example overleaf, which I
lately purchased of a dealer in old iron at Lewes, is
ornamented with the arms of the family of Thatcher,
and was probably cast for the hall of their fine old

mansion, Priesthawes, in the parish of Westham.
The one at its side is one of a pair in the possession
of Mr. William Harvey.[46]   The upper portion of the
andiron is a *demy* human figure, in the costume of
temp. James I, holding a tobacco-pipe in the right
hand, and in the left a jug or tankard.   The bird on
the shield is perhaps intended for a phœnix.   The
columnar andiron (which may belong to the close of
the preceding century) is at Hammond's Place, Clayton, the property of Colonel Elwood.   This house
was a seat of the Michelbornes, but the initials I. T.
upon the andirons prove them to have belonged to
some other family; perhaps the Turners of Old Land,
in the same district.   The next, belonging to Mr.
Hassell, of Waldron, is a remarkably clean and deli-

[46] I avail myself of this opportunity of acknowledging the kind
assistance of Mr. Harvey, in calling my attention to the Burwash
slab, and to many of the other productions of the Sussex furnaces,
which illustrate this essay.

cate piece, of casting. It bears the date of 1640, and
a coat of arms, which I have not been able to appropriate. It is traditionally reported to have been cast
in the parish of Waldron. A pair of *monster* andirons, of about the same date, is in the possession of
Mr. A. Playsted, of Wadhurst. They are 39 inches
in height, and their style is Egyptian. The heraldric
bearing, which is much defaced, appears to be " a
cross between four martlets."

The chimney-backs of the seventeenth century are
likewise exceedingly various in point of design. Many
of them exhibit the royal arms, and the arms of noble
and other families belonging to the county; others,
classical stories, as Venus and Adonis, the Thief and
Dog, from Æsop, &c.; some are ornamented with
Scripture histories, particularly Abraham offering up
Isaac, the Queen of Sheba, Christ and the woman of
Samaria, &c.; and some with designs of a much more
objectionable character. On a back at Maresfield is

an equestrian figure of Charles I, with the initials
C. R.; and Mr. Ashby of East Dean possesses a very
curious one, adorned with an oak tree bearing acorns,
and the same initials, Among the branches are three
crowns, and on a scroll surrounding the trunk, the
words "THE ROYAL OAK"—allusive to the incident of
Charles II, the possessor of three crowns, taking
refuge in the oak at Boscobel.

From the early part of the seventeenth century,
down to the extinction of the manufacture, our foundries produced numbers of monumental slabs, which
are still remaining in the churches of Sussex and
Surrey. At Wadhurst there are no less than thirty
examples, ranging between the years 1625 and 1799.
The inscriptions and armorial decorations are in
general of very rude workmanship, and, as the slabs
lie upon the pavement of the nave and aisles, in somewhat inconveniently bold relief. The persons commemorated by them comprise individuals of the
families of Bucher, Porter, Fowle, Dunmoll, Barham,
Luck, Atwells, Braban, Holland, Saunders, Benge,
and Playsted, many of whom were connected with the
trade in this parish.

In 1643, after the taking of Chichester and Arundel
by the Parliament's forces, the iron-works belonging
to the crown and to royalists, in the western division
of Sussex, were destroyed by a detachment of the
army commanded by Sir William Waller.[47]

The mode of making iron in Sussex in the seventeenth century is detailed by John Ray, the celebrated
naturalist, in two papers appended to his 'Collection
of English Words.' "This account of the whole process of the iron-work," he says, "I had from one of
the chief iron-masters of Sussex, my honoured friend,

[47] Dallaway's Western Sussex.

Walter Burrell, of Cuckfield, Esq., deceased." The particulars of the *modus operandi* of the manufacture, furnished from so authentic a source, are of sufficient value to warrant their introduction in this place.

"THE MANNER OF THE IRON-WORK AT THE FURNACE.

" The iron-mine lies sometimes deeper, sometimes shallower, in the earth, from four to forty [feet] and upward.

" There are several sorts of mine, some hard, some gentle, some rich, some coarser. The iron-masters always mix different sorts of mine together, otherwise they will not melt to advantage.

" When the mine is brought in, they take small-coal [charcoal] and lay a row of it, and upon that a row of mine, and so alternately S.S.S., one above another, and setting the coals on fire, therewith burn the mine.

" The use of this burning is to mollify it, that so it may be broke in small pieces; otherwise if it should be put into the furnace as it comes out of the earth, it would not melt, but come away whole.

" Care also must be taken that it be not too much burned, for then it will *loop*, i.e. melt and run together in a mass. After it is burnt, they beat it into small pieces with an iron sledge, and then put it into the furnace (which is before charged with coals), casting it upon the top of the coals, where it melts and falls into the hearth, in the space of about twelve hours, more or less, and then it runs into a *sow*.

" The hearth, or bottom of the furnace, is made of sandstone, and the sides round, to the height of a yard, or thereabout; the rest of the furnace is lined up to the top with brick.

" When they begin upon a new furnace, they put fire for a day or two before they begin to blow.

"Then they blow gently and encrease by degrees 'till they come to the height in ten weeks or more.

"Every six days they call a *founday*, in which space they make eight tun of iron, if you divide the whole sum of iron made by the foundays: for at first they make less in a founday, at last more.

"The hearth by the force of the fire, continually blown, grows wider and wider, so that at first it contains so much as will make a sow of six or seven hundred pound weight; at last it will contain so much as will make a sow of two thousand pound. The lesser pieces, of one thousand pound, or under, they call pigs.

"Of twenty-four loads of coals, they expect eight tun of sows: to every load of coals, which consists of eleven quarters, they put a load of mine, which contains eighteen bushels.

"A hearth ordinarily, if made of good stone, will last forty foundays, that is forty weeks, during which time the fire is never let go out. They never blow twice upon one hearth, though they go upon it not above five or six foundays.

"The cinder, like scum, swims upon the melted metal in the hearth, and is let out once or twice before a sow is cast.

"THE MANNER OF WORKING THE IRON AT THE FORGE OR HAMMER.

"In every forge or *hammer* there are two fires at least; the one they call the *finery*, the other the *chafery*.

"At the finery, by the working of the hammer, they bring it into *blooms* and *anconies*, thus:

"The sow they, at first, roll into the fire, and melt off a piece of about three-fourths of a hundredweight, which, so soon as it is broken off, is called a *loop*.

" This *loop* they take out with their shingling-tongs, and beat it with iron sledges upon an iron plate near the fire, that so it may not fall in pieces, but be in a capacity to be carried under the hammer. Under which they, then removing it, and drawing a little water, beat it with the hammer very gently, which forces cinder and dross out of the matter; afterwards, by degrees, drawing more water, they beat it thicker and stronger 'till they bring it to a *bloom*, which is a four-square mass of about two feet long. This operation they call *shingling the loop*.

" This done, they immediately return it to the finery again, and after two or three heats and workings, they bring it to an *ancony*, the figure whereof is, in the middle, a bar about three feet long, of that shape they intend the whole bar to be made of it ; at both ends a square piece left rough to be wrought at the chafery.[48]

" *Note*. At the finery three load of the biggest coals go to make one tun of iron.

" At the chafery they only draw out the two ends suitable to what was drawn out at the finery in the middle, and so finish the bar.

" *Note* 1. One load of the smaller coals will draw out one tun of iron at the chafery.

" 2. They expect that one man and a boy at the finery should make two tuns of iron in a week : two men at the chafery should take up, i. e. make or work, five or six tun in a week.

[48] The definition of *ancony* given in this paragraph is adopted by Bailey in his Dictionary (folio, 1730). In common with several terms employed in anatomy and architecture, it seems to be derived from the Greek word ἄγκων.

" 3. If into the hearth where they work the iron sows (whether in the chafery or the finery) you cast upon the iron a piece of brass, it will hinder the metal from working, causing it to spatter about, so that it cannot be brought into a solid piece."[49]

An interesting relic of the manufacture is preserved at Howbourne, in the parish of Buxted.   This is the

old *hammer post*, which exists *in situ* near the extremity of the once extensive but now drained pond.   It is formed of an oak tree, and if not wantonly injured will stand for many years longer.   Its height above ground is nine and a half feet.

The greatest existing remains of Sussex iron are the balustrades which surround St. Paul's Cathedral.

[49] Ray's English Words not generally used (originally published in 1672), 4th edit., printed in 1768, p. 134 et seq.

They were cast at Lamberhurst furnace, and their weight, including the seven gates, is above 200 tons. Their cost, according to the account-books kept at the furnace, was £11,202. 0s. 6d.[50] It may be mentioned that the annual consumption of wood at this furnace was about 200,000 cords! This establishment was subsequently called Gloucester Furnace, in honour of its having received a visit from the princess (afterwards queen) Anne, and the Duke of Gloucester.

If we may credit the general report of the parish, the cannon cast at Gloucester Furnace were not always employed for the use of the British navy, but were conveyed by smugglers to the coast, and there shipped for the service of French privateers, in the war then waged against England. This villany was detected, and the parties engaged in it were fined to a large amount. The government contracts were of course withdrawn; and from this period we may date the decline of these works.

The iron-founders to King Charles II were Alexander Courthope, .Esq., of Horsmonden, co. Kent, and George Brown, Esq., of Buckland, co. Surrey: their foundries were at Ashburnham, Hawkhurst, Horsmonden, Barden, and Embden. Their correspondence, contracts with the commissioners of ordnance, &c., are in the possession of G. Courthope, Esq., of Whiligh.[51]

The manufacture continued to flourish with almost unabated vigour through the seventeenth century, and even in 1724 it was considered the chief interest of the county. In that year was published Budgen's Map of Sussex, a very useful document, as showing

[50] Topog. Libr. Sussex.
[51] Ex inf. W. Courthope, Esq., Rouge Croix.

the sites of the still existing works. The ornaments surrounding the title of it consist of emblems of the trade, Vulcan with Venus and Cupid, Cyclops at the anvil and forge, &c.

Besides the illicit exportation of cannon above-mentioned, much heavy ordnance was shipped in the eighteenth century from the ports of Rye and Newhaven. Some seems to have been sent to our Asiatic colonies. When the late Major Fuller entered on his first campaign in India he found with mingled pleasure and surprise some of the old artillery there inscribed with the name of his native village " Heath-field ! "

We owe many of our finest sheets of water to the iron manufacture. In other instances, the meadows which were converted into " ponds and pools," have again been drained and restored to their former use, or appropriated as hop-gardens and osier beds. The sites of many of the " hammers " are now occupied by corn-mills.

In choosing sites for the works, our iron-masters of course sought spots which were at once contiguous to the beds of ore and to some convenient water power. The places chosen for artificial ponds were generally the vales through which streams and rivu-lets flowed. Across these were thrown great dams of earth, usually known as " pond-bays," with a con-venient outlet of masonry for the supply of water, by means of which the wheel connected with the machinery of the " hammer " or the furnace was set in motion. A valley of moderate width was generally selected, as the narrow ravine and the broad level were equally objectionable, the former requiring too lofty, and the latter too long and expensive a pond-bay. All the Sussex rivers and their tributary streams within the first few miles of their course, are well adapted by nature for this useful purpose.

Upon the "decline and fall" of the trade few words are necessary. The amazing consumption of wood rendered the production of iron in this district more expensive than in those localities where the coal-mines and the ferruginous strata are in close proximity to each other. Upon Sir Roderic Murchison's authority, our wealds still contain a much greater quantity of iron-ore, and that of richer quality, than many of the coal-fields of England; but for the reason alluded to, competition with those districts was hopeless. In spite, however, of the invention of "charking"sea-coal, alluded to as a desideratum by Fuller,[52] Sussex still maintained its position as a seat of the iron trade long after the establishment of that process;[53] and many families were enriched by the alchemy of transmuting iron to gold so lately as the middle of the last century. Conspicuous among these was that of Legas, one of whose members, John Legas, Gent., "by his industry and diligence in the iron-works of this county, acquired a handsome fortune, with great credit and reputation. He died the 22d May, 1752, aged 62 years."[54] Even in the days of our grandfathers, cannon continued to be cast in some places, and the great hammer's "occupation" was not wholly "gone."[55]

[52] Worthies, vol. iii, p. 53, ed. 1840.

[53] So recently as 1754, it appears that a Staffordshire ironmaster could profitably engage in the manufacture of Sussex iron; since in that year Sir Whistler Webster, Bart., of Battel Abbey, let his Robertsbridge furnace to a Mr. John Churchill, of Hints, co. Stafford. The iron of the south, wrought with charcoal, was probably found serviceable for mixing with the pit-coal iron of the lessee's home manufacture.

[54] Mon. Inscr. in Wadhurst Church.

[55] From parliamentary papers quoted in the 'Encyclopædia Bri-

By degrees, however, the glare of the furnace faded, the din of the hammer was hushed, the last blast was blown, and the wood-nymphs, after a long exile, returned in peace to their beloved retreats! Farnhurst, in Western, and Ashburnham, in Eastern Sussex, witnessed the total extinction of the manufacture.

Some strange instances of the fluctuations of fortune are connected with the history of this trade in the South. The two following, relating to the parish of Wadhurst, one of the principal seats of the iron-works, are worthy of a special record.

At Riverhall, in Faircrouch quarter, there were a furnace and a forge worked by the Fowles, a family of considerable note,[56] whose prosperity rose and fell with the iron manufacture. Nicholas Fowle, who carried on these works, built in 1591 the fine mansion of Riverhall, which still exhibits traces of its former grandeur. His son, William Fowle, had a grant of free-warren from King James, over his numerous manors and lands in Wadhurst, Frant, Rotherfield, and Mayfield. The fourth in descent, and heir male of this personage, left Riverhall, and kept the turnpike-gate at Wadhurst. His grandson, Nicholas Fowle, a day-labourer, emigrated to America in 1839, with his son, John Fowle, a wheelwright, and a numerous young family, carrying with them as a family relic, the royal grant of free-warren given to their ancestor.

Brookland Forge and Ferredge Forge, on the borders of Frant, were worked by the Barhams of Butts, and Shoesmiths. John Barham of Butts, in

tannica,' it appears that in 1740 there were 59 furnaces in England, of which 10 were in Sussex. In 1788 there were 77, only 2 of which were in Sussex. In 1796 the total was, for England 104, for Sussex *one.*

[56] They were descended from a brother of Bartholomew Fowle, alias Linsted, last prior of St. Mary Overie, in Southwark.

Wadhurst, second son of a younger son of Henry Barham, Esq., lord of Barham, &c., co. Kent, a descendant (according to the Kentish historian and genealogist, Philipot) from Robert de Berham, son of Richard Fitz-Urse, and brother of the murderer of Thomas à Becket, was the founder of several branches of the Barhams inhabiting the mansions of Great Butts and Shoesmiths, the former of which has disappeared and been replaced by a miserable little house. His descendant, John Barham, resided there till about 1713, when he sold the remnants of his paternal inheritance. He died in obscurity in 1732, aged seventy-five. John Barham, grandson of the above-named John Barham of Great Butts, erected or rebuilt, about 1630, the beautifully-situated and spacious mansion of Shoesmiths, and worked Bartley Mill and Brookland Forges. His grandson was high-sheriff of the county, 14 William III, but at his decease his family fell into obscurity.

Scragoak works were formerly carried on by the Mansers, and afterwards by the Barhams; and Snape Furnace, the property of the Barhams, was worked by the Culpeper family about the middle of the seventeenth century. David Barham built the greater portion of the present house at Snape about 1617. He died in 1643, and is interred in the south aisle of Wadhurst Church, beneath an iron slab of very curious workmanship. This estate afterwards passed to the Barhams of Scragoak, who worked the furnace there, and this line of the Barhams terminated with Nicholas Barham, who died in the workhouse in 1788, aged eighty-two. The representative of these once distinguished families, now resident at Wadhurst, is Nicholas Barham, a wheelwright. [57]

[57] Ex inform. W. Courthope, Esq.

The day may not be far distant when Sussex iron shall again be called into use. If anthracite fuel were brought to the south coast, and some of the richer veins of ore near the eastern extremity of the county were re-opened, it is calculated that the smelting might be advantageously and profitably carried on here. Within the last few years, the attention of several gentlemen, practically connected with the iron trade in distant parts of the island, has been directed to this subject.

WINCHELSEA'S DELIVERANCE;

OR,

THE STOUT ABBOT OF BATTAYLE.

The Argument.

"THE Frenchmen came to the town of Winchelsey, where understanding the Abbot of Battell was come to defend it, they sent him word to redeeme the towne: unto whom the abbot answered, he needed not to redeeme the thing which was not lost, but willed them to desist from molesting the towne upon paine of that which might follow. The French exasperated at this answer, requested him that if hee would not have peace, hee would send forth to fight man to man, or more in number if he would, to trye the matter in view of armes; but neyther would the abbot admitte the one request or the other, saying he was a religious man, and therefore (ought) not to admitte such petitions, and that he came not hither to fight, but to defend and preserve the peace of the country. These things being heard, the Frenchmen, supposing the abbot and his people wanted courage, they assaulted the towne with such instruments of warre as cast forth stones far off, not ceasing from noone till evening; but by the laudable prowess of the abbot and such as were with him, the French prevailed nothing, but left it as they found it."—*Stowe's Chronicle*, pp. 278-9.

This happened in the year of grace 1377, the first of Richard II. Hamo de Offington was Abbot of Battel from 1364 to 1383. Battel Abbey was dedicated to St. Martin; and St. Thomas and St. Giles were the patrons of Winchelsea, in which town the Alards were a distinguished family. Brother Dunk is not wholly an imaginary personage, for the Chronicles inform us, that a short time previously to the attack of Winchelsea, the French, in one of their marauding excursions, captured *a monk of Battayle clad in complete armour*. None but the hypercritical will doubt that this was the identical brother who figures to so much advantage in the ensuing verses.

FYTTE YE FYRSTE.

IT was Midsummer time, at the season of prime,
    When many a knock and a shout
Did fiercely assail the great gate of Battayle,
    And call forth the warder so stout.

" Saynt Martin ! for sure ! " as he opened the door,
   Says he, " 'tis the young Squire Alárd,
From fair Winchelsee—as it seemeth to me,
   Good syr, you have ridden full hard."

" I have not ridden slow, as my gelding doth know,"
   To him said the right gallant youth:
" Now to the lord abbot I pray thee to go,
   And tell him this word from my mouth :—

" The Frenchmen are coming to burn Winchelsee,
   Are coming with tall galleys ten,
And unless we have aid, I am sorely afraid
   'Twill go hard with the Winchelsee men."

Now, hearing the rout, my lord abbot came out,
   And without any needless delay,
Bade summon his men, two hundred and ten—
   A goodly and doughty array.

" Brother Clement," he said, " go fetch my good
     blade,
   That hangeth up in the great hall ;
There's my jacket of mail hard by on a nail,
   And my greaves and my helmet withal.

" And, Sacristan Gower, hie thee to the tower,
   And ring out Saint Martin's great bell !
The men of Battayle for sure will not fail
   To know what *that* meaneth right well."

He bade a tall groom bring horses forth soon—
  He said, and the thing it was done;
For no order in vain gave he to his men,
  Stout Hamo, surnamed Offingtón.

Without the great gate his coming did wait
  Of tenants a sturdy long row,
In doublets of leather; in each cap a feather,
  In each hand a trusty yew bow.

There were yeomen and hinds from the forest so wide,
  And men from the mill and the forge;
And Alard did ride by the abbot his side,
  With the pennon of bold Saint George.

Knights and squires one or twey had taken their way,
  To lead on the valorous crowd,
While old Clement Dunk, a tall, sword-loving monk,
  Chanted *paters* and *aves* aloud.

The abbot on horse showed the footmen their course
  Through many a green glade and lea,
And in a short space, by 'r Lady's good grace,
  They were come unto fair Winchelsee.

FYTTE YE SECONDE.

Now the Frenchmen were coming full fast to the town,
  Were coming full fast to the wall,
When a herald did blow a *terly-lo-lo*,
  And loud on the abbot 'gan call.

"*Monsieur Abbé,*" said he, on his low-bended knee,
  "A word with my lord *s'il vous plait ;*
'Tis our *capitaine*'s will you should ransom *cette ville*
  With red gold, and then he will away !"

Then the abbot out said : " By Saint Martin's sword-
    blade,
  Bid thy maister to hold in his boast ;
Methinks, by the masse, he must deem me an asse,
  To ransom what never was lost !"

This angered the foe, both noble and low,
  And chiefly the grand capitaine,
Who swore a great oath by Saint Sepulchre's tooth,
  And sent forth his herald again.

"*Le grand Chevalere,* milord, sends me here,
  To challenge you forth to the fight ;
He biddeth me say, you will suffer this day
  The loss of full many a wight."

But Hamo of Offington meekly replied :
  " Carnal weapons, as holy writ saith,
'Vail little, and I, as a son of the Church,
  Fight only the good fight of Faith."

Brother Dunk, who stood by, rather turned up his
    eye,
  As he thought of the helmet and sword
He had fetched from the hall, at the good abbot's
    call,
  That morning—but said not a word.

The herald went back, and the Frenchmen, not slack
   To curse the lord abbot's reply,
Called him cowardly knave, and declared he should
   have
   Good space to repent by-and-bye.

So their engines they fetch, and their cables they
   stretch,
   To bring up each mighty machine;
The catapults all they put nigh to the wall,
   With battering-rams set between.

The portsmen prepare to perform well their share,
   In defending their gates from the foe:
The young Squire Alárd, too, is setting the guard;
   Brother Dunk runneth swift to and fro.

The abbot hath donned his bright raiment of steel;
   Saint Martin defend his old head!
The men of Battayle will never him fail,
   While life-blood remains to be shed.

Huge stones fly about, and the Frenchmen all shout:
   "Work the catapults!" "Rams to the breach!"
But good brother Dunk (that most valorous monk)
   Replies with hot lead and burnt pitch.

Now Saint Thomas defend! and Saint Giles his aid
   lend!
   Burning houses and dead men are here;
But the brave young Alárd is fighting full hard,
   And bidding the portsmen good cheer.

FYTTE YE THYRDE.

" But where is the abbot? and where is the monk?
  And where are the men of Battayle?
They are gone every one, and we're surely undone;
  Well-a-day when such brave men turn tayle.

" Alas and alas, that this cometh to pass ! "
  Said the Winchelsee men—all but one;
The young squire well knew that the abbot was true,
  Though he knew not for why he was gone.

But listen ! a shout from the town walls without,
  Saint Martin! Saint Martin's the cry.
From a low-sunken trench at the rear of the French,
  Ten-score of bright arrow shafts fly.

For the abbot so bold (and as true as fine gold),
  With his bowmen two hundred and mo',
By a postern hath sped, and hath gallantly led
  Them, unseen to the back of the foe.

Saint Martin ! Saint Martin ! again is the word,
  And again, all at once, bend the yew;
The cloth-yards have fled, and a Frenchman lies dead
  'Neath each arrow so keen and so true.

The foes in amaze right ruefully gaze
  On each other awhile, till at last
A trumpet is blown, and the Frenchmen are flown
  To the shore and their galleys in haste.

Then up, stalwart Offington ! up, gallant Dunk !
   And forth come ye portsmen so free !
For, thanks to the deeds of the abbot and monk,
   You 've gotten a brave victorie.

Now rest thee, lord abbot, till morning's fair light,
   Then betake thee to Battayle again,
And let loud *Te Deums* be chanted aright
   At the holy Saint Martin his fane.

Alárd, may God save thee, thou gallant young squire,
   And thy kindred in fair Winchelsee :
Let masses be said in Saint Thomas's choir
   For the foes whom the bowmen did slee !

THE SOUTH DOWNS—A SKETCH.

"To freedom, thought, and peace, how dear!
To freedom, for no fence is seen:
  To thought, for silence soothes the way;
To peace, for o'er the boundless green
  Unnumbered flocks and shepherds stray."—*Bloomfield*.

WHO, from Cornwall to Caithness, from Kent to
Cardigan, has not heard of the South Down hills?
Who that loves travel has not at some time or other,
like White of Selborne, expatiated on their broadly-
extended slopes and rounded summits? or, like John
Ray, admired the goodness of the Creator in spreading
this ample, this sweetly-undulated, verdant carpet for
the foot of man? "I have heard of them," the
gourmand may perhaps reply, "and I like the mutton
which they produce better than any other." "And I,"
the languid pleasure-seeker may adjoin, "why, I have
seen them two or three times when I have been
'down at Brighton;' but I must say I thought them
remarkably dull—nothing but turf and ploughed land,
ploughed land and turf, everywhere; no trees, no
hedges—all one monotonous brownish-green waste!"
Hold there, good friend; stay awhile; look again.
Take a few turns with us over their broad sides;
ascend with us a few of their plastic promontories;
dive with us into their wondrously secluded valleys;
let us examine in company their historic sites, their
curious natural productions, animate and otherwise;
pore over their romantic associations, and listen to

the folk-lore of their denizens—to tales of smuggler
and fairy, and quaint legends of ancient days, as they
come, in unsophisticated Saxon phrase, from plough-
man and shepherd ; and when we have so " perlus-
trated, investigated, and expatiated " over their unen-
cumbered expanse, then, and not till then, let us
decide whether the South Downs are in any sense
dull, dreary, and monotonous.

To avoid the suspicion of prejudice, let us say, *in
limine*, that we claim not our birth-place among these
hills. The chain which is said so sweetly to bind
mortals to their natal soil enthrals us not. We are
free to admire whatever is beautiful or majestic
wherever found ; we have no patron to serve, no lands
to sell, no "eligible building leases " to glorify,
while we challenge on behalf of the South Downs
an amount of interest scarcely to be claimed by any
like district in the realm.

Noble hills! mountains in miniature ; but not
mountains either. The rugged sublimity attaching
to that idea they do not possess. Grandeur they
have, and much beauty. Hear dear quaint old Gilbert White, no bad authority on such a question : " I
think," says he, " there is something peculiarly sweet
and amusing in the shapely figured aspect of chalk
hills in preference to those of stone, which are rugged,
broken, abrupt, and shapeless." A cursory view of
them would lead one to pronounce the absence of two
elements generally considered essential to the picturesque—wood and water—as damnatory of any
rightful claim to the eye of taste. But we maintain
that, in any point of view, the South Downs, despite
this absence of sylvan and aqueous features, still
demand our notice and admiration. We look upon
them with somewhat of the same feeling which pos-

sesses the sea-going traveller, who, with only two elements of the picturesque—sky and salt water— finds infinite pleasure in all that his eyes behold. Nor is the supposed analogy unapt; for the wavy ever-varying contour of our Downs presents the very diversity of surface which gives a charm to the sea-view. There is, however, this difference; that while the latter pleases from the restlessness of its undulations, these " everlasting hills " gratify and soothe the mind by their calm and immoveable repose. The two things differ from each other as does a giant in action from a giant asleep !

One great source of the charm which attends these hills is doubtless their delicate turf, so agreeable to the traveller whether he employs two legs or four. There is none like it under the sun—so soft, so dry it is—so smooth and gentle beneath the foot, equine or human. The next source of pleasurable sensation is the almost boundless expanse over which we may wander and gallop without obstruction. No bluff game-keeper interposes with his " Take care of your dog," — no uncourteous wooden-headed intimation that there is "No thoroughfare" obtrudes itself upon the notice of the by-passer. All around seems to say, " Go where you like—make yourself at home—glad to see you. Would you like to lie down a bit? Or take off your coat for the sake of coolness ? Do so by all means; we are not particular. We have no hedges hard by to engender snakes. Toads never come up here. Take your ease—you are welcome ! " The traveller may deviate from the beaten path, and go " up hill, down dale " without the least offence to crusty land-owners, or the slightest danger to his neck. Some of these advantages might, it is true, be predicated of an Arabian desert, but no desert anywhere can say of itself what we boldly affirm of the South Downs, namely, that go where you please over their ample area, you shall most certainly never see two spots alike,—never feel annoyed by the monotony of the prospect. In their sweet undulations there are continually changing curves and indents, which vary as they may—from the precipitous valley down which a confident horseman would scarcely urge his courser, to the gentle declivity where the most delicate lady (in imitation of the fairies which of old haunted it) might dance—are always "lines of beauty," such as we confidently believe have nowhere else an existence, except, perhaps, in some graceful island group of the Pacific.

What a charming picture of quiet English life does a South Down village present! You may traverse these hills unconscious of the proximity of human habitations, and with a feeling almost amounting to we, wondering at the solemn stillness of the scene, and tempted to ask yourself whether you are really in busy, teeming, railway-traversed England, and within a league of that great "highway of the nations," the English Channel, when, lo, the top of an adjacent brow is gained, and suddenly a scene unfolds itself such as no country save England, and no county except Sussex, can yield. Lying at your feet, two or three hundred yards distant, as if put there for your own proper delectation and joy, is a cluster of lowly habitations, some thatched, some tiled, some abutting the street, some standing angularly towards it, but all built of flint or boulders. Here a barn, a stable, a circular pigeon-house, centuries old, with its denizens (direct descendants of the old manorial pigeons which lived here in the days of the Plantagenets), and an antique gable or two, covered with Horsham stone, peer

out among tall elms, and show you the habitation of
the farmer, who with much of patriarchal simplicity
rules the destinies of a little community of husbandmen
and shepherds.   A pretty place this farm-stead generally is, with its high-walled garden behind, and its
smooth lawn and flower-beds in front.   The house is
an old one, built of flint, with stone window-frames,
and door-cases, and a high-pitched roof crowned with
a stack or two of old-fashioned chimneys of elaborate
and fantastical design.   This was a gentleman's house
once, and it is still called "the Court," or "the Place,"
or some other name indicative of its olden importance.
The present occupant is probably as wealthy, or nearly
so, as the ancient owner who put in the stone window-frames and built the antique chimney-stacks, and
in all likelihood possesses as strong a claim to being a
"gentleman" in the true sense of the word as he
did; he is, however, as the phrase goes, a "gentleman-
farmer" only.   It may chance, too, that he can
boast of as respectable an ancestry as the other; for
he is in possession of "capital" derived from a long
line of thrifty progenitors, members of an aristocracy
of agriculturists, who have been occupants, "time out
of mind," of that very South Down mansion and
farm.   We know several men of this class, whose
ancestors have been tenants of the same fertile acres
from the time of the Maiden Queen; and Sussex can
produce many instances of the tillers of the soil
having a more permanent interest in that soil than
the proprietors themselves.   For two or three centuries, in spite of the fluctuations of agricultural affairs,
these men have maintained their standing as tenants
of land, which, from reverses of fortune, or the extinction of families, has frequently changed owners. . . .
Close to the garden wall stands the church, a little

grey edifice, with a diminutive tower of flint, and a low tiled spire, surrounded by its cemetery, in which "the rude forefathers of the hamlet sleep." The architecture of this humble house of prayer was originally good, though simple and unpretending, but it has generally been queerly deformed by a slate roof, and perhaps by a sash-window, painted white, in the chancel; still, in spite of these obvious defects you look upon it with far more favour than yesterday you did upon the gimcrack, pinnacled, and crocketed thing, called a "district church," upon Cobbley Common in the Weald. At the base of yonder opposite hill are a snug little school-house in the Elizabethan (or, as a quaint friend of ours calls some of these erections, Eliza-*beastly*) style, and some more straggling cottages, intermixed with gardens, forming the lane leading up to the parsonage-house, which, with its stuccoed front and young plantations, tells of recent re-erection, and suggests comfortable reflections upon the bounty of Queen Anne. Higher up you get a view of ox-teams and horse-teams, plodding lazily over the furrow-streaked "laines," and a shepherd guarding his fleecy charge. As you descend into the "Dean," whose surrounding hills shut out the rest of the world from this pleasant picture, you cannot help thinking that, if the slated roof, and the sash-window, and the stuccoed front, were away, you might easily imagine yourself pushed back into the middle of the reign of Elizabeth, and forget that newspapers and railways existed.

Then again, the air of these hills is among the purest in the world. The chalky soil absorbs all moisture, and stagnant water cannot exist upon it. The demon malaria cannot show his baleful front on these breezy plains, and it is only where an occasional gross disregard of cleanliness in the vicinity of houses prevails that he sometimes puts in his appearance. It is impossible to traverse the South Downs without a sensible elevation of the animal spirits. Horses as well as men seem to participate in this feeling, and manifest their pleasure in fifty quiet ways. Then look at the sheep; what a manifest difference they present to their congeners of the lowland meadows. There is almost as great a disparity between the two families as between the wild fowl and the tame, the pheasant and the barn-door chicken. It is to the fine climate, and sweet short grass of their *habitat*, rather than to any structural peculiarity, that we owe the finest mutton in existence. With regard to the absence of wood, it should be remembered that this is owing more to the neglect of its cultivation than to any inability of the soil to produce it. Wherever we find a gentleman's seat, we see timber flourish, especially beech, elm, and fir. In the *holts*, as small groves are locally designated, ash, hazel, and even oak succeed very well. Among shrubs, furze,[1] heath, juniper, and box are natives of the South Downs, though the last two are of rather rare occurrence. Our favourite in the South Down arboreticum is the hawthorn. See that cluster of them in the *combe* below us. Venerable trees they are, with their grey stems, the growth of ages, perhaps of centuries, contrasting beautifully with their fresh green foliage of the last month's growth—an emblem of Nature herself, always old, yet constantly rejuvenescent.

The South Downs afford a fine field for the naturalist as well as for the sportsman. One cannot but regret, however, the extinction of some of the animals which they formerly nourished, particularly

---

[1] Furze is locally called *hawth*, and sometimes *fuzzes*.

that fine indigenous bird, the bustard or wild turkey. The grandfather of the present writer was among the last who joined in the sport, about the middle of the last century, of hunting down the last remains of the species with dogs and bludgeons. The badger is now extremely rare; but this is not, considering the mischievous character of the tribe, so much to be regretted. The wheatear (*Sylvia Œnanthe*) is becoming much less numerous than heretofore, to the great loss of the shepherds. The T-shaped incisions or traps in the turf, are still seen, however, at the proper season, and many a timid, inoffensive bird still subjects itself to "capital punishment" in the horse-hair noose insidiously concealed within. In the neighbourhood of Mount Caburn a single shepherd is recorded to have caught eighty-four dozen in one day—but this was nearly a century ago. Even a greater number than this must have fallen to the share of a shepherd remembered by a friend of ours. This man, after having filled a large bag and his wife's apron with the game, was fain to take off his "round frock," and to fasten the neck and sleeves of that rustic garment by way of sack, which he filled to repletion with his delicious victims. It was formerly a lawful, and rather a common, practice, for wayfarers, on coming to a wheatear trap, to take out the bird, and to leave a penny as a "*quid* pro quo," which it often literally was—as this small pecuniary deposit was commonly appropriated to the purchase of tobacco. We are afraid that a lower tone of morals in this respect is now prevalent. The wheatear is reckoned no way inferior to the Ortolans of Southern Europe. Fuller, in his 'Worthies' (iii, 240), gives the following account of it:—"Wheatears is a bird peculiar to this county—hardly found out of it. It is so called

7 §

because fattest when wheat is ripe, whereon it feeds [incorrect], being no bigger than a lark, which it equalleth in the fineness of the flesh, far exceedeth in the fatness thereof. The worst is, that being only seasonable in the heat of summer, and naturally larded with lumps of fat, it is soon subject to corrupt, so that (though abounding within forty miles) London poulterers have no mind to meddle with them, which no care in carriage can keep from putrefaction. That palate-man shall pass in silence, who being seriously demanded his judgment concerning the abilities of a great lord, concluded him a man of very weak parts ' because he saw him at a great feast feed on chickens when there were wheatears on the table !' "

One of the most interesting objects which the naturalist will find upon the South Downs are the numerous fairy-rings or " hag-tracks" as they are sometimes called. They are perhaps not only more abundant, but better defined on these hills than elsewhere. They are sometimes of great size, measuring fifty or sixty feet in diameter. Sometimes they appear and disappear in the course of a year or two, but we have known instances in which they have retained a distinct and unvarying form for many successive years. Their origin is a matter of some uncertainty. It has been ascribed to that *dernier ressort* of many of the arcana of nature, electricity. Our own belief is that the cause is to be found in the growth of various species of mushrooms,[2] which are invariably found in these bright green circles—a theory which has received the sanction of Drs. Hutton and Wollaston. It is

[2] Besides the edible agarics there are several varieties of toad-stools and puff-balls. The latter are known among shepherds as "Satan's snuff-boxes." The common table mushroom grows in great quantities on the Downs. A friend of ours sold the produce of a field of eleven acres one summer for twenty-five pounds.

Hutton's opinion, based upon the positions which these fungi occupy, that they are formed by a progressive increase from a centre. " I thought it not impossible," says Wollaston, " that the soil which had once contributed to the support of fungi might be so exhausted of some peculiar pabulum, necessary for their production, as to be rendered incapable of producing a second crop of that singular class of vegetables. The second year's crop would consequently appear in a small ring surrounding the original centre of vegetation, and at every succeeding year the defect of nutriment on one side would necessarily cause the new roots to extend themselves solely in the opposite direction, and would occasion the circles of fungi continually to proceed by annual enlargement from the centre outwards. An appearance of luxuriance in the grass would follow as a natural consequence, as the soil of an interior circle would always be encircled by the decayed roots of fungi of the preceding year's growth." The Doctor's subsequent observations and experiments went far to substantiate this ingenious theory.[3]

[3] Old Aubrey, the Wiltshire antiquary and naturalist, one of the most credulous men of his credulous age, has a wondrous theory upon the subject. " In the yeare 1633-4, soone after I had entered into my grammar at the Latin Schoole at Yatton Keynel, our curate, Mr. Hart, was annoyed one night by these elves and fayries. Comming over the downes, it being neere darke, and approaching one of the fairey dances, as the common people call them in these parts, viz. the greene circles made by those sprites on the grasse, he all at once sawe an innumerable quantitie of pigmies or very small people dancing rounde and rounde, and singing, and making all manner of small odd noyses." So much for the *fact*—now for the theory, which we hope the reader will find more intelligible than we have done . . . . " As to these circles, I presume they are generated from the breaking out of a fertile subterraneous vapour, which comes from a kind of conical concave, and endeavours to get out at a narrow passage at the top, which forces it to make another cone inversely situated to the

It is not, however, our intention, in this sketch, to invade the realms of science, or to trouble the reader with botanical researches. We should be more at home with the poetical superstition, hardly yet extinct, that these mysterious rings are formed by the feet of the fairies in their nocturnal dances. An age or two back, before Penny Magazines and Mechanics' Institutions were invented, this was the universal belief among the ploughmen and shepherds; and no inconsiderable amount of " folk-lore" of this kind might still be collected from the mouths of the older denizens of the secluded Deans and Combes, as the valleys of the South Downs are denominated; though the rehearsal would probably be prefixed by some phrase strongly implying a want of faith, or at least of sufficient courage to avow it, such as " They used to say when I was a boy," or, " My old uncle Tuppen used to tell us youngsters." As in the case of ghosts, however, the love of the wonderful to this day outweighs with some the suggestions of reason; and the sceptical air only serves to conceal a lingering faith in a species of mythology which has been handed down from Saxon forefathers through the lapse of thirty generations.

In the days of our grandfathers, some rustic Will Fowington, or some ancient Dame Boxholt, would entertain a group of unlettered village children by the hour with the marvellous adventures which some of their forefathers or former acquaintance had experienced with the *Pharisees*, as fairies were always

other, the top of which is the green circle . . . . If you digge under the turfe of this circle, you will find at the rootes of the grasse a hoare or mouldinesse . : . . Mem:—that pidgeon's dung and nitre steeped in water will make the fairy circles : it drawes to it the nitre of the aire, and will never weare out."—*Halliwell's Fairy Mythology*, p. 122.

locally designated. Indeed the popular superstition was supposed to be sanctioned by scriptural authority. Pharisees were mentioned in the Bible, and that was a proof of their existence ! " Besides," old Fowington would argue, " though I have never seen any of 'em, my grandmother, who was a very truthful woman, has, time and often. They was liddle folks not more than a foot high, and used to be uncommon fond of dancing. They jound[4] hands and formed a circle, and danced upon it till the grass came three times as green there as it was anywheres else. That's how these here rings come upon the hills. Leastways so they say; but I don't know nothing about it, in tye,[5] for I never seen none an 'em; though to be sure it's very hard to say how them rings do come, if it is'nt the Pharisees that makes 'em. Besides there's our old song that we always sing at harvest supper, where it comes in—' We'll drink and dance like Pharisees.' Now I should like to know why it's put like that 'ere in the song, if it a'nt true."

This folk-lore has, as we have said, been handed down from ancient times, and believed in by a race of simple-minded folk, independently of the sanction given to it by our poets of the sixteenth and seventeenth centuries; and it is curious to observe how it coincides with the orthodox creed of those poets. Shakespeare, in the ' Midsummer Night's Dream,' makes one of the " liddle folks " say—

> " I serve the fairy queen
> To dew *her orbs upon the green*."

And again, Titania to Oberon—

> " If you will patiently *dance in our round*,
> And see our moonlight revels, go with us."

---

[4] This is the Sussex preterite of the verb " to join."
[5] *In tye*—not I.

In the ' Life of Robin Goodfellow ' (Halliwell's ' Fairy Mythology ') we have—

> " Little fairyes
> That doe fillch, blacke, and pinche mayds of the dairyes
> Make *a ring on the grasse with your quicke measures :*
> Tom shall play, and I'll sing for all your pleasures."

In an ' Episode of Fairies ' in the same collection—

> " Round about, round about, *in this fine ring-a*
> *Thus we dance,* thus we dance, and thus we sing-a,
> Trip and go, to and fro, over this green-a,
> All about, in and out, for our brave queen-a."

Further, our favourite Drayton, in his ' Nymphidia '—

> " And *in their courses make that round*
> In meadows and in marshes found,
> Of them so call'd the fairy ground,
> Of which they have the keeping." [6]

But to return. Several well-connected fairy stories were current, from ancient tradition, towards the close of the last century; and we are enabled, through the aid of one, who, himself a native of the South Downs, has now passed the " three-score and ten " of life, to preserve one or two of these all but obsolete legends, which we shall take the liberty of relating, as nearly as may be collected, in the *verba ipsissima* of the Master Fowington aforesaid. With regard to the first of these stories, I have only to premise that Burlow Castle formerly stood on an elevated spot near the little river Cuckmere, which is the western boundary of the easternmost group of the Downs.

" When I was a liddle boy and lived with my gurt uncle, old Jan Duly at—, dere was a old place dey used to call Burlow Castle. It wa'nt much ov a

[6] For these citations, some of which were new to us, we are indebted to the " Antiquities and Folk-lore of Worcestershire," by J. Allies, Esq., F.S.A.

castle—onny a fow old walls like—but it had been a
famous place in de time when dere was a king in every
county.[7]   Well, whatever it had been afore, at the
time I speak an, it was de very hem of a place for
Pharisees, and nobody didn't like to goo by it ahter
dark for fear an um.   One dee as Chols Packham,
uncle's grandfather (I've heerd uncle tell de story a
dunnamany times), was at plough up dere, jest about
cojer [8] time, he heerd a queer sort of a noise right
down under de groun dat frightened him uncommonly
sure-lie.   ' Hullow,' says Chols to his mate, ' did you
hear dat, Harry?'   'Yahs,' says Harry, ' what was
it?'   ' I reckon 'twas a Pharisee,' says uncle's grandfather.   ' No 'twa'nt,' says Harry, ' dere a'nt no
Pharisees now.   Dere *was once*—at Jerusalem; but
dey was full-growed people, and has been dead hun-
derds o' years.'   Well, while dey was a talkin', Chols
heerd de noise agin.   ' Help! help! help!'   Chols
was terribly afeard, but he plucked up heart enough to
ax what was wanted.   ' I've been a bakin,' said de
liddle voice, ' and have broke my peel,' (dat's a sort o'
thing dat's used to put loaves into de oven wud) ' and
I dunnow what upon de airth to do.'   *Under* de
airth, Chols thought she ought to a said, but howsonever he didn't say so.   And being a tender-hearted
kind of a chap dat didn't like any body to be in
trouble, he made answer without any peramble,
' Put it up, and I'll try and mend it.'   No soonder
said dan done; dere was a chink in de groun', for
de season was dryish, and sure enough, through dat
chink dere come up a liddle peel not bigger dan a
bren-cheese knife.   Chols couldn't hardly help

[7] It is a common notion in the South that every county once had
its king.

[8] A Sussexism for luncheon taken about eleven o'clock.

laughin', it was such a monstus liddle peel, not big
enough to hold a gingey-bread nut hardly ; but howsonever he thought 'twas too seerous a thing to laugh
at, for he knowed of old how dahngerous 'twas to
offend any of dem liddle customers. So he outs wud
a tin-tack or two as he happened to have in his weskit
pocket, and wud de help ov his cojer knife for a hammer, and his knee for a bench, he soon mended de
peel and put it down de chink again. Harry was
back-turned while dis was a gooin on, and when he
come back Chols up and told him all about it; but
Harry said 'twas all stuff, and he didn't believe a
word consarnin' ant, for Master Pettit, de parish clerk,
had told him 'twas all a galusion, and dere wa'nt no
Pharisees now-adays.

" But howsonever he proved to be wrong more ways
dan one ; for de nixt dee at cojer time when Harry
was back-turned agin, Chols Packham heerd de voice
as afore a comin' up out ov de chink and a sayin',
' Look here ! ' Well Chols turned roun', not quite so
much frightened dis time, and what should he see
standin' close agin de chink but a liddle bowl full of
summut dat smelt a hem-an-all better dan small beer.
' Hullow ! ' thinks Chols to his-self, ' dis is worth
havin', he thinks. So he tasted it, and at last drunk
it all up; and he 'llowed, dat of all de stuff *he* ever
tasted dat was de very best. He was a gooin to save
de liddle bowl to show Harry that dere certainly *was*
fairies, but whelst he was a thinking about it, all of a
sudden de bowl slipped out of his hands and deshed
itself into a hunderd pieces ; so dat Harry onny
laughed at him, and said 'twas naun but a cracked
basin. But howsonever Harry got sarved out for
bein' so unbelievin', for he fell into a poor way, and
coudn't goo to work as usual, and he got so tedious

'ɔad, dat he fell away to mere skin and boän, and no
doctors couldn't do him no good, and dat very day
twelmont he died, at de very same hour dat de Pharisees was fust heerd, and dat he spoke agin 'em.

"An ol' brother of my wife's gurt gran'mother *see*
some Pharisees once, and 'twould a been a power
better if so be he hadn't never seen 'em, or leastways
never offended 'em. I 'll tell ye how it happened.
Jeems Meppom—dat was his naüm—Jeems was a
liddle farmer, and used to thresh his own corn.   His
barn stood in a very *elenge* lonesome place, a goodish
bit from de house, and de Pharisees used to come
dere a nights and thresh out some wheat and wuts for
him, so dat de hep o' threshed corn was ginnerly bigger in de mornin dan what he left it overnight. Well,
ye see, Mas' Meppom thought dis a liddle odd, and
didn't know rightly what to make ant.   So bein' an
out-and-out bold chep, dat didn't fear man nor devil,
as de sayin is, he made up his mind dat he'd goo over
some night to see how 'twas managed.   Well accordingly he went out rather airly in de evenin', and laid
up behind de mow, for a long while, till he got rather
tired and sleepy, and thought 'twaunt no use a
watchin' no longer.   It was gittin' pretty handy to
midnight, and he thought how he'd goo home to bed.
But jest as he was upon de move he heerd a odd sort of
a soun' comin' tóe-ards the barn, and so he stopped
to see what it was.   He looked out of de strah,
and what should he catch sight an but a couple of
liddle cheps about eighteen inches high or dereaway
come into de barn without uppening the doores.   Dey
pulled off dere jackets and begun to thresh wud two
liddle frails as dey had brung wud em at de hem of a
rate.   Mas' Meppom would a been froughten if dey
had been bigger, but as dey was such tedious liddle

fellers, he couldn't hardly help bustin right out a laffin'. Howsonever he pushed a hanful of strah into his mouth and so managed to kip quiet a few minutes a lookin' at um—thump, thump; thump, thump, as riglar as a clock.

"At last dey got rather tired and left off to rest derselves, and one an um said in a liddle squeakin' voice, as it might a bin a mouse a talkin':—' I say Puck, I tweat; do you tweat?" At dat Jeems couldn't contain hisself no how, but set up a loud haw-haw; and jumpin' up from de strah hollered out, ' I'll tweat ye, ye liddle rascals; what bisness a you got in my barn?" Well upon dis, de Pharisees picked up der frails and cut away right by him, and as dey passed by him he felt sich a queer pain in de head as if somebody had gi'en him a lamentāble hard thump wud a hammer, dat knocked him down as flat as a flounder. How long he laid dere he never rightly knowed, but it must a bin a goodish bit, for when he come to 'twas gittin dee-light. He could'nt hardly contrive to doddle home, and when he did he looked so tedious bad dat his wife sent for de doctor dirackly. But bless ye, *dat* waunt no use; and old Jeems Meppom knowed it well enough. De doctor told him to kip up his sperits, beein' 'twas onny a fit he had had from bein' a most smothered wud de handful of strah and kippin his laugh down. But Jeems knowed better. ' Tā-ünt no use, sir,' he says, says he, to de doctor; ' de cuss of de Pharisees is uppán me, and all de stuff in your shop can't do *me* no good.' And Mas' Meppom was right, for about a year ahtawuds he died, poor man! sorry enough dat he'd ever inta-fēred wud things dat didn't consarn him. Poor ol' feller, he lays buried in de church-aird over yender— leastways so I've heerd my wife's mother say, under de bank jest where de bed of snowdraps grows."

The conclusion of this legend reminds us of a custom which we think peculiar to the South Down churchyards—that of planting snowdrops in them. We have noticed beds of this flower, particularly in those of the eastern portion of the range; and their effect in early spring, scattered over the tombless graves of the lowly, is peculiarly affecting. It was under such an impression that the following lines first saw the light:—

SONNET

Suggested by the sight of a bed of Snowdrops growing in the Church-
yard at Jevington, Sussex, Feb. 16, 1850.

Sweet flower, say wherefore hast thou thus become
(Commingling with the grass beneath our feet)
A resident in awful Death's retreat.
Leaving the garden, thy more natural home,
Art thou become a mourner—dost thou show,
With downcast head and face as pale as snow,
A sorrow for the dead? Or, rather, dost thou give
A lesson to the living—emblem fair
Of things beyond the tomb, in regions where
The dead who sleep in Jesus ever live?
Emerging gently from the darksome sod,
Where erst in wintry days thou hast been laid,
In purest white of innocence array'd,
Thou *liv'st again* with joy, before the face of God!

The last half century, which has done so much to alter and generally to ameliorate the condition of society all over these realms, has not overlooked—that is to say, if a half-century can either look at or overlook anything—the population of the South Downs. The shepherds and ploughmen who inhabit these hills are a far less unsophisticated race than they were a couple of generations back, and in an equal degree less interesting. Understand, if you please, gentle reader, we are, to speak generally, no Tory—no advocate of a stationary condition of life and manners; but still we cannot but regret in some little degree the loss of that primitive and almost patriarchal simplicity which formerly characterized the inhabitants of the South Downs. Let us look for a moment at a shepherd such as our grandfathers well knew, and we shall find some traits of character and condition which have disappeared, but which we could almost wish to see restored. The shepherd of our grandfathers' times was not a mere hireling who could be turned off by an ill-tempered or imperious master at a week's notice. His settled wages, indeed, were very small—ten or fourteen pounds a year, perhaps—but then he had some thirty or forty ewes of his own, for which he had to pay down some golden guineas when he took the place. These ewes ran with the flock and fared as the rest did, and when any sheep were sold he always received a proportionate share of the money; and the same with the wool after sheep-shearing; so that he was a sort of humble partner with his master. In those days the farmer had little to do with his flock, but left everything to his shepherd, who was always a steady, trustworthy, man. Now, the sheep-breeder takes the oversight himself, and the man who carries the crook is in reality only a kind of under shepherd, with few motives for exertion but such as are common to hirelings. As an old shepherd once remarked to us, "It made great odds to a shepherd's trying his best when he knew that every pound he earned for his master put a sixpence into his own pocket. That's what my father used to call 'having a stake in the hedge.' This plan made the shepherds more thoughtful, and gave them more *forecast* about things than they seem to have now. The shepherds then were not common day-labourers, but were looked upon as rather respectable folks in their way . . . . Old Mr. S. used to treat my father more as a kind of friend than as a mere servant, and always asked his mind about what land he should sow with turnips, and what ground he might break up for corn without hurting the 'run' of the flock; and so there was always a good understanding between master and man, more such as the scripture gives us an account of than what we see now."

The comparative respectability of the shepherd in old times is shown by the custom, formerly prevalent on the South Downs, of their being small landholders. "Shepherds' acres" are found in many places; but only the name remains, the property having been absorbed by some neighbouring farm. Often, too, under the peculiar system known as "Tenantry" the shepherd held by inheritance one or more parcels of land in the manor, which he usually let to his master. Many of the existing shepherds of the Downs, though they cannot as of old account themselves men of property, are notwithstanding men of *family*, and might, if so disposed, by the help of parish registers, easily prove their descent from the days of the Charleses through an unbroken line of pastoral progenitors, although the observation that families below patrician rank seldom remain more than three generations in one parish holds good of them. But though they remove from place to place, they rarely forsake their great habitat —the South Downs. Like certain plants, they only thrive well upon this chalky soil. For "ages and generations" the names of Tuppen, Duly, Dudeney, Carter, Thomas, Pettit, Bussey, and others, have been thus associated with the shepherd's crook.

But the same thing may be said in a still greater

degree of the shepherds' masters, the South Down
farmers—we beg their pardon, *agriculturists*—many
of whom are likewise proprietors of land. For two,
three, four, or even five centuries, they have adhered
to that soil of which they may almost claim to be
autochthones — earth-born sons. The Farncombes
were " of that Ilk" near Brighton, in the days before
Crescy and Poictiers, and they still hold on ' the even
tenour of their way' in the locality, occasionally in the
lapse of generations furnishing branches to higher
social grades and to other pursuits. One of this name,
of whom Sussex may well be proud, lately filled the
civic chair of the metropolis of these realms. The
Beards of Rottingdean are of equal antiquity, and
have supplied the rank of gentry with more than one
prosperous offshoot. Ridges, Ades, Scrases, Lambes,
Saxbys, Coopers, Verralls, Woodhamses, Rogerses,
Kings, Hodsons, Bynes, Marchants, Bulls, Turners,
Blakers, Olivers, Bushbys, Dukes, Penfolds, and Bot-
tings, flourish well on the Downs, and if they are found
elsewhere, they are but the exceptions that establish
the rule of their destiny, which fixes them to these verdant hills and valleys. Not many years since, a landed
proprietor who served the office of high sheriff of the
county selected the whole body of his javelin-men
from his own tenantry, and from the name and family
of Botting, all denizens of the Downs.

But *revenons à nos moutons*, or rather to those who
kept them—the South-Down shepherds of old times.
A truly primitive folk they were a hundred years back
—those orthodox pastors who lived when our grandfathers were boys. They were not exactly Arcadian
in manners. Our northern clime had robbed them
of the poetical outside of classic Damons, and the
stern and responsible duties of pitching the fold,

and caring for the flock amidst the snows of winter, rendered them anything but the *beaux ideals* of the stage, and of lackadaisical sonnetteers. They were fond, it is true, of the pipe, an instrument which afforded them high gratification whenever they played upon it, and which poured forth volumes, not of sweet melody indeed, but of fragrant smoke. In brief, it was not the pipe of the Arcadian deity,—

> "disparibus septem compacta cicutis
> Fistula,"—

but the pipe of *tobacco* which afforded them solace. Perhaps we could not, in our desire truly to depict the olden South Down shepherds, do better than quote the very words of one now dead, who had himself carried the shepherd's crook, and worn the shepherd's "great coat" for many a year on these hills.

"The life of a shepherd in my young days was not the same as it is now. Many things have been altered a good deal, besides what I was a speaking of just now. You very seldom see a shepherd's hut on our hills in these times, but formerly every shepherd had one. Sometimes it was a sort of cave dug into the side of a bank or *link*, and had large stones inside. It was commonly lined with heath or straw. The part above ground was covered with sods of turf, or heath, or straw, or boughs of hawth. In rough, *shuckish* weather, the shepherd used to turn into this hut, and lie by the hour together, only just looking out once in a while to see that his sheep didn't stray too far. Here he was safe and dry, however the storm might blow overhead, and he could sit and amuse himself as he liked best. If he could read, so much the better. It was in *my* hut, over in the next bottom to this, that I first read about Moses and his shepherding life, and about David's killing of the lion and the bear. Ah, how glad I felt that we hadn't such wild beastés to frighten, and may-be kill, our sheep and us. The worst we ever had to fear were the foxes that sometimes killed a young lamb or two. But there was otherwhile[9] a crueller thing than that. If a yoe[10] happened to get overturned on a lonesome part of the hill,[11] the ravens and carrion crows would come and pick out her eyes before she was dead. This happened to two or three of my yoes, and at last I got an old gun and shot all the crows and ravens I could get nigh. Once I shot an eagle— but that was the only eagle I ever saw. Since the hills have been more broken up by the plough, such birds are but seldom seen. There haven't been any wild turkeys either for many a year : I have heard my father say he killed two or three, no great while before I was born : they used to call them bustards. There used to be a good many buzzards on the hill when I was a boy. They did no hurt to the sheep, but they destroyed the game and the chicken. Once I set up a pair of *clams*[12] for one, in a thorn-bush in Box-holt Bottom, and when I went to look the next morning I found my bird catched by the legs. He was such a great fellow that I was afraid to tackle him, and was obleeged to fetch him several raps over the head with

[9] This excellent old adverb is now obsolescent.

[10] '' *Yoe*''—ewe.

[11] It is to be remarked that the natives of the South Downs do not seem to recognize the appellation *Downs*. They always speak of " the Hill," in contradistinction to the great Weald below. The folk of the Weald, too, always speak of what newspapers call " Agriculturists of the South Downs" as " hill-farmers."

[12] A trap of small size, an exact miniature of " man-traps." So called, perhaps some ingenious etymologist may say, because placed upon any spot (*clam*) " without the knowledge of " the animal intended to be caught !

my hook, which brought him sprawling, clams and all, to the ground; and I had a great 'to do' before I could kill him. Matthy Simmonds, a shepherd's boy that I knew once, put a long bit of string with a running knot to it round a buzzard's nest that he'd found in the hawth upon Norton Top, and when he saw her a-coming he got ready, and as soon as she was settled he pulled the string, and catched her round both legs.

"I have often thought," my simple but intelligent friend went on to say, "that a shepherd's life, as it went in my young days, was the happiest life that could be; there was so much to make a man think of the goodness of God; so much to admire on every hand; and so little to disturb him and to tempt him to do bad things. The greatest temptation that shepherds used to have was from the smugglers. There was a deal of smuggling done over these hills fifty or sixty years back. Luggers, loaded with silk, and tea, and spirits, and tobacco, used to come ashore at the *gaps*,[13] and the gangs met them to 'work' the goods. Time and often I have seen as many as a hundred men a-horseback with led horses, all loaded with tubs of spirits and bags of tobacco. Very often they would come to this part of the hill and hide their things among the hawth, or dig great pits to put them in. I would never have anything to say to them, though they very often wanted me to it, and would have paid me well for my pains. They were bad folks, and very cruel if anybody offended them. It went again' my conscience to know how they broke the laws, and yet I didn't dare inform again' them for fear of being hurt or killed. They kept all the country round in fear, especially the Hawhurst Gang, who

[13] *Gaps.* Openings in the cliffs.

8

killed several folks, but at last some of them came to
the gallows; though that was a goodish bit before my
time.   They used to have captains as they called them,
who made a good deal of money at times, though it
never did them much good; for 'what is got over the
devil's back is mostly spent under his belly,' as uncle
Caleb used to say.   There was old Sam Rookhurst;
he had so many old guineas and six-and-thirty shilling
pieces that he didn't know what to do with them; so
his wife made a lot of little canvas bags and hung
them on the iron rod of the bed, under the vallance.
But somehow Master Rookhurst's money didn't wear
well, for he died in the workhouse after all.   The
smugglers used to think it a fine joke to play a trick
upon the excise-officers.   There was Nick Cossum the
blacksmith; he was a sad plague to them.   Once he
made an exciseman run several miles after him, to take
away a keg of *yeast* he was a-carrying to Ditchling!
Another time as he was a-going up New Bostall, an
exciseman, who knew him of old, saw him a-carrying of
a tub of hollands.   So he says, says he, 'Master Cossum,
I must have that tub of yours, I reckon!'   'Worse luck,
I suppose you must,' says Nick in a civil way, ' though
it's rather again' the grain to be robbed like this; but,
however, I am a-going your road, and we can walk
together—there's no law again' that I expect.'   ' Oh,
certainly not,' says the other, taking of the tub upon
his shoulders.   So they chatted along quite friendly
and *chucker* [14] like till they came to a cross road, and
Nick wished the exciseman good bye.   After Nick
had got a little way, he turned round all of a sudden and
called out: ' Oh, there's one thing I forgot; here's a
little bit o' paper that belongs to the keg.'   ' Paper,'
says the exciseman, 'why, that's a *permit*,' says he; 'why

[14] *Chucker;* in a cheerful, cordial manner.

didn't you show me that when I took the hollands?'
' Oh,' says Nick, as saucy as Hinds, ' why, if I had
done that,' says he, ' you wouldn't a carried my tub
for me all this way, would you ?' "

Scores of stories connected with the contraband trade
might be related, were they fully pertinent to our subject.
Many a fearful fray and desperate encounter have these
hills witnessed between the 'free-traders' in hollands
and tobacco, and the revenue ' protectionists.' To the
honour of our shores and the credit of the present
efficient coast-guard system, it can now be said that
smuggling is numbered amongst the things that were.
Independently of fiscal considerations, this is matter of
satisfaction of no ordinary kind, since the traffic had
a most demoralizing effect upon the rustic population,
whose sympathies almost universally ran with the
smuggler in opposition to the government official.
Neither was the leaning towards the law-breakers confined to the humbler classes. The country squire, and
even the village clergyman, connived to a certain extent
at the doings of the illicit trader, and stories are ·
current of justices of the peace having been called
upon by a culprit to pay for " that last tub of brandy"
in order to enable him to discharge the fine levied
upon him by their worships—for smuggling !

To the lover of a combination of the bold and
beautiful in nature, the scenery of the Downs affords a
rich and varied source of enjoyment, though it is not
a little singular that few painters have done it justice.
We are not sure, indeed, that any artist of mark, except
Copley Fielding, has treated South-Down subjects, with
entire success. What we have said of the *form* of
these hills, in their ever-varying contour, also applies
to their *colour*, and the effects of light and shade upon
them. You rarely see them twice of the same precise

hue. Viewed from the Weald, at the distance of from five to fifteen miles, their tint is cerulean of Claude-like excellence, forming a most exquisite back-ground to the sylvan beauty of that noble vale. But a nearer prospect furnishes every variety of tint that can stain the pencil, from the saddest green to the most gorgeous purple. We have remarked that the Downs seldom afford sufficient abruptness of outline to entitle them to the character of mountains, but there are points which must be excepted from that remark. Such are Beachy-Head, fatal to seamen, as well as the bold eminences known as Firle Beacon, Ditching Beacon, Mount Caburn, Cissbury, Chanctonbury, Wolston-bury, and others. The views from these over the Weald of Sussex and the adjoining counties, and on the sea-board towards the Isle of Wight, are hardly to be surpassed in their kind. Nor are the valleys less remarkable. We may instance in particular two—*the* Combe, as it is called *par excellence*, near Lewes (whose deep recess the low-going wintry sun hardly visits—its shortest day being briefer than that of Iceland[15]) and the Devil's Dyke, north-west of Brighton. The latter, especially, with its sharp, steep declivity, looks more like a trench cut by the hands of a band of giant ex-cavators than a natural indent of geology. It is to this peculiarity that its designation refers. A popular legend attributes its formation to the Author of Evil, who, looking with suspicion upon the numerous churches of the Weald, as so many fortresses reared against his rule in the world, 'once upon a time' began to dig this trench through the Downs in order to let in the waters of the English Channel to sub-merge them. This legend has been pleasantly

[15] It is so stated in some magazine of the last century which we have seen.

turned into verse, by the late accomplished William Hamper, F.S.A., and we introduce it here without apology, although it has been often printed.

" Five hundred years ago or more,
   Or if you please, in days of yore ;
That wicked wight y'clept *Old Nick*,
Renown'd for many a wanton trick,
With envy, from the Downs, beheld
The studded Churches of the Weald ;
(Here Poynings cruciform, and there
Hurst, Albourne, Bolney, Newtimber,
Cuckfield, and more, with towering crest,
Quæ nunc præscribere longum est ;)
Oft heard the undulating chime
Proclaim around 'twas service time.
" Can I, with common patience, see
These Churches, and not one for me ?
Shall I be cheated of my due,
By such a sanctimonious crew ? "
He mutter'd twenty things beside ;
And swore *that* night the foaming tide,
Led through a vast and wondrous trench,
Should give these pious souls a drench !
Adown the West the Steeds of Day
Hasted merrily away,
   And Night in solemn pomp came on,
Her lamp a star—a cloud her throne ;
The lightsome Moon she was not there,
But deck't the other hemisphere.

   Now with a fit capacious spade,
So large, it was on purpose made,
Old Nick began, with much ado,
To cut the lofty Downs in two :
At every lift his spade threw out
A thousand wagon loads, no doubt !
O ! had he labour'd till the morrow,
His envious work had wrought much sorrow ;
The Weald, with verdant beauty graced,
O'erwhelmed—a sad and watery waste !

   But so it chanced, a good old dame,
Whose deed has long outlived her name,
Waked by the cramp, at midnight hour,
Or just escaped the night-mare's power,

Rose from her humble bed, when lo!
She heard Nick's *terrible ado!*
And by the starlight, faintly spied
This wicked wight, and Dyke so wide!
She knew him by his mighty size,
His tail, his horns, his saucer eyes;
And while with wonderment amazed,
At workman and at work she gazed,
Swift cross her mind a thought there flew,
That she, by stratagem, might do
A deed which luckily should save
Her country from a watery grave;
By his own weapons fairly beating
The father of all lies and cheating!

Forth from her casement in a minute,
A sieve, with flaming candle in it,
She held to view :—and simple Nick,
Who ne'er suspecting such a trick,
(All rogues are fools) when first his sight
A full orb'd luminary bright
Beheld—he fled—his work undone—
Scared at the sight of a *new Sun ;*
And muttering curses that the day
Should drive him from his work away!

Night after night, this knowing dame
Watch'd—but again Nick never came!
Who now dares call the action evil
To hold a Candle to the Devil?"

To the antiquary the South-Downs afford a fine field
for investigation. Some of the churches nestled in
their Deans and Combes, remote from well-travelled
roads—though generally plain and unpretending in
outward style—possess features full of interest for the
ecclesiological explorer, and exhibit specimens of all
the architectural features that have prevailed from the
days of the Confessor and the Conqueror.

But it is among the earthworks and tumuli which
break the smooth surface of their broad backs, that the
retrospective taste now so rife finds its choicest pabulum. From the deeply-intrenched circular hill-forts

constructed before the name of Cæsar was known, and which strikingly mark such prominences as Caburn and Cissbury, and the well-defined lines of Roman castrametation—from the barrow in which repose in inverted urns the ashes of the primitive Celt, accompanied by the rude implement of flint, which was his only weapon and his only tool—from the cemetery of the Roman cohort, rich in sepulchral vase and unguentarium and lachrymatory—from Saxon resting-place of the days of Hengist and Ella and the grave of the marauding Sea-king—from all these the archæologist may gratify his longing curiosity as to the habits and customs of those ancient races who successively lived and moved upon, and found a long repose beneath, the soft turf of these hills. Among medieval antiquities in immediate contiguity to the Downs, we must not overlook the baronial fortresses of Arundel, of Bramber, and of Lewes—all fraught with rich historical associations. Least of all must we forget, that it was upon one of their capacious slopes that constitutional right aimed its deadliest blow at monarchal tyranny, when De Montfort with the confederated Barons overthrew the truce-breaking Henry at the Battle of Lewes. ' Mount *Harry*' still carries in its name a memorial of an event which will always be associated in the mind of patriots with that safeguard of a rational liberty, a representative form of government.

The geologist who surveys these hills looks upon such relics and such events much as other men look upon an old newspaper. His mind's eye is only content in wandering back to the periods when the world was young, when these green hills and dales were the slimy bed of ocean, and received their form from the plastic force of rushing waters. It was here that one of the greatest of modern geologists, and one who did more to popularise his sublime science than all other writers besides—the late Gideon Mantell—began his investigations, almost unassisted, upon the chalk formation and its numerous fossils, which resulted in the publication of his valuable ' Geology of Sussex,' and ' Fossils of the South Downs.'[16]

We happen to be in possession of an anecdote of Mantell, which, as it shows how incidents very trifling in themselves often give direction to genius and produce important results to science, will be interesting to every reader. While yet a mere youth, Mantell was walking one summer evening with a friend on the banks of a stream communicating with the Ouse, when his observant eye rested upon an object that had rolled down from a marly bank which at the particular spot overhangs the stream. He dragged it from the water and examined it with great attention. "What is it?" was the natural inquiry of his friend. " I think, Warren," he replied, " that it is *what they call a fossil !* I have seen something like it in an old volume of the Gentleman's Magazine." The ' curiosity,' which proved to be a fine specimen of the Ammonite, was borne home in triumph by the two friends; and from that moment young Mantell became a geologist. There is at all events a sermon, and a wholesome, edifying one too, in *that* stone !

We have spoken of old feudal fortresses which once overawed the simple bondmen of the Downs. We might say more of Lewes, where the royally-allied and potent De Warennes reigned, and at whose foot

[16] Dr. Mantell's collection of chalk and other fossils which he amassed during his residence at Lewes and Brighton, now forms an important feature in the geological department of the British Museum.

existed the majestic priory, the resting-place for ages of the distinguished dead, until it fell beneath the stroke of that *malleus monachorum*, the vicar-general Cromwell. We might weave, too, a little romance of the fair Gundrada, the Conqueror's child, who, with her husband, De Warenne, founded the priory, and was buried if not exactly in the 'odour of sanctity,' still with more solid and saintly virtues than many a one canonized by sovereign pontiffs. We might tell of her tomb of black marble, long severed from her grave, till lovingly restored to a spot not far from it by a great fautor of 'hoar antiquitie' four-score years ago—of the discovery of the bones of this "Stirps Gundrada ducum, nobile germen," a few years since, by the pickaxe of the railway excavator—and of the re-entombment of those relics side by side with those of her consort in a shrine of costly work beneath the same old well-preserved memorial which had originally covered them in the goodly fane of St. Pancras. Though 𝔒rate pro animabus, as applied to the dead, forms no part of our creed, we would fain invoke a blessing upon those living worthy men who 'of their charitie' executed this graceful pious deed of homage to the long-departed !—We might tell more also of Bramber, of which one solitary fragment stands like the tall tombstone of the mighty race of Braose—and more of thrice-besieged Arundel, of equal interest to painter and to historiographer.—And leaving these tangible memorials of other days we might linger upon sites once renowned, but where not one stone is left upon another to call to mind the high achievements of Poynings and of Pierpoint, albeit the one race have bequeathed to posterity a noble cruciform church, and the other have imprinted their name upon their old abode. We might

8 §

dwell upon spots which are yet cherished in historic memories and which are still the abodes of perennial prosperity—upon Ratton, where the old Roundhead Parkers dwelt—upon Firle, where the name of Gage still survives in undecayed splendour—upon Glynde, where Morley, distinguished in civil wars, had his seat —upon Danny, where dwelt Goring the partizan (equally zealous and perhaps more conscientious) of the opposite cause—upon Wiston, ever memorable as the birth-place of the three Sherley brothers who in the old Elizabethan days were the common boast of Christendom—upon Glyndebourne, the seat of the poetic muse—upon Folkington, Stanmer, Rowdell, Parham, Compton Place, Patcham, Preston, Street, Michelgrove, Friston, Plumpton, Findon, and many more, now or once of name in national annals, the histories of which would be ' longe to reherse !' We might pore, moreover, upon that quaint gigantic effigy upon Wilmington Hill, eighty yards long, and balance the probabilities of its having been cut by lazy monks in Plantagenet days, or by Celtic hands twenty centuries or more ago ; or endeavour to guess who it was that carved erewhile in the turf in front of Plumpton Hill that now almost effaced cross—pious memorial of some forgotten deed. But we forbear ; nor will we tarry long to expatiate upon the pleasant towns and villages which nestle lovingly on the bosom, or at the foot of, the Downs. The time would fail us to tell of that marine Babylon, Brighton,—of its rise from a town of fishermen to be the abode of the wealthiest and the gayest—of the days when huts and barns stood in its busiest streets, and how now and then the simple men of ' Brighthelmston' builded boats upon the Steyne ;—of pleasant Lewes, full of old historic remembrances ;—of fashionable Worthing with its pleasant environs;—of Eastbourne, prettiest of southern sea-resorts;—of Seaford with its picturesque environs and political, if not poetical, associations;— of Newhaven, noticeable for the landing, in '48, of the fallen king of the French;—of Rottingdean, a plea- santer place by far than its *corrupt* name imports;— of Hurstperpoint, its scenery and its antiquities;—of Ditching with its cruciform church and streets (as milliners say) 'to match;'—of Steyning, hallowed in the days of saints and Saxon kings;—and last—not least—of Arundel, the historical and the picturesque.

We might tell too of invasions and hostile landings on the sea-ward foot of the Downs: how John de Cariloco, prior of Lewes, armed his dependents in the days of Richard the Second to resist the French, and how after what Lord Berners calls a "*sore scrimysshe*" on Rottingdean Hill the holy man and two of his knightly friends were borne off into captivity;—of the invasion of Brighthelmston in Henry the Eighth's days by "talle shippes and galeyes," and of the burning of the town by the French;—of the attack of Seaford soon after, and its gallant and successful defence by Sir Nicholas Pelham and his tenants and friends. Many a tale might likewise be remembered of dis- astrous shipwreck and of bloody smuggling adventure, were such scenes to our taste or pertinent to our sub- ject. From risk of foreign invasion, and from illicit trading, these shores are now happily free, and, thanks to advanced science, shipwrecks are much less fre- quent than in days of old. Many a harrowing scene would Beachy-Head—graceful and beautiful as its sum- mit looks in summer weather—have to account for, were it a sentient thing. Acroceraunia, and Scylla, and all the rocks dreadful to the mariners of antiquity, were harmless and innocent in comparison to this gigantic pile of white chalky cliffs—fit type of many other *apparently* fair and lovely, but *really* dangerous and destructive things !

> " Come on, sir ; here's the place ! stand still.—How fearful
> And dizzy 'tis, to cast one's eyes so low !
> The crows and choughs that wing the midway air
> Show scarce as gross as beetles : Half-way down
> Hangs one that gathers samphire ; dreadful trade !
> Methinks he looks no bigger than his head.
>
> * * * * * *
>
>   the murmuring surge,
> That on the unnumber'd idle pebbles chafes,
> Cannot be heard so high :—I'll look no more ;
> Lest my brain turn, and the deficient sight
> Topple down headlong."

These well-known verses are far more applicable to Beachy-Head than to the so-called Shakspeare's Cliff at Dover, which is more than a hundred feet less lofty, as well as much less precipitous. Samphire (*crithmum maritimum*) grows here as abundantly as upon the Kentish cliff: but, however associated with danger that humble plant may have been in the poet's mind, it once became, like Noah's olive-branch, the indication and the pledge of safety from the furious and devouring wave. In Burnet's ' Introductory Lecture to the Medico-Botanical Society ' occurs the following highly interesting narrative in relation to it : " During a violent storm in November, 1821, a vessel, passing through the English Channel was driven on shore near Beachy-Head, and the whole of the crew being washed overboard, four escaped from the wreck only to be delivered, as they thought, to a more lingering and fearful, from its being a more gradual and equally inevitable, death ; for, having in the darkness of the night been cast upon the breakers, they found, when they had climbed up the highest of these low rocks, that the waves were rapidly encroaching on

their asylum; and they doubted not that, when the
tide should be at its height, the whole range would be
covered with water. The darkness of the night pre-
vented anything being seen beyond the spot upon
which they stood, and which was continually decreas-
ing by the successive encroachments of each advancing
wave. The violence of the storm left no hope that
their feeble voices, even if raised to the uttermost,
could be heard on shore; and they knew that amidst
the howling of the blast their cries could reach no ear
but that of God. What human arm could give assistance in such a situation? Even if their distresses
were known, how vain was the help of man! The
circle of their existence here seemed gradually lessen-
ing before their eyes; the little span of earth gradually contracting to their destruction. Already they
had receded to the highest points, and already the
infuriated waters followed them, flinging over their
devoted heads the foremost waves, as heralds of their
speedily approaching dissolution. At this moment,
one of these wretched men—while they were debating
whether they should not, in this extremity of ill, throw
themselves upon the mercy of the waves, hoping to
be cast upon some higher ground, as, even if they
failed to reach it, a sudden would be better than a
lingering death: in this dire extremity, one of these
despairing creatures—to hold himself more firmly to
the rock, grasped a weed, which, even wet as it was,
he well knew, as the lightning's sudden flash afforded
a momentary glare, was not a fucus, but a root of
samphire, and he recollected that this plant never
grows under water. This then became more than an
olive-branch of peace—a messenger of mercy; by it he
knew that He who alone can calm the raging of the
seas—at whose voice alone the winds and the waves

are still—had placed his landmark, had planted his standard here; and by this sign, they were assured that He had said to the wild waste of waters, ' Hitherto shalt thou come, and no further ! ' Trusting, then, to the promise of this angel of the earth, they remained stationary during the remainder of that dreadful, but then comparatively happy, night; and in the morning they were seen from the cliffs above, and conveyed in safety to the shore."

The erection, within the last thirty years, of a light-house upon *Belle-Toute*, a lofty eminence adjoining the Head, has been the salvation of many a precious life, and of vast treasures of merchandise and art. It seems strange that this measure of safety should not have been thought of ages before. The only attempt previously made to avert shipwrecks was by a philanthropic, though eccentric personage, Jonathan Darby, vicar of the adjacent village of East Dean. Upwards of a century and a quarter since, this gentleman, influenced by motives of humanity, excavated the cavern at the base of Belle-Toute, which still retains the name of " Parson Darby's Hole." It consists of two apartments, a good deal mutilated by the storms of six-score winters, but still sufficiently capacious to contain, as it often has contained, a group of shipwrecked mariners; to say nothing of incautious travellers (among whom we must include ourselves), who in venturing to "round the Head" upon the beach, have been overtaken by the rising tide. The apartments, in the formation of which some thousands of cubic feet of solid rock chalk had to be removed, are said to have been excavated by Mr. Darby's own hands. Hither, when the Herculean labour was finished, he used to betake himself on stormy nights, and to hang out a light, not so much perhaps as a beacon to prevent shipwreck, as a guide for the shipwrecked to a temporary asylum. There is a tradition that his humane exertions were once rewarded by the preservation of twelve sailors, the crew of a Dutch merchantman, which had been driven upon the opposite rocks. Another tradition asserts that the good vicar was partly impelled to his pious task by the turbulent temper of his wife, and that his cavern sometimes served him as an asylum from connubial objurgations, which were more distasteful to him than the howling of the winds and the dashing of the waters. According to the parish register of East Dean this lady's tongue was stilled by death in the month of December, 1723. Her husband survived a few years longer, still dividing his time between his parochial duties and his cave, until his health at length failed from long exposure to damp and cold, and he was gathered to his fathers, October 25, 1728.

We know not whether there is in the fine climate of the South Downs anything that generates eccentricity of character. Certain it is, however, that few districts have produced a greater number or variety of human oddities—odd parsons, odd clerks, odd millers, odd farmers, odd peasants. Only the pen of a Dickens could do them justice. We are sorry to say that the traditional history of the district tells rather against *the cloth,* as it existed a couple of generations ago. We will not therefore blot our page by telling how Parson W—, whose grace before meat was " Let us eat and drink, for to-morrow we die ! "—was stumbled over one dark night close to his churchyard, and how, on turning his face " upward to the stars," he observed that " they had put him to bed in a remarkably high-pitched room ! "—nor how Parson

F— once preached with a blackened eye, and his right arm in a sling, the result of a pugilistic encounter with a justice of the *peace ;*—nor of Parson P—, who in default of a congregation on wet Sundays took his clerk to the ' Wheatsheaf,' where they stayed till both master and man were internally well drenched with " dog's-nose." But *on a changé tout cela*—and we believe that a more zealous or respectable class of clergymen is nowhere found than the existing generation of South Down ministers.

From parson to clerk is a very natural transition ; and the parish clerk, everywhere more or less an oddity, seems to have come to the perfection of his species on these hills. Innumerable are the traditions relating to the old Bens, old Sams, old Jans, and other " old " clerks (for it is to be noted that a parish clerk, be he eighty years of age or twenty-five, is always *old*) who have " done duty " beneath the little dove-cot steeples of the South Down churches. A few years ago, a violent gale occurred during the afternoon service at ——n church, which unroofed several barns, and blew down a windmill. The clerk's position was the only one which commanded, through a little Norman window by his desk, a full view of this damage. It was time for the psalm before sermon, when the clerk rose as usual, and astonished the whole congregation by the words :—" Let us sing to the praise and glo—Please, sir, Mus' Cinderby's mill is blowed down ! " The announcement was of course followed, not by singing, but by a general *exeunt* of the congregation. A still more ludicrous announcement was made by the clerk of an adjoining parish not long since. One wet Sunday, the clergyman in crossing the Downs had the misfortune to receive a fall from his horse upon the wet turf. As his dress was almost saturated with water, he told the clerk to apprise the people that, in consequence of a slight accident he had met with, he should be unable to preach a sermon that day. Accordingly, after prayers, the clerk rose and said, " Ye be to goo now." The congregation, not understanding this laconic hint, retained their seats, when the clerk exclaimed at the top of his voice, " Ye be to *goo*, I say. Passon ant a gooin to praich to-dee—acause he's wet his-self ! " But the standard joke against the South Down parish clerk is the following—the precise period and locality of which, however, I have not been able to ascertain. Perhaps some musical antiquary may be more successful.

One dark Sunday afternoon in winter, the " old " clerk—really old in this case—after wiping his " sparticles " and vainly striving to read off the first line of the psalm, looked helplessly towards the singers who were standing in the gallery, and said in an apologetic tone, *" Mine eye's so dim, I cannot see ;"* upon which they, taking the words for the first line of a ' varse,' immediately struck up—

Mine eye's so dim, I can - not see,

The old man, astonished at this proceeding, now expostulated with them by saying, *" I cannot give it out."* This also the choristers took as a genuine portion of the psalm, and continued—

I can - not gi - ive it out;

Master clerk now began to vent his impatience, by angrily adding, "*Tarnation fools, ye all must be;*"—and this also was duly responded to, with many a repetition of the offensive title—

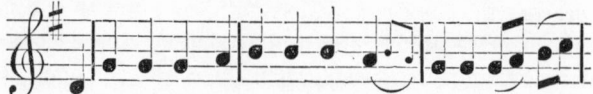

Tar -na-tion fools, Tar-na-tion fools, Tar - na-tion fools, Tar-

na - tion fools ye a - - ll must be;

The poor old fellow, teazed beyond endurance, now unconsciously completed his common-metre stanza, by furiously demanding, "*What be ye all about?*" This was also received in good faith by the folks in the gallery, who at length got through the weary windings of another stave in manner following :—

What be - e - e - e - e - e - e - e ye all a - bout?

But lest we should be considered invidious towards the Church, let us turn to the eccentricities of some of the *laity* of our Downs. If the village church is frequently associated with some droll anecdote, so is also the village windmill. We rather like millers. They are a quiet, well-disposed race—useful members of the commonwealth, and frequently better read and better informed than their neighbours. They are generally ingenious mechanics, and they sometimes dabble a little in the arts of music, drawing, and poetry, although these accomplishments may not often extend far beyond the playing of a few dusty tunes upon the German flute or clar'net, a "draught of our mill in full sail," or a "copy of varses" laudatory of the grinding trade. From a production of the latter class, which we remember having seen— fairly copied (though badly spelt) and affixed to a mill-post, we quote a specimen :—

> "The windmill is a Couris thing
> Compleatly built by art of man,
> To grind the corn for man and beast
> That they alike may have a feast.
>
> "The mill she is built of wood, iron, and stone,
> Therefor she cannot go aloan ;
> Therefore, to make the mill to go,
> The wind from some part she must blow.
>
> "The *motison* of the mill is swift,
> The miller must be very thrift,
> To jump about and get things ready,
> Or else the mill will soon run empty."

Most sea-side health or pleasure-seekers have heard of the "Miller's Tomb" on High-down-Hill, near Worthing. Upon one of the most beautiful eminences on the range of South Downs, the eccentric "Master Oliver" prepared an altar-tomb, which he inscribed with scripture texts and "verses of his own composing," surrounding the whole with an iron fence. In this tomb this singular character was deposited in the year 1793—the eighty-fourth of his age. His funeral, which is still remembered by some old persons, was as quaint as his choice of a burying-place, and attracted thousands of spectators, not from the hills only, but from distant places. The persons who carried the body to the grave were dressed in white, and many young women in garments of the same hue preceded and followed the coffin. On arriving at the spot, one of the girls read a sermon over the grave. We should like to know more of this eccentric being and his motives for eschewing consecrated ground. He is stated to have been an ingenious mechanic and to have constructed several singular *automata,* which were affixed to the roof of his house and moved by the wind. While on the subject of eccentric millers, we will, with the reader's leave, step aside a little from the Downs to record a very curious tradition of one, whose mill stood, however, within four or five miles of the range; of a portion of which it commanded a fine view. At Chalvington there once resided, as the villagers tell us, *the only honest miller ever known.* About a century since, this person, finding success in business impossible, in a fit of despair hanged himself in his own mill, and was buried—as was then the practice with suicides—in a neighbouring " crossways." An oaken stake driven through his body grew into a tree, and threw a singular shrivelled branch, the only one it ever produced, across the road. It was the most singular abortion of a tree we ever saw, and had something extremely hag-like and ghostly in its aspect. The spot was of course haunted, and many a rustic received a severe shock to his nerves on passing it after nightfall. The tradition was always received by the intelligent as a piece of superstitious *folk-lore* and the story of the only honest miller looked upon as fabulous, until about twenty-seven years ago, when a labourer employed in digging sand near the roots of the scraggy oak discovered a human skeleton. For this part of the history we can vouch, having in our boyish days seen some of the bones. One remarkable physiological peculiarity is said to have belonged to our honest miller—to wit, a tuft or "tot" of hair growing in the palm of each hand! [17]

But the queerest miller commemorated in the traditions of the Downs was Master Coombs, a descendant of a race of men who carried on the same trade in the days of Edward the First. It was his boast that his antique little mill, not far from Newhaven, had belonged to his ancestors from the days of Henry the Eighth. Master Coombs once made a strong asseveration as to a statement he had put forth, that if it were not true he would never enter his mill again. Upon the statement being proved incorrect, he kept his word; he would spend hours every day upon the upper step of the mill-stairs, but never, to the end of his life, did he venture to enter the building. One of Master Coombs's oddities was the *painting* of his mill-horse. Mounted on this steed he would astonish the denizens of some neighbouring village, who had never before set eyes upon a *yellow horse!* The next week a whole market-town would be startled from its propriety by the apparition of the miller's horse in a coat of *green*. By another metamorphosis the poor thing looked *blue*, then rose-pink, and so on through all the varieties of tint *im*proper to the equine race. In Master Coombs's days, some four-score years ago, millers' carts were almost unknown, and the village

[17] The substance of this anecdote was communicated to *Notes and Queries*, vol. iv.—The 'tot of hair' is said to be the external denotement not of such a miller as Chaucer's—

"Wel colde *he* stelen corn and tollen thries,—"

but of one who deals justly by his customers—grinding their corn only, not themselves. A north-country miller who was regarded as somewhat deficient in understanding was once accosted by a would-be wit with—"Well, miller, you're not an honest man; where's the bunch of hair in your palm?"—"Oh," said the miller, "it's there safe enough, only it taks an honest man to see't!"

grists were carried home upon the back of a horse.
When to the weight of several flour-bags that of the
miller himself was superadded, the poor beast had no
light load to carry, especially in the then miry condition of the roads. So Master Coombs, taking this
into consideration, whenever his horse had an unusually
heavy burden, instead of dismounting, used to take
one of the bags upon his own shoulders, at the same
time observing with great complacency, " The marciful man is marciful to his baste ! " Like Parson
Darby, poor Coombs was rather unhappy in the con-
jugal relation; but he acknowledged that it was in
some measure his own fault, as he had received a
supernatural warning against the match. " As I was
a gooin' acrass Excete laine to be married at W——
church, I heerd a voice from heaven a-saying unto
me—' Will-yam Coombs ! Will-yam Coombs ! if so
be that you marry Mary———— you'll always be a
miserable man.' . . . . And so I've always found it,"
he added, " and I *be* a miserable man." Many other
traits of Miller Coombs might be added, but as they
would tend to put both his veracity and his honesty
into a bad light, in charity to his memory we will only
say, that he bore a strong general resemblance to
Chaucer's miller, and that no ' tot ' of hair is known
to have grown in his palm.

The notice of the stranger on his first visit to the
South Downs is generally arrested by those great
excavations in the escarpment of the hills—the chalk-
pits, presenting as they do a perpendicular cliff-like
appearance of almost snowy whiteness, in strong contrast to the green turf of the hills out of which they
are scooped. We well remember the surprise of a
little American girl on first viewing a chalk-pit. Her
delight at " a whole mountain " made of this, in her

estimation rare, material was unbounded. To use a slang phrase of her compatriots, it exceeded all her preconceived notions—"by a long chalk!" These hills are perforated in several places by railway tunnels of considerable length. During the formation of a short one which runs almost immediately beneath Lewes Castle, a laughable incident occurred. It was frosty weather, and the water-pipe in a cottager's kitchen being frozen up, the old lady of the house requested her next-door neighbour, a cobbler, to procure her some water from a disused well close at hand. Master Crispin, who was a kind-hearted man, laid down his "lapstone" and proceeded at once to comply with her wish. The old well-bucket was duly lowered, turn after turn, until at last it reached the length of its rope, when he felt a sudden jerk as if something heavy had been thrown into it, while sounds of loud and unearthly laughter rose echoing through the shaft. Crispin, frightened out of his wits, left his hold of the winch, and ran into the cottage, exclaiming,—" The Devil is in the well—I heard him roar, and felt him tugging at the chain— oh dear me!" The cause of his consternation, however, was soon ascertained. The bottom of the well had been cut off in the formation of the tunnel. The jerk had been caused by the throwing into the descending bucket of a great lump of chalk, while the roar which accompanied the feat proceeded not from Pandemonium, but from some half-a-dozen excavators who had witnessed the act of one of their comrades and given vent to their merriment in a loud and long-continued peal of laughter.

"As old as the hills" is a common proverb, but "as old as the chalk-pits" would imply a pretty respectable degree of antiquity, since if Solinus is correct, the Romans imported some of their chalk from South Britain.   On the modern utilities of the chalk-pit it is unnecessary to expatiate, as it affords us lime for the mortar of our houses, and the manure of our lands, while its flint supplies us with bottles for our wine, and its magnesia with medicine for our ailments.

Full easy it were to multiply legend and anecdote, and to jot down a hundred sweet reminiscences of our favourite hills.   But we have done.—We have far exceeded our original design, which was simply to rebut the charge of dulness and insipidity often brought against the South Downs.   We feel conscious of our inability to do full justice to our theme.   Oh that some heaven-inspired son of song loved it as well as we do ! [18]

[18] One or two attempts to do honour to the subject in the voice of poesy have been made; such as Hay's ' Mount Caburn,' Dunvan's ' South Downs,' and some fugitive pieces.   We may add, that in an article on ' South Down Shepherds and their Songs,' by R. W. Blencowe, Esq., M.A., in the second volume of the ' Sussex Archæological Collections,' there are several interesting traits of olden pastoral life to which we have not alluded in the foregoing sketch.   The autobiographical notice of John Dudeney, the South Down shepherd and philosophical schoolmaster, which accompanies that article, is, we venture to assert, hardly to be surpassed in its way.

ON YEW-TREES IN CHURCH-YARDS.

It is a common question, " Why were yew-trees first planted in church-yards ?"—but I have never seen it satisfactorily answered. The popular notion is, that it was for a supply of bows, in the times when archery was not merely a pastime but a very necessary art. But this is untenable; for in the first place the religious feeling of those days would have been violated by the removal of boughs from a tree standing within consecrated precincts. Then again the foresight of our ancestors must have been extraordinary indeed, if it induced them to plant for such a purpose, a tree which, at its exceedingly slow rate of growth, would be at least half a dozen generations old before it could supply an equal number of branches adapted for the making of bows, the removal of which would besides have spoiled the tree. Now although in some districts the yew is comparatively rare, yet there was probably in the middle ages a sufficient quantity of it growing upon unconsecrated ground to answer the demands of the archer. Another prevalent notion is, that yews were planted in church-yards as a shelter for the sacred edifices ; but here again the slow growth of the tree presents itself as an objection; for the building would grow old long before the tree attained such maturity as to offer any material defence against destructive winds, whereas many other species of timber would, in the course of a very few years, reach a sufficient height to be helpful in this respect. It must be noticed, too, that church-yard yews often stand

9

at such a distance from the building and in such situations as to render this supposition as unwarrantable as the other.

Why, then, were yew-trees first planted in church-yards? I think the reason must be sought in the veneration in which the yew, in common with some other evergreen trees, was held in times antecedent to the introduction of Christianity, not only among the classical ancients, but also among the barbarians of the north. It has been held sacred to funereal rites among nearly all nations—and it was in special esteem with the Druids. The great age of these trees in some church-yards forbids the idea of their having been planted subsequently to the erection of the buildings, or any others consecrated to the same forms of faith that may have occupied their sites. According to the eminent botanist, Decandolle, the yews at Fountains Abbey and Crowhurst are each 1200 years old,—that at Fortingal, in Scotland, 1400,—while a fine specimen of the *Taxus baccata* at Braborne in Kent must, according to the same authority, have been contemporary with Solomon's temple, having reached what Fuller would have called the " stupendous antiquitie " of thirty centuries. We know that it was the temporising policy of Augustine and the Roman missionaries to connive at many of the pagan superstitions which they found on their advent into Britain. Predilections for sacred sites and objects were indulged. Thus a Druidical fountain lost none of its virtues in the popular mind if dedicated as a holy well to some saint, and many of the earliest churches arose upon spots previously dedicated to pagan worship, as within a Druidical circle. I think it is highly probable, therefore, that from this feeling some churches may have been built in immediate proximity to sacred yews, and that afterwards—a symbolical meaning having been attached to the tree—it became customary to plant them in church-yards generally. Whether my theory be right or wrong, the great age of some of the specimens referred to sufficiently proves that in those particular instances the church must have been brought to the tree, and not the tree to the church. At the same time, I willingly admit that the yew is one of the liveliest of all symbols of eternity, and therefore no inappropriate tenant of every Christian cemetery. Its evergreen foliage and its great longevity beautifully typify that "world without end," which is the ultimate aspiration of the Christian soul. In some cases this tree is even rejuvenescent. I have seen one entirely hollow, next to nothing of it but its rugose venerable bark and a few green boughs remaining; in the midst of which springing from the central roots there is a fair young stem which may some ages hence expand itself to a diameter that will burst asunder the tegument of the parent tree, and live on again, a fair and stately yew, till dynasties shall have changed, and many generations of mortal men have found a long repose beneath its umbrageous arms!

A LYTTEL GESTE OF A GREATE EELE.

ॐ Memorandum.

THE following ballad is based upon an incident related in Dr. Andrew Borde's 'Merry Tales of the Wise Men of Gotham,' first published in the reign of Henry the Eighth. I have elsewhere[1] adduced arguments to prove that these gibes were written in order to lampoon the proceedings of a public body connected, not as some writers have imagined, with the village of Gotham in Nottingham-shire, but with another place of the same name on the southern coast. A Sussex tradition, now nearly obsolete, connects this particular jest with the ancient town of Pevensey, so noticeable for its historical associations, and its venerable Roman and medieval castle. This is confirmed by the known fact that the learned, facetious, and eccentric physician for some time practised his science at that place.

Like many of its neighbour towns, Pevensey had greatly declined from its olden importance, and was hardly more than the shadow of its former self. Its charter of privileges as a Cinque-Port was, however, retained in Borde's time—and is so even at the present day. A person of "old Andrew's" temperament would therefore be extremely likely to seize upon the sayings and doings of the freemen of such a small municipality for the purpose of raising a laugh at their expense. Hence in all probability it is, that while some traditionary jests redounding little to the wisdom of the officials of other decayed corporations are extant, the number of such stories related of Pevensey should be unusually large. They are, however, generally of so very puerile a description as to be scarcely worth recording; and even did they possess more point, it would be anything but fair towards the constituents of this ancient corporation, who are quite equal in intelligence and wisdom to their neighbours.

The point of the jest before us lies in the *drowning of an eel!* Now this is evidently an allusion to the old municipal practice, which obtained at Pevensey and some of the other Cinque-Ports, of destroying criminals by casting them into deep water. In the Custumal of

---

[1] Archæologist, and Journal of Antiquarian Science, 184. p. 129. Sussex Archæological Collections, vol. vi, p. 207.

Pevensey, as copied about the middle of the fourteenth century, we read :—

"In judgments of the crown, if a man be condemned to death, the port-reeve, as coroner, shall pronounce judgment, and, being seated next the steward shall say, ' *Sir, withdraw, and axe for a priest ;* ' and if the condemned be of the franchise, he shall be taken to the town bridge at high water, and drowned in the harbour; but if he be of the geldable [*i.e.*, liable to taxes, which the freemen were not], he shall be hung in the Lowy, at a place called the Wahztrew."

On this singular mode of punishment, and still more singular form of sentence, the Rev. Lambert B. Larking observes :—"I do not remember ever before to have seen any Saxon form of sentencing a criminal to death. How courteous and considerate to the feelings is the gentle " Sir, withdraw, and axe for a priest ;" and how coarse and rude by contrast with it is "You shall be taken hence to the place from whence you came, and thence to a place of execution, there to be hanged by the neck till you are dead"—a sentence only fit for a dog. The scene must have lost half its terrors by this gentle courtesy in announcing the doom of the law; but, deny it who will, our Saxon ancestors were highly civilized, and gentlemen in all they did; why, what a gentlemanly death was that reserved for the privi- leged burgess, to be slid off the port into the sea. Clarence and his Malmsey-butt is vulgarity itself compared with a "header" down to the "rocks where corals grow : "—

> "Nothing of him that doth fade,
>   But doth suffer a sea change
> Into something rich and strange ;
>   Sea-nymphs hourly ring his knell."

. . . Highly privileged were ye, ye men of Pevensey. "O for- tunati sua si bona norint!"[2] But to our legend—

¶ In daies when Popyshe governmente
    Ordayned, agaynst our wishe,
That men sholde, duryng time of Lent,
    Bothe dyne and suppe on fysshe—

There liv'd a verie honest wight,
    A free-man of this porte,
Who by his neyghbours Perkyn hight.
    (Hys other name was Shorte.)

[2] Sussex Archæological Collections, vol. iv, p. 210.

Now Perkyn never could awaie
    With dyet slyght and meane;
No man on thys fatte lande, they say,
    In better case was seene.

Hys mutton and his marsh-fedde beefe
    Hee picked unto yᵉ bone,
Untyl he stoode in bolde releefe
    A man of twentie stone.

A ryght goode catholyke was hee,
    And dulie payd his tythe,
From cowe, and pigge, and fowle, and bee,
    From syckle and from scythe.

But yet one item of hys creede
    Went sore ageynst the wishe
Of hys confessour, Father Speede—
    He colde not dyne on fysshe.

And in yᵉ drearie tyme of Lente,
    By commonlie transgressinge
The rule—on beefe or mutton bente—
    Hee loste the father's blessyng.

Tyll by adventure on a daye,
    Whyle wyth a neyghbour faring,
Hys heart was muche releeved, thei saye,
    By tasting a redde-heryng.

Had Perkyn beene a learnyd wight,
   And knowne a bit of Greek, a
Case more than likelie 'tis hee might
   Have cride alowde, *Eureka !*

But since of Latine and of Greek
   Hee nought at alle dyd knowe,
As sone as joie wold let hym speake
   He onelie sayd *"Hullowe !*

" Why this is somethyng like a fysshe,
   " A relysshe new and gustful !
" And Holie Churche of this same dishe
   " Wyl nevere be distrustfulle.

" Noe more I'll fret o'er Lenten chere—
   " Wyth eyght or tenne of these,
" Wasshed down with goode Octobyr beere,
   " Ile dyne and suppe with ease."

Arryved at home hee told hys wyfe
   His newe discovered pleasure ;
Hee nevyr hadde, in al hys lyfe,
   Of joie so fulle a measure.

Sayes Perkyn—" Roger, ryde our nagge
   To Hasting, for to chuse
Of these same ffysh a pretie bagge,
   To breede them uppe for use."

Y^e groome went foorth and soone was backe,
  (None colde have rydden faster)
Wyth fulle three bushels in a sacke,
  And gave them to hys maister.

" Judyth," says Perkyn to his spouse,
  " My lovinge dame and fonde ;
" We'll eate two busshels, and we'll put
  " One busshel in owre pond.

" When Lent comes next there sure will be
  " Of ffyshe a large incresse—
" Enow for me and eke for thee,
  " For everie daie a messe."

So from the sacke thei straightway drew
  Of heryngs all the best,
Y^e whiche into theyr ponde they threw—
  For foode reserved the reste.

¶ *Heere endyth ye fyrst parte of the jeaste of y^e*
Eele, and here doth folowe the seconde parte of the
same jeste.

Agayn is Lenten tyme come round,
  And layd aside is beefe ;
Syr Perkyn trustith from hys ponde
  To drawe a goode releefe.

Sayes Perkin, " Wife, my angles fetch,
  And eke my rodde and lyne,
I goe some heryng for to cacche,
  Methinks they'll prove full fyne."

Unto his pond in blythesom sort
  Doth Perkyn hie, but, marry!
Fulle colde ye weather for that sporte,
  At th'ende of February.

Sayes Perkyn, "Tis a fyshe that's shie,
  And verie slowe to byte;
So I a nette must even trye,
  And dragge the ponde outright."

So Roger, John, and Hykke he bade
  To bryng his fysshynge nette;
But 'twas in vayne—with all theyr aide,
  No heryng he colde get.

Sayes Perkyn, "Thys wyl never doe;
  I e'en thys ponde must drayne—
Pull up the sluice!" The water through
  Then foamed and dashed amayne.

Eftsoones ye ponde is draynéd right
  Of water every dele;
But nought appeares to Perkyn's sight
  Save one Greate Wrygglynge Eele!

"Marry!" says Perkyn then, "I wis
  "My lucke is surely evyll—
"Yon villaine Eele hath eate my fysshe;
  "—Beshrew thee, ravenous Devyl!"

Now Perkyn, takyng uppe the theefe,
  In ireful moode did saie :—
"Thou shalt be punysshed to thy grief ;
  "For thou must dye streyghtwaye !"

"Goe hange hym, Maister," Roger sayd ;
  "Choppe off hys head," quoth Hykke ;
"Naye, burne hym, Syr," says honest John,
  "For this soe knavysh trycke !"

¶ Eche servaunt hadde a severall wysshe ;
  Roger a theefe dyd view hym—
And as a traytour worthy Hykke
  Looked on hym.—"A foule heretyke,"
Said John, "he is, to steale Lent fysshe,
  "By'r Ladye—I beshrew hym !"

¶ "Peace ! fooles," says Perkyn, "for tis writ,
  "And in our Charter founde—
"That hee who murther dothe committe,
  "I' the haven must be drownde."

Soe to yᵉ bridge thei bare hym fast,
  To dye for that hys slawghter,
And, withowte more adoe, thei cast
  Yᵉ Eele into the water ! !

¶ To Father Speede the worthie deede
  Dyd Perkin then reherse,
As hath beene either sunge or sayd,
  In our foregoing verse.

" Pax tecum ! 'twas well done," quoth hee ;
  " And now, for thy releefe,
" (By paying Holie Churche a fee)—
" From fasting thou absolved shalt be
  " *Go dine alle Lent on beefe !*"

Soe heere's an ende to Perkyn stout,
  And eke to Father Speede ;
The Eele his punisshement (noe dowte)
  Thought *capytalle* indeede !

Portrait of Dr. Andrew Borde, from his "Boke of the Introduction of Knowledge."

A DISCOURSE OF GENEALOGY.

Γενεαλογια—the tracing of one's descent—the finding out of one's progenitors, *avi, proavi, abavi,
atavi, tritavi,* grandfathers, great-grandfathers, great-
great-grandfathers, and *their* fathers and grandfathers—is a passion inherent in the human family.
Under all circumstances of civilization—whether in
Judæa, Greece, Rome, England, China, or New
Zealand—it has been cherished with a fondness
second only to the preservation of one's own personal
honour and reputation. It is a theme that has employed alike the pen of the classic poet, and the
tongue of the barbarian bard and scald. It was the
ambition of most heathen princes and chieftains to
deduce their descent from the gods, as it is of modern
potentates and nobles to trace up their lineage to the
renowned and mighty men of far by-gone ages—and
naturally; for in spite of the hackneyed Ovidian
sentiment—

> " — genus, et proavos, et quæ non fecimus ipsi,
> Vix ea nostra voco,——

there must of necessity be a pleasure and a pride in
the assurance, or even in the probability, of a descent
from distinguished progenitors. Men estimate the
value of things by their rarity. Some excel in
knowledge, others in power, others in wealth. These
are all extraordinary advantages, attainable but by
the few; honoured and respected, if not aimed at,
by the many. But a man, duly gifted and favoured,

may become wise, rich, and influential, and yet want the qualification of a good or noble descent. It cannot be bought with money, or acquired by wisdom or by power. The poor may become wealthy, the ignorant wise, the feeble potential; but no man may reverse the decrees of fate and make his dead progenitors what they were not. Nobility of birth is transmissible to an idiot; but the wisest, the richest, the mightiest, has no more to do with the selection of his ancestry than he has with the origination of his own existence.

Among the democratic tendencies of our own times none is more striking to the thoughtful mind than a disposition to despise pedigree. Titular rank and a good descent are held in little estimation by the multitude. The sentiment of Burns—

> " The rank is but the guinea's stamp,
> The gowd's the gowd for a' that,"

is a favourite one, and when made use of before a plebeian auditory is sure to secure a large amount of applause. And why? Because it flatters the self-love of every man, worthy or unworthy, and places him, in his own conceit, upon a level with the greatest. But how often, in these cases, is there the want not only of the stamp, but of the precious metal too. Burns himself, in spite of his genius (and that by the way is much overrated by his countrymen), was sadly deficient of both the one and the other. It is not the least among the defects of his moral nature that he too often delights in representing the great as the " natural enemies" of the poor. Accepting his creed, we should imagine that every human virtue is associated with poverty—all that is base in our nature with the possession of rank and its concomitant wealth.

To what bad passions does he pander in such effusions as this :—

> " See yonder poor o'erlaboured wight,
>   So abject, mean, and vile,
> Who begs a brother of the earth,
>   To give him leave to toil ;
> And see his lordly fellow-worm
>   The poor petition spurn ;
> Unmindful though a weeping wife
>   And helpless offspring mourn ! "

Happily for the peace of society, such sentiments are daily losing ground, and the wider diffusion of the principles of a sound political economy will, I trust, ere long dissipate the monstrous idea that the great and wealthy are from the nature of their position necessarily wanting in sympathy towards their less-favoured brethren.

But to return : those who affect to despise rank closely resemble the fox in Æsop, which thought the grapes that grew hopelessly beyond his reach particularly sour. The people who sneer at ancestral honours, and deride heraldry as a by-gone folly, are always those who have no genealogical roll to fall back upon— no " family evidences" to prove that *their* forefathers had a coat (armorial or otherwise) to their backs ! Let their philosophy go into partnership with that of the poor wretch who pronounces learning useless, because he himself cannot read, and despises, or affects to despise, wealth, when he has not half-a-crown in his pocket.

The truly wise man is a truly contented one. If he is poor, he does not covet affluence—if he lacks influence, he is not ambitious. So also, if he is not of gentle birth, he does not repine at the want of gentilitial distinctions. But because he does not possess the first, the second, or the third, he is not therefore

necessarily insensible to their inherent value. We
have never known a man whom in our judgment we
could pronounce wise or judicious who despised a good
descent. We never yet met with one who did not, on
the contrary, feel a degree of pleasure in being able
to point to well-born ancestors, and regard pedigree
as quite as essential a thing in himself as in his own
horses !

"Well," perhaps the caviller will say—"I stand
upon my own merits; what matters it whether my
predecessors were wise or foolish, poor or rich, gentle
or simple?" Stay, my friend ! Do you call yourself
a patriot ? Can you consistently say with Terence,
"Homo sum?" If you stand entirely upon the
pharisaical platform of your personal excellences, it
matters little whether your forefathers were Englishmen, Turks, Laponese, or Bushmen,—whether they
were made in the likeness of God, or in the degraded
image of the oran-outang or the baboon. For to be
a patriot you must have a national pride, which is in
a modified sense to be proud of your descent—to be
proud of your manhood, you must felicitate yourself
upon the fact of your not having been hatched by a
vulture or spawned by a toad !

Again; is there any man so besotted as to be re-
gardless whether his progenitors were brave, healthy,
virtuous, honest—or whether they were mean, pitiful
scoundrels, the scum and offscouring of the earth?
No, verily. Tell your self-sufficient reviler of pedigree
that his grandfather was dishonest, or his great-grand-
mother unchaste, and he recoils at once with indignation from the impeachment, be it mere calumny or
plain, undeniable truth. The evil fame of base ancestors
he feels to be a reproach—an *injury* to himself. The
truth is that he, in common with all mankind, respects

descent as a matter of feeling, however slightingly he may *affect* to regard the qualification of a good and unblemished ancestry in his ordinary conversation.

I will therefore reiterate the sentiment with which I set out; namely, that a love of ancestry is a passion belonging to our common nature. It is deeply seated in every virtuous mind, in spite of the modern cant which pretends to despise it, and treat it as a thing of nought. Men not unfrequently by a perversion of reason, like that which induces some to boast of their own vices, profess to disregard that which they in reality respect. Were an illustration in proof of this observation required, I could adduce from a recent "autobiography" some very sarcastic remarks on family history and the futility of genealogical honours and long lines of descent, with not a few sneers at " griffins, mermaids, and other monsters which ought to be exploded from modern education, and from the language of science and art." But that the writer is attempting to expel with a fork that nature which *will* reassert herself is rather ludicrously shown on the self-same page, where he tells his readers, with no little complacency, " A family coat of arms I could display, fully emblazoned, from an old stone authority, and might use it as the —— Arms ; but this would subject me to taxation, and my taxes are already more weighty than pleasant." It is an easy matter to flourish rhetorically upon this subject, and to quote such hackneyed couplets as—

> " What can ennoble sots, or slaves, or cowards ?
> Alas! not all the blood of all the Howards "—

but it is by no means an equally easy thing really to scorn a derivation from a noble, historical, and virtuous race, or to regard a man as something the

worse for such a descent. It is only when he post-
pones honour, morality, and every excellent attribute
to the pride of ancestry, that he becomes truly worthy
of our contempt; and it is willingly admitted that he
who rests his sole claim to the consideration of society
upon the musty evidence of a parchment scroll, however elaborated by heraldric art, is a truly despicable
object. I know not which is the greater fool—the
man who has nothing to boast of but a good descent,
and who makes no effort to support in his own person
the dignity of worthy ancestors, or he who despises
pedigree *in toto.* Fool the First would be a better man
were the axe laid to the root of his genealogical tree,
and he rendered oblivious of the past : Fool the Second
should never plant such a tree; for how can one who
takes no pride in ancestral virtues expect to be ac-
tuated by those ennobling principles which should
make him a model and pattern for his descendants?

But I have been in some degree carried away from
the object of this discourse, which is not intended so
much as an apology for what is called " good blood "
or gentilitial distinctions, as an inquiry into the interest and utility of genealogical investigations as a
science—a science which, I venture to predict, will
ere long occupy the intellect and the pens of many by
whom it has hitherto been to a great extent neglected.

It is a vulgar and very unreasonable mistake to
suppose that a love of pedigree (or, more properly
speaking, the genealogical taste) relates solely to the
illustration of ancestries that have played a conspicuous part in the history of our species, or that have
been distinguished by the possession of broad lands
and transmissible honours and titles. *It is not so !* As
the naturalist expatiates with equal delight upon the
structure and habits of the beetle and those of the

elephant, so the true genealogist feels as much pleasure in searching out the records of a yeomanry stock, or in tracing the descent of the humblest plebeian, as in imparting additional lustre to the coronet of nobility. He would as gladly see the Family Bible of every intelligent cottager adorned with the registers of birth, marriage, and death, for a few generations, as he would endeavour to throw light upon the deeds, titles, and alliances of the peer. For my own part I would wish every family to preserve their pedigree as the ancient Jews did, irrespectively of social position and the possession of riches.

The moral benefits of such a practice would be very great, for men would learn—or rather would not be permitted to forget—by how many ties of consanguinity the families of a district, a county, or a nation are connected. It would then appear that many who now toil and plod at the base of the social mountain, earning every day's bread with the sweat of their brow, are the collateral kinsmen of those who range its summit in all the splendour of wealth and distinction. It would also be shown how some families have ascended from the vales of poverty to the high places of the earth, and how others, by a decadence more or less gradual, have descended from positions of influence and wealth to those of insignificance and penury.

Old Camden has well remarked, that "the High are descended from the Low, and contrariwise the Low from the High." Not a few of the peers of this realm spring from graziers, bakers, barbers, and day-labourers. On the other hand, some men now ride on the box whose ancestors rode inside the carriage, while others serve in the kitchen whose progenitors commanded in the hall. In the veins of many a poor country gentleman flow Plantagenet blood and the ichor of heroes.   Indeed there are few families of respectable antiquity who do not in some way or other, through female ancestors,

> " deduce their birth
> From loins enthroned and princes of the earth ; "

and claim equally with Mæcenas the *atavis edite Regibus*.   Well may Shakspeare demand—

> " What ! will the aspiring blood of Lancaster
> Sink in the ground ? I thought it would have mounted."

Mr. Charles Long, in his ' Royal Descents,' observes that " when once you are enabled to place your client in a current of decent blood, you are certain (by a slight Hibernicism) to carry him up to some one of the three great fountains of honour, Edward the Third, Edward the First, or Henry the Third ; and in families of good, or even partially good, descent the deducing of a husband and wife from *all* the children of Edward the Third, and *all* the children of Edward the First, has been successfully established by perseverance and research."   On the other hand, Mr. Long satisfactorily shows the right of a carpenter, a gravedigger, a saddler's apprentice, a shoemaker, and a tailor, to quarter the royal arms as lineal descendants of Edward the Third ; while a still greater disparity presents itself in the descent of George Wilmot from King Edward the First.   Poor George in 1845 kept the turnpike-gate at Cooper's Bank, near Dudley, almost contiguous to ' the very walls of those feudal towers that gave name to the barony' of which he was a genuine and indisputable coheir.

The following considerations will serve to show how wonderfully men and families are knit together by the ties of blood.   When one reflects that his ancestry doubles in every ascent, or, to speak more correctly, increases in a two-fold geometrical progression, he will easily see this. Thus, as everybody has one father, two grandfathers, four great-grandfathers, eight-great great-grandfathers, and so on (the case being of course the same on the female side), if we go back to the time of King John, which (allowing three generations to a century) would be about nineteen generations, we shall find that in the space of little more than six centuries, every one of us can boast of the astounding number of five hundred and twenty-four thousand, two hundred and eighty-eight ancestors; that is to say, that the blood of more than half a million of the human race flows in our veins. This calculation supposes, however, that all one's male ancestors have married strangers in blood, which has probably not been the case in any instance. A few matches with cousins, near or remote, vastly reduce the number. Blackstone, long since, called attention to this multitudinousness of ancestral relations, in his 'Commentaries,' where he gives a table of numbers extending to the twentieth genealogical remove. At the fortieth remove, a period extending over about sixteen or seventeen hundred years, the total number of a man's progenitors amounts to more than a *million millions!* The same eminent lawyer also shows, from the most satisfactory data, that "we have all now subsisting nearly two hundred and seventy millions of kindred in the fifteenth degree; and if this calculation should appear incompatible with the number of inhabitants on the earth, it is because by intermarriages among the several descendants from the same ancestor, a hundred or a thousand modes of consanguinity may be consolidated in one person, or he may be related to us in a hundred or a thousand different ways"—and that without our being aware of it!

It is thus that I account for the extraordinary resemblance, both personal and mental, often occurring between persons not recognised as kinsmen. We know how both physical and intellectual characteristics are often transmitted by overleaping several generations and reappearing at intervals like a comet. A due consideration of these facts would be of great moral advantage to mankind, as serving to induce a kindliness of feeling to all, whether lowly or exalted, since we know not by how many ties of blood they may be connected with us,—in a stronger sense than is usually affixed to the words, "All men are Brethren."

I may append here a little illustrative anecdote. About seventy or eighty years since, a shepherd named Tuppen was sent by his master, who resided near Eastbourne, Sussex, to drive some sheep into South Devon. The man having discharged his commission was returning homewards from his somewhat toilsome pilgrimage, when, on passing a cottage at least two hundred miles from his own habitation, and on a spot which he had never before visited, he was greeted with the familiar words, "How d'ye do, Master Tuppen?" The shepherd with a rather bewildered air turned round and found that the salutation had been addressed to him by a peasant's wife, the tenant of the cottage, a person of whom he had not the slightest knowledge. He told her as much; whereupon she apologized by saying that she had mistaken him for one Master Tuppen, a man who lived in a neighbouring hamlet, but of whom the Sussex shepherd had never heard. There can, however, be no doubt of the common origin of these two "Master Tuppens," though all remembrance of kindred was lost.

To return—All ancient nations seem to have preserved genealogies, of at least their more powerful families, with a scrupulousness little regarded among the most civilized nations of the present day; and even now some of the barbarous peoples of the East and of the southern ocean, though ignorant of any graphic art, preserve by oral tradition the names of their ancestors for many generations.   It would be far from fair to infer from this, that a love of genealogy is a feeling more adapted to barbarians than to civilized men; for we find that the greatest nations of antiquity, the Greeks and the Romans, cherished it as well as the rudest.   How often do we meet in the classical writers of history and biography expressions implying the respect in which a good descent was held. Perhaps the reason why in modern times so much less respect has been paid to it lies in this.   The feudal system of the middle ages having acted oppressively upon the lower orders of society—on the abolition of that system, the plebeian part of mankind, regarding genealogical honours as one of the prerogatives of their ancient oppressors, and possessing little power to discriminate between cause and concomitant— between what was essential to the existence of the old misrule, and what was merely a harmless offshoot of it—viewed them with positive dislike.   Another cause of the unpopularity of genealogy may be the arrogant tone of the majority of its advocates in old times. After feudalism had passed away, and the revival of literature, consequent upon the invention of the printing-press, had revolutionized society by the abrogation of old stereotyped forms of thought, there arose a department of literature hitherto scarcely known, the design of which was to assert the super-excellence of lofty birth, and to degrade plebeianism to the dust.   All the old heraldric writings from Dame

Juliana Berners' 'Boke of St. Alban's' down to John Guillim's 'Display,' are more or less tinctured with this supercilious contempt of whatever relates to humility of birth and position. Between the " gentylman " and the " un-gentylman" these writers attempt to fix a great and all but impassable gulf—a barrier based upon assumptions as ridiculous as those which divide the Castes of Hindostan. In this they were but pandering to a pride really entertained by too many of their patrons ; for the proprietor of an estate in Carolina or Virginia, in our own days, scarcely carries himself more haughtily towards his negro slaves, than did many of the " noblesse " of those times towards their humble, though now manumitted, neighbours.

With a contempt (among right-minded men of all classes) for such arrogant pretensions, there not unnaturally arose, among plebeians, a dislike of the external denotements of nobility ; and heraldric distinctions began to be viewed as the symbols of a worn-out and obsolete *wrong*. This feeling is still entertained by many intelligent persons, who do not seem to have sufficiently reflected upon the distinction which I am anxious to establish between the mere pride of high birth, and the real interest attaching to scientific genealogy. In order to make my meaning fully understood, it may be well to glance at the origin of heraldry, and to vindicate it from the sneering definition that has been applied to it, viz : " The science of fools with long memories."

Notwithstanding the extravagant antiquity ascribed to heraldry by the writers of the sixteenth and seventeenth centuries, who assigned armorial bearings to all the distinguished persons of the earliest ages, there is not any evidence to prove that the science existed until within the last seven centuries. According to the best modern authorities, the latter half of the twelfth century furnishes us with the first actual specimens of the armorial shield. Mr. Planché, who is the latest, as he is unquestionably one of the best, writers upon the subject, after the research of many years, cannot discover one instance of a shield decorated with heraldric insignia before the year 1164, when the lion-rampant of Philip I, Count of Flanders, occurs upon his seal. "There is, we repeat, no proof of the existence of heraldry—by which we mean an arrangement of the lines, colours, and figures, that make up what are called coats of arms by a certain fixed and systematic code of laws—until the twelfth century. Even our honoured national ensign, which is boastfully described as having borne the brunt of breeze and battle for a thousand years, has only enjoyed that honour for some six centuries and a half; the three golden lions-passant-guardant appearing for the first time upon the great seal of Richard Cœur de Lion, in the year 1195. We do not say that shields and banners were not decorated with certain symbolical figures at a much earlier date; there is abundant evidence that they were from the remotest periods so adorned. Art in some respects as well as Nature may be said to abhor a vacuum. The broad face of a well-formed shield, and the graceful expanse of a floating banner, invited ornamentation, and accordingly we find the buckler of the Homeric hero and the earliest flag of the barbarous chieftain alike enriched with apposite devices; but these, beyond perhaps the suggestion of the original idea, had no relation to the hereditary armorial compositions of the middle ages. Feudalism, the Crusades, and the adoption of fixed hereditary surnames in the families

of the great, may have all had some hand in the
origination of heraldry, as they all certainly promoted
its growth; but we search in vain among the records
of the times for the first germ of a science or practice
—call it what you will—which adds so much of the
picturesque and the romantic to the days of the
Plantagenets and Tudors, and which led to the production of some of the most extraordinary books that
exist in the whole circle of European literature." [1]

Early heraldry, it is hardly necessary to state, was
always connected with war. In the older times the
eagle had been the standard of imperial Rome, and
Saxons and Danes had respectively flocked around
their banners of the white horse and the raven.
Under feudalism every baron and well-landed knight
was a petty sovereign, and as such had his own particular banner, and this not so much as a matter of
ostentation as one of actual necessity, for the better
rallying of his dependents upon the battle-field, where
many of these little feudal armies were aggregated
against the common foe. It was not until the banner
of a particular race had been rendered conspicuous by
the prowess of its successive owners in Crusade or
other remarkable war, that it began to be regarded as
the symbol or external sign of the virtues of a family,
and to be looked upon as a thing which elevated it
above the general mass of mankind. Thus what had
been among the indispensable accessories of medieval
warfare soon became almost equally indispensable as
a guarantee of social status. The *armiger* or " arms-
bearer," however remotely descended from the head
of his race, counted himself as a gentleman : all other
men were reckoned plebeians, churls, servi, villani,
bondmen ; in one word—in the phrase of the ' Boke

[1] M. A. L. in Retrospective Review, Feb. 1853.

10

of St. Alban's'—"ungentylmen." So originated the distinction between the upper and the lower classes of European society; for what is called the middle class was throughout the middle ages very unimportant, and it has only been fully developed within the last two centuries.

But as society advanced, and the cramping influence of feudalism was removed, many persons of humbler birth emerged by the force of their wealth or talents, or both, from the undistinguished mass of the people, and took up a position among the families of ancient blood. A *novus homo* was looked upon then as in old Roman times, or in our own, *naso adunco;* but the fault of a plebeian origin is one that cures itself in time, since each successive generation conduces to the antiquity of a race, and helps to throw into obscurer distance the circumstances of its beginning. And thus, in course of time, war, merchandise, learning, law, physic, divinity, philosophy, and other less honourable means, each added its quota of families to the patrician side; and all these new additions came in a short time to be regarded (by the majority at least) as upon a par with the oldest Norman and Plantagenet blood.

Now, these families, both old and new, embraced nearly all the persons of moderate education in England. (I speak of this country only, but the observation applies equally to others.) Few besides persons of gentle birth knew how to read. The common people had few incentives to intellectual pleasures. The romance attaching to a long descent was disregarded or unappreciated by them. The gentry, on the other hand, were all more or less pleased with pedigree, and no gentleman's education was supposed to be finished until he had become expert in the technicalities of heraldry. The practice of heraldic Visitations also tended much to encourage such tastes. About three or four times in a century, the heralds, upon the authority of their College and with the sanction of the Earl-Marshal, visited every county, and, taking up their quarters (after the manner of "revising barristers" in our times) in the principal towns of the county, summoned all the resident gentry of each district, on a certain day and hour, to appear before them to prove, by sufficient documentary evidence, their right to bear arms; as also to furnish data for the establishment of their pedigree, which was duly registered in the visitation-books, and attested by the signature of the representative of the family. This custom originated in the reign of Henry the Eighth, and was continued till that of James the Second. It seems to have fallen into disuse in consequence of the great dislike of the nation generally to the unconstitutional powers exercised by the officials. These men, under the sanction of a royal commission, promoted by the Earl-Marshal, went so far as to "reprove, controul, and *make infamous* by proclamation at courts of assize," all persons who unwarrantably assumed the title of Esquire or Gentleman. This was in the reign of Charles I; and although things were not driven to such extremities under his sons Charles II and James II, the heraldic prerogative, with its invidious distinctions and heavy fees, was considered inconsistent with the rights of the subject, and these inquisitorial Visitations fell into disrepute. The truth is, that since the days of the Tudors the old Norman blood had wellnigh become extinct in male lines, and the existing aristocracy had become a *mélange* of ancient houses and families of comparatively recent growth, so that the old exclusive idea, of which so much has been said, had almost died out. It could no longer be said with one of our oldest poets—

> "Of the Normans be these high men that dwell in this land,
> And the low men of Saxons."

The spirit of "John Bull-ism" had been much fostered by two great political events—the revolutions of 1642 and 1688. Class distinctions were to a very large extent merged in the vital question of civil and religious freedom. On both occasions men of very opposite birth and position had fought the battle of great principles under a common banner, and had felt how necessary each was to each—a feeling never fully admitted before. Thenceforward the slang expressions "Tory" and "Whig" may be said to have occupied the antagonistic positions erewhile assumed by the so-called gentle and ungentle.

In the abolition of great injustices and abuses, mankind are very apt to do away with some harmless or even useful things, simply because they have been associated with those evils. Thus, in the Protestant Reformation of the sixteenth century, the cross, the very symbol of our common Christian hope, because it had been prostituted to idolatrous uses by the Romanists, came to be regarded by many sincere-minded, but (*me judice*) mistaken, men, as a thing to be avoided and spurned at. So, because feudal tyranny had wrought great and manifest wrongs, heraldry and genealogy—which were, as I have already said, not merely harmless concomitants, but really and in themselves (as I shall further attempt to prove) useful things—came to be considered as shreds of a rotten and injurious system.

That a taste for family history may exist without any degree of what is called aristocratic pride is evident to every one at all acquainted with general society. I could mention some of the yeomanry class and others of similar rank, men of moderate educational attainments, who are skilful genealogists, and know a great deal more of their ancestry for a few centuries upwards than do the generality of the titled classes themselves. But while this taste for the science of genealogy is cultivated by many, a much larger number unscrupulously assume that external mark of a good descent, a coat of arms, without the least regard to ancestry whatever. That vulgarly *"genteel"* class of people, who, not content with the honest names of Smith and Taylor, metamorphose themselves into Smythes and Tayleures, boldly assume the armorial ensigns of well-known ancient families, and hope by this transparent piece of trickery to impose upon the incurious part of society. As soon as people reach the sunny side of the "middle class," they usually assume, along with other consequential airs, a coat of arms, which they parade upon every carriage-panel and teapot in their possession. Instead of acquiring this distinction in a fair, honest way, at the Heralds' College, at a cost of some fourscore pounds, they either call to their aid some seal-engraver, by whom arms are "found," or consult a dictionary of heraldry, and without any compunction of conscience adopt the family ensigns of others with whom in all probability they are in no way connected. Happily for these people the heraldic Visitations have ceased to be; for I believe that not a fourth of the armigerous class of the present day can prove their right to the arms they bear.

Others, who wish to adopt "ensigns of honour," go about their acquisition in a more honourable way, and pay the £78. 15s. to the King of Arms and his

official subjects, for a *new coat*. But this straight-
forward conduct, instead of being regarded in its
proper light (as an honest avowal that the purchasers
are *novi homines*), exposes them to the contempt of
the class which they aspire to join, no less than to the
envy of that which they are quitting, and thus, like
the bat in Æsop, they get flouted on every hand.

Now I should like to see the practice of bearing
arms largely extended. Every family choosing to
bear arms should have liberty to do so upon payment
of a small annual tax for the privilege, as at present,
to Government. This should be done as no matter of
vanity, but purely, as in the earliest days of heraldry,
as one of *distinction*—of genealogical, not of aristocratic, discrimination. Stubbs, and Boaks, and
Timpkins, and Joblings, should have their own proper
coats as well as Neville, and Beauchamp, and Chol-
mondeley. This may seem a somewhat startling
proposal, but it is far more feasible than at first sight
it may appear. To some it may seem that heraldry
is unable to admit of so large an expansion—that the
multiplication of coats armorial to such a degree
would exhaust the stock of heraldic materials. But
this is by no means to be feared. With one half of the
charges now borne in arms, variously combined,
according to the existing rules of heraldry, every
respectable family in Christendom might be supplied
with its peculiar ensign. By a principle somewhat
analogous to that of arithmetical *permutation*, a comparatively limited number of simple elements might
be so disposed as to produce an infinite variety of
armorial designs. And in order that this plan should
be successfully carried out, I would have it regulated
by a central body of scientific heralds like that now
composing the College of Arms, who, for a *small* fee,

should devise and register every coat. To all the various branches of a family bearing a common surname, and within a traceable degree of kindred, I would of course assign a common coat of arms. This would greatly reduce the number of new bearings requisite.

By the adoption of this plan the dishonest assumption of other people's property above adverted to would be abolished; but other and more practical advantages would accrue from it. Without any profound acquaintance with heraldry we should be enabled to distinguish from each other, persons bearing a commonly-occurring name. Thus instead of discriminating several Wilsons belonging to a particular circle by "Tall John," "Lawyer John," "Spectacled John," and such-like uncomplimentary phrases, well-informed people would distinguish neighbours by some prominent feature in their family bearings, such as "William Smith (fleur-de-lis)," "Thomas Jones (cinquefoil)," "James Browne (portcullis)," and "Henry Robinson (red cross)." This may be deemed picturesque trifling, but, even conceding this, there remains a real and tangible advantage which cannot be gainsaid—I mean the impulse which my plan would give to the study of genealogy, and the comparative facility with which after the lapse of a few generations family relationships might be traced. How many tedious and harassing chancery suits, more or less injurious to all concerned in them, might have been avoided, had some such simple practice been long ago adopted. We have known instances where a pedigree was satisfactorily established up to a certain point, when all hope of carrying it further was suddenly cut off by the occurrence, in parish registers or other public documents, of two persons of the same Christian name and surname living contemporaneously in the same place, but who were perhaps not in the slightest degree connected by the ties of consanguinity. Everybody acquainted with genealogical investigations is aware that a coat of arms is a much safer guarantee of kindred than the orthography of a name.

But long before this, some of my readers will have asked " Would it not be absurd for the middle class to assume distinctions which were formerly accorded only to gentlemen? " Let me endeavour to answer this question. The expression *gentleman* is perhaps one of the vaguest in the language ; as all men who wear decent apparel, from duke to draper's assistant, from ambassador to journeyman, from archbishop to parish-clerk, are, in the courtesies of the age, " gentlemen." Every man, in short, who in virtue of any supposed qualification considers himself entitled to the respect of his neighbours, accepts the application of the phrase to himself without scruple, and applies it without hesitation to his acknowledged equals. But without admitting so great a latitude to the term, it is a matter of no small difficulty to ascertain what really constitutes a gentleman. The lawyer will tell you, after Sir Thomas Smith and Blackstone, that he " who can live idly, and without manual labour, and will bear the port, charge, and countenance of a gentleman, shall be called *master*, and shall be taken for a gentleman." Hence in official lists and legal documents, persons who, from inability or disinclination, adopt no trade or profession, although their yearly income should not exceed a hundred pounds, are styled gentlemen, while their opulent neighbours possessed of twenty times as much, if engaged in mercantile affairs, are designated by the name of their trades; and hence it sometimes happens that a spend-

thrift or imbecile son who cannot be trusted in his
father's counting-house or behind his counter is styled
" gentleman," while his respectable and worthy parent
is described as " merchant," " draper," "printer," or
as the case may be. If we turn to the authority of the
herald, although we find the use of the word a little
more restricted, there is still much vagueness in its
application. " Gentlemen," says my author, " have
their beginning, either of blood, as that they are born
of worshipful parents—or, that they have *done something worthy* in peace or war whereby they deserve to be
accounted gentlemen." [2] So then, the sailor who took
a fort in Hindostan by his individual prowess, or any
" common hind " who has saved a fellow-creature
from drowning, ought to be considered a gentleman.
According to the same authority " a gentleman of
what estate soever he be, *although he go to plough and
common labour for his maintenance, yet he is a gentleman*." [3] Such is the deliberate opinion of a " judicious herald" as promulged in a goodly folio under
the " cavalier" period of the Stuarts !

" Done something worthy ! " Why, then, whoso-
ever hath introduced some useful invention—written
some good book—established some benevolent insti-
tution—painted some beautiful picture—erected some
noble building—constructed some convenient highway—built some commodious bridge—fulfilled some
onerous office for the common good—reformed some
vicious character—annihilated some ancient abuse—
promoted the well-being of his native town — or
" done something (that is *anything*) worthy," is a
gentleman ! So be it, Master Herald ; may *such* gentlemen increase and multiply. Amen !

[2] ' Guillim's Heraldry,' edit. 1679, part ii, p. 154.
[3] Ibid. p. 155.

10 §

Now this is high heraldic authority; and it is therefore clear that the number of families entitled to coats of arms is much greater than the number actually bearing them. For that must be a base and brutish stock indeed that has never owned as its head a man who has " done *something* worthy ; " and since it is argued that gentry is inextinguishable— that the offspring of a gentleman, " even although they go to plough," must be gentlemen too, it should follow that we are all, or nearly so, " gentlemen of blood," and therefore entitled, if we choose, to use armorial distinctions.

Again, if we look at the " stuff " gentry was made of in old times, we may assert for the many a claim to be in all material respects upon a ground of equality with the gentlemen of the middle ages. According to the vulgar estimate, three things are essential to the being of a gentleman—" money, wit (that is knowledge), and manners." Now if we compare the nineteenth century with the fourteenth, or even with the seventeenth, we shall find that large section of our commonwealth known as the middle class far richer, better educated, and of more polished carriage and demeanour than the gentlemen of those older periods. If the claim to gentility be made to rest upon a *comparative* basis, then the " gentle " must always bear about the same numerical proportion to the " ungentle," as it did in the days of the Planta-genets and Tudors; but if, on the contrary, gentility be a *positive* and inherent thing, and the " law of developement " applies to this as well as to other subjects, the proportion of the truly " gentle " must become much greater as society advances in wealth, knowledge, and refinement.

I hope my reader will not consider these remarks

inconsistent with those with which I set out. I wish
to be understood that I esteem every person of "good
conduct, guidance, and conversation"—possessed of a
fair income, whether from realized property or from
actual exertions—and enjoying the advantages of fair
education and general intelligence—a gentleman.
But while I claim this distinction for a numerous
class to whom it is not usually conceded, far be it
from me to hold in disesteem the additional advantage
of descent from an ancient family. While those
qualities constitute what is essential to the true gentleman, *this* is an additional ornament. In the one
case we have (to employ an architectural figure) the
simple characteristics of the Tuscan pillar—in the
other those of the elegant Corinthian or elaborate
Composite. But be the capital plain and simple, or
be it gorgeous and ornate, the pillar is still a pillar,
and equally calculated in either case usefully to
uphold the fabric of society, and to be an essential
part of every noble state and polished commonwealth.

That a love for genealogical knowledge may exist
to a large extent where rank and title are out of the
question—that it may be cherished like any other
branch of science for its own sake—is evidenced by
the Americans. It is well known that a taste for it
prevails in the United States to a degree little
dreamed of by the revilers of pedigree in England, and
that not only among what is termed the "Upper Ten
Thousand" or republican aristocracy, but among the
learned and intelligent of every class. Such a book
as Farmer's 'Genealogical Register of the First
Settlers in New England' (Boston, 1829) is a goodly
and tangible proof, not only of the existence of the
taste, but of the zeal and ability with which genea-

logical researches are pursued beyond the Atlantic. In his preface the editor remarks : " We are all curious to know something respecting those who have preceded us on the stage of action ; and ti.ere has been a curiosity among many of the present generation to trace back their progenitors in an uninterrupted series to those who first landed on the bleak and inhospitable shores of New England. And it is not improbable that the arrival of our puritan fathers will form a more memorable epoch in history than the Conquest of England does in that country, and that posterity, a few centuries hence, will experience as much plea- sure in tracing back their ancestry to those colonists, as some of the English feel in being able to deduce their descent from the Normans." The Americans too have succeeded in an attempt which has until quite recently failed on our side the water, namely, the establishment of Genealogical Societies. I have before me, ' An Address to the New England Historic- Genealogical Society,' delivered last year by a vene- rable correspondent, Dr. William Jenks, some extracts from which will better exemplify than any observations of my own, the feeling entertained on this subject by many of our Transatlantic cousins.

" The feeling [the love of pedigree] is natural. I belongs to our very self-hood. It is a modification, doubtless, of self-love. But how much more liberal than the boast of riches, or the oppression of power ! How far more purifying and ennobling !—since he who values his descent from an ancestry distinguished for any of the virtues, inherits also with this affec- tion, most generally, a disposition adverse to practices of a contrary character. ' Dedecorant bene natos culpæ,' said the Roman poet, as if he had cautioned thus : ' would you maintain the respect your predecessors have acquired, abhor every mean and dishonourable thing.' It becomes an axiom.

"Then, again, as population advances, the relations of kindred seem gradually to become more and more faint. A brother is but what a cousin was in former times, when the population was sparse and its numbers few. Now whatever tends to bring men happily together, and unite them in bonds of mutual regard, has an effect to purify and advance civilization, and render to society an antidote to the ruder and merely selfish propensities. This does the much-abused science of Genealogy."

Again—

"We require pedigrees of horses—we inspect with great care those of cattle—to ascertain the genuineness of their descent; and the keen-sighted, experienced breeders of them acquire with the farmer, the sportsman, the independent gentleman, an almost enviable fame—but, is it not to be feared [in regard to human pedigree] that in multitudes of instances, as in the old countries of Europe, the pecuniary consideration outweighs immeasurably that which is merely physiological? . . . .

"I will pursue this subject further. The very hardships which are encountered by settlers, in such scenes as our country first exhibited to Europeans, call for energy, inforce self-denial, demand frugality and good economy, strengthen the constitution, give health and vigour to the mind, and tend to prolong life. It has been said that a voyage across the Atlantic adds ten years to a man's life. How this may be, I will not undertake to determine. But it is a fact that descendants of younger branches of noble families, obliged to look out for themselves, and therefore claiming often the footless 'martlet' as their peculiar heraldric designation, have been found in America, among the sons of industry if not of want. Yes, when riot and debauchery, or high, luxurious living and indolence, have caused a 'noble' family to become extinct—the offshoot, neglected and exposed, has grown to be a sightly tree. The heir of the illustrious and ancient house of DE COURCY was discovered in a hardy seaman, sailing, nearly a century ago, out of the harbour of our own Newport; and in my own time, the legitimate owner of the immense estates of the GROSVENORS in a poor farmer of New York. The latter never inherited. The descendant of the former now possesses the family title and estates." . . . . .

And further :—

" Many of our immigrants have, a long time since, and onward, brought badges of distinction with them, and still indulge the harmless vanity—am I to call it? —of keeping them. The badges to which I allude are coats of arms; which have indeed their use, and an important use when authentic, in identifying families and proving descents. In these, our friends of New York are advanced far before us already, and have a system, brief however, published and in circulation. And, if its representations are admitted, our WASHINGTON was not only of noble but royal lineage ; and an admirable representative, it must be acknowledged, of regal dignity—' one of Nature's nobles.' "

As to George Washington's descent from nobility or royalty, I have not at hand the means of verifying the statement, though it is highly probable; as he was descended from a good family in the county of Northampton. Like Oliver Cromwell, the American patriot was fond of genealogy, and corresponded with our heralds on the subject of his own pedigree. Yes, this George Washington, the man who gave sanc-

tion, if not birth, to that most democratical of sentiments—that "all men are free and *equal*," was, as the
phrase goes, a gentleman of blood, of ancient line,
and of coat armour; nor was he slow to acknowledge
the fact. When the Americans, in their most righteous
revolt against the tyranny of the mother country, cast
about for an ensign by which to distinguish themselves
from their English oppressors, what did they ultimately
adopt? Why, nothing more nor less than a gentleman's badge—a modification of the old English coat
of arms borne by their leader and deliverer. A few
stars and stripes had in the old chivalrous times distinguished his ancestors from their compeers in tourna-
ment and upon battle-field : more stars and additional
stripes (denoting the number of States that joined in
the struggle) now became the standard around which
the patriots of the West so successfully rallied. It is
not a little curious that this poor out-worn rag of
feudalism—as many would count it—should have thus
expanded into the bright and ample banner which now
waves upon every sea!

It is to me a pleasing reflection that our American
cousins, in spite of their great tendency to "go ahead,"
should now and then exhibit a strong retrospective
taste also. Their novelists and poets, in common with
our own, go back to olden days for subjects whereon
to feast the imagination and refine the taste. The
author of ' Bracebridge Hall ' is as much at home in
the depicting of ancient scenes and the delineation of
obsolete manners, as our own Sir Walter Scott; and
there are touches in the best of recent American poets
that equal, in allusions to by-gone things, the happiest
strains in Marmion. To adduce an instance from
Longfellow's ' Flowers :'

"Not alone in Spring's armorial bearing,
   And in Summer's green-emblazoned field,
But in arms of brave old Autumn's wearing,
   In the centre of his brazen shield;

"Not alone in meadows and green alleys,
   On the mountain top, and by the brink
Of sequestered pools in woodland valleys,
   Where the slaves of Nature stoop to drink;

"Not alone in her vast dome of glory,
   Not on graves of bird and beast alone,
But in old cathedrals, high and hoary,
   On the tombs of heroes, carved in stone.

"In the cottage of the rudest peasant,
   In ancestral homes, whose crumbling towers,
Speaking of the Past unto the Present,
   Tell us of the ancient games of Flowers."

One also notes with pleasure that a taste for the retrospective in the direction of genealogical research is manifesting itself in a people among whom even less than among the bustling denizens of the West it would be looked for—I mean the Society of Friends. The disparity between the emblazoned surcoat and crested helmet of old times, and the sober drab and broad brim of our own, which this allusion will call up, may suggest a smile, but to the thoughtful mind it suggests something besides. It is an additional illustration of the doctrine that "extremes sometimes meet," or rather of that higher one, that human nature will assert herself under all circumstances.

"Naturam expelles furcâ, tamen usque recurret,
   Et mala perrumpet furtim fastidia victrix."

A love of ancestry is a passion of the human breast, whether that breast be encased in uncomfortable gilded armour, or in supple broad-cloth of the soberest hue. For my own part I do not see why the sister Rachels and Rebekahs of the nineteenth century should not embroider a cushion with their family badge, with as good a grace as did the lady Isabels and Alionoras an armorial scarf for their champion knights in the fourteenth. The "coat of arms" has lost its association with deeds of blood, and is become a mere mark of family distinction, to which the Quaker has as good a right as the Commander-in-Chief.

Let me now say a few words upon the pleasures derivable from genealogical investigations. To those whose sordid temper leads them to disregard everything not immediately conducive to the accumulation of wealth or the gratification of appetite, the search after one's ancestors among damp tombstones, musty registers, and antiquated wills, may appear the ultimatum of human folly. But he who engages in the pursuit with intelligent zeal has an intellectual pabulum of which such men little dream—a pleasure far surpassing the excitements of the chase, the gratification of the palate, or the aggrandizement of riches. Apart from the accumulation of mere names, dates, and alliances, and the barren chronicle of births, deaths, and marriages, there is a *poetry* in the study of genealogy such as is to be found in no other pursuit, except, perhaps, in the investigation of external nature. Some little hint occurs in an old will or in a time-worn epitaph, upon which the pedigree-hunter dwells with delight, and out of which he frames a theory which may indeed be erroneous, but which is still harmless, and productive of a pleasurable feeling hard to describe—a joy with which the uninitiated stranger cannot intermeddle.[4]

[4] There is perhaps scarcely a more amusing narrative in the English language than one which seldom falls into the hands of general readers—Bell's Huntingdon Peerage. It details the parti-

It is not intended in this rambling dissertation to lay down any regular system of rules upon which genealogical investigations should be based. Still it may interest those of my readers who have not yet paid attention to the subject, if I submit a few hints for their guidance.

In the first place, I would say—in this, as in all other inquiries, let Truth be your great object. Few things are easier than to " vamp up " a pedigree, and to deduce yourself from ." high blood." There is little difficulty in setting forth a genealogical tree which shall convince your ordinary associates and friends that you have all manner of noble blood in your veins —that all the Percys and the Howards are your kinsmen. This may be done—nay, *is* very often done without the remotest intention of trickery or fraud, by the simple and easy process of putting mere probabilities in the place of proven truths. How often do our genealogical writers of a certain class illustrate this remark ! A family of respectability happens to bear a name distinguished in the annals of our nation —a name which figures in that apocryphal document the Roll of Battel Abbey, in the Chronicles of the Barons' wars, in the muster-rolls of Crescy, or of the conflicts of the Roses,—and by a series of ingenious and impalpable dove-tailings they are made descendants of all that is noble and chivalrous from the " coming in of the Conqueror " to the present day. Mere coincidences in Christian names are made to assume all the force of proved identities; and, worse than this, surnames are twisted out of all etymological propriety, and by the omission or insertion of a

culars of a series of adventures engaged in, in making good a title to an ancient peerage on behalf of the author's client, which was brought to a successful issue about thirty-three years since.

letter or two, the veriest plebeianism is engrafted
upon ancient nobility. I will not undertake the invidious task of proving this by examples, which are
scattered thickly enough over the pages of works
produced for the twofold purpose of gratifying the
vanity of *parvenus,* and filling the purses of the flat-
terers. I shall say no more upon this disagreeable
topic, but merely remark, that " the strength of a
chain is the strength of its weakest link," and that
consequently no pedigree is a sound one unless *every*
link of descent is proved by evidence such as would
satisfy any intelligent jury of impartial men. I willingly admit that there are cases genealogical, as
well as legal, where, in the very nature of things, circumstantial evidence must be accepted in the absence
of direct proof. For example, if I find, in title-deed
or other record, evidence that two persons of the
same family name were possessed, in succession, of
the same estate, I conclude with little hesitation that
they were of the same stock, although there may be
no means of ascertaining whether son succeeded to
father, brother to brother, or nephew to uncle. Nor
does this much matter (provided only that some
mark of the dubiety be acknowledged), since the
proof of a common stock is sufficient. Our baron-
ages will furnish abundant illustrations of my
meaning.

Secondly, my suggestion is—" Begin at the right
end." Let no considerations of vanity lead you to
jump to a conclusion that you are descended from the
high-born and mighty. If you can establish this by
a succession of proofs, like the steps in a geometrical
proposition, well and good ; but pray remember, what
has before been hinted at, the true intent of genealogy
is to show who and what your real ancestors were—not

to gratify personal vanity. Should they prove to
have been men of humble position, do not therefore
relinquish your investigations, or cast aside your
labour as fruitless. The hunting of the hare sometimes proves better sport than the chase of the wild-
boar or the stag. By beginning " at the right end,"
I mean, let your inquiries be *retrogressive*—trace
upwards from yourself—not downwards from somebody else. The latter course will almost certainly do
for some other person, in whom you have not the
slightest interest, what you designed to do for yourself, and so in the end be really a loss of labour;
whereas the opposite procedure will certainly result
in some gratifying fruits, and—to pursue an analogy
just now mentioned—if you do not succeed in forging
a *long* chain of precious metal, you will at all events
have a *strong* and satisfactory one, though it may be
of limited length and of less glittering material.

Assuming that one knows comparatively nothing
of his descent—not even perhaps the parentage of
his grandfather—the best method of procedure is, first
to examine with diligence any paper, book, or other
like relic that may have come down from that
ancestor. A title-deed of real property, however
small, frequently assists in carrying back a pedigree
from some generations; while an old Family Bible
often furnishes not only the direct line of descent but
collateral branches also. Next to such sources of
information, inquiries of one's oldest surviving rela-
tive should be resorted to. By this means the inves-
tigator may, in ordinary cases, with comparatively
little trouble (or rather with no trouble at all, for
the maxim, *Labor ipse voluptas*, applies here), ascertain his ancestry for at least five descents, or to the
grandfather's grandfather. All such oral information

should, if practicable, be verified by searches in the baptismal registers of the parishes where the respective progenitors have resided, and in this research much collateral information respecting marriages and ancestors in female lines is almost certain to turn up. In making inquiries of aged people, care should be taken to note down remarkable incidents and anecdotes which occur in the course of conversation. By this means the dull recital of names, dates, and residences, will be enlivened, and suggestions of a useful character for subsequent investigations will sometimes result. What will most strike the observant inquirer is the fact that he not unfrequently finds himself connected by comparatively few links with remote circumstances and events in a way of which he little dreamed. For example, the writer of the present pages (forty years old in this year of Grace, 1853) can show traditionary evidence of the existence of the Great Plague in London in 1665, with the intervention of only two generations, through whom it has been handed down. His grandfather, who was born in 1735, was personally acquainted with an aged woman who had that dreadful disease in her early youth, and who survived it to reach an extraordinary age. The writer's father is therefore able to make the somewhat startling assertion—"My father knew a person who had the plague one hundred and eighty-eight years ago!" Several equally remarkable instances are upon record.[5] To return: it sometimes happens that your antiquated informant, through decay of memory, has lost the Christian names of some still older members of the family, and can only recollect the place of their residence. A search in

[5] See the early volumes of 'Notes and Queries' for a variety of them, furnished by different contributors.

the parish registers of the place indicated will generally supply the desired information, and perhaps
afford the means of adding several links to the upper
end of your chain. An old tombstone or two in
some neglected corner of the churchyard may also
serve you with valuable subsidiary testimony.

Having exhausted these sources of evidence, one
should next have recourse to the registries of wills
preserved in every diocese, or, on failure there, to those
of the archiepiscopal prerogative courts. Sir Harris
Nicolas, in the Preface of his 'Testamenta Vetusta,'
observes:—"Of all species of evidence, whether of the
kindred or of the possessions of individuals, perhaps
the most satisfactory is afforded by their wills; and
in many cases also these interesting documents exhibit traits of character which are more valuable,
because more certain, than can possibly be deduced
from the actions of their lives. Suggestions of interest, prejudice, and not unfrequently motives of
revenge, may induce a witness either to misstate facts,
or to give a colouring to them, which, although it
may not violate truth, is, nevertheless, far from being
strictly in accordance with it. But the corporeal
suffering under which a man often labours when he
makes his last testament—the solemn invocation with
which it commences—the associations which it cannot fail to excite—and, above all, the recollection
that the important document will not see the light
until he is removed from that sphere where alone
falsehood can be successful, or vice be triumphant—
tend to render the statements in wills of unquestion-
able veracity."

But a will, especially one of old date, is valuable on
other grounds than the sincerity of the sentiments
which the testator puts upon record. Better than

any other source of evidence, it illustrates habits of
thought, modes of living, and the articles of furniture
and of costume in use at different epochs.   It also furnishes valuable hints as to obsolete customs, venerated
shrines, and the like.   To the genealogist it supplies
the most correct information as to the property and
social status of the testator, and above all as to his
collateral relations and descendants.   A single will
sometimes proves by its references three, four, or
even five descents of a pedigree.

From these two principal sources, parish registers
and wills, then, one may, with a moderate degree of
genealogical zeal, succeed in ascertaining his pedigree
for a considerable number of descents.   Many parish
registers commence with the year 1538, and in most
parishes where they have been carefully preserved
they will be found to extend back to the beginning
of Queen Elizabeth's reign, 1558.   The will-registries
generally are of earlier date—several going back to
the fourteenth century ; but they are rarely indexed
for more than a century or two, and a search in some
of the courts is an almost hopeless task, by reason of
the want of arrangement which prevails.

Much additional information connected with pedigrees is contained in various public records—particularly the 'Inquisitiones post Mortem,' and the
'Escheat Rolls.' As these documents furnish the names
of the deceased's relatives, and mention his real property, they are of the utmost value and interest.   An
eminent legal authority, Lord Mansfield, very justly
remarks, that since the disuse of this species of inquiry in the seventeenth century, it has become more
difficult to establish a pedigree for a hundred years,
since that time, than for five hundred years before it.
Then there are the Heralds' Visitations of the various

counties preserved in the College of Arms and in the British Museum,[6] some of which contain elaborate pedigrees, deducing the families from the earliest periods of genealogical record. There are likewise the curious rolls of arms of the reign of Edward I, and later, which are of great value, as showing the true original heraldric bearings of the few whose privilege it was in those early times to make use of such distinctions. Numerous other sources of genealogical materials might be mentioned; but should my reader desire to pursue the subject, I cannot recommend a more pleasant, or a more skilful, guide than Mr. Grimaldi, whose *Origines Genealogicæ* will afford all the information that can reasonably be desired.

Here these desultory observations must close. Some of them have been expressed with more warmth than I intended, and I may appear to be somewhat of a zealot in the advocacy of a study which many of the oracles of the day decry and condemn. I trust, however, that I have not invalidated any argument by proving more than I intended, and that I have not attached to the science of Genealogy any greater amount of importance than in the mind of the dispassionate reader it may appear to deserve.

[6] Sims's Index to the Pedigrees and Arms contained in the Heralds' Visitations in the British Museum, 8vo, London, 1851, is a work of great value to the genealogical inquirer, and prevents the loss of much useless labour. I hear also with satisfaction, that Mr. Sims is preparing for publication a work similar to the *Origines* —but on a more extended scale.

AN ANTIQUARIAN PILGRIMAGE IN NORMANDY.

Normandy! To what numberless historical associations does the mere mention of this word give rise. By what a variety of ties is that province connected with our own Fatherland! Separated by a mere strip of Ocean's domain from the land of our nativity, it is the very first foreign shore that a great proportion of English travellers set foot upon; and upon historical grounds, particularly, it is the very first that they *ought* to visit! It is a fair and pleasant land; and, though widely differing in many important respects from England, is one where the well-disposed tourist can always succeed in making himself at home.

The interest which I had long felt in the history of the distinguished family of De Warenne, whose alliances with royalty, great territorial possessions, and remarkable deeds in Anglo-Norman history, give them a prominent place in our annals, was considerably increased by the discovery, under rather unwonted circumstances, of the remains—enshrined in little leaden coffers, inscribed with their names—of William, Earl of Warenne, the first settler of his race in this country, and his countess, Gundrada, a younger daughter of William the Conqueror. This occurred in 1845 on the site of Lewes Priory, a once magnificent establishment, which had been founded at the foot of their baronial castle by the noble pair themselves for their souls' health, and which became,

11

in the course of the two or three succeeding centuries, during which they flourished in pristine splendour, the "long home" of their descendants. The discovery having been to some extent associated with my own humble name, the feeling alluded to, growing by what it fed upon, induced me during one of my brief summer visits to Normandy, to seek out the original *habitat* of so venerable a race. I had seen their grave, and was now anxious to visit their cradle.

Accordingly, on a delightful morning towards the close of June, 1849, I found myself seated in the capacious *voiture* of my friend Monsieur P., who had kindly consented to become my guide and companion from *la ville fidèle*, the town of Dieppe (so interesting for many an ancient reminiscence both English and French) to Bellencombre—a small *bourg*, situated about six leagues to the s.s.e. of that place—which in times anterior to the Norman Conquest had been the *cunabula* of the mighty race in whose fortunes I felt so great an interest. An hour's drive along the broad roads and over the unenclosed fields of the district brought us to La Chapelle, the residence of Monsieur de Breauté, member of the Institute, and a perfect type of the *gentilhomme Français*, by whom we were courteously received, and treated with a view of his noble and comprehensive library. Here we met my friend M. l'Abbé Cochet, the learned antiquary, who was to accompany us for the rest of the journey, and who had been on a visit of some days at the château. La Chapelle is situated in a pleasing country. The mansion is principally of brick, apparently of the date of the early part of the eighteenth century, and, as usual in this part of France, is approached by a straight avenue of lofty beech-trees.

Taking leave of this abode of learned leisure and polished hospitality, we soon made our way to the town of Longueville, a spot intimately associated with Anglo-Norman annals, and calculated to awaken many emotions of regret in the retrospective mind of the antiquary. On entering the town one is struck by the appearance on every hand of fragments of columns, capitals, and other architectural remains, built into the houses. Should you enter a *café* you are likely enough to find it partly paved with medieval tombstones, the spoils of the once famous abbey of Longueville. At the entrance of a druggist's shop your eye will rest upon a stone incised, in characters of the fourteenth century, with the legend, " Here lies the Lady Isabel .... pray God for her soul."— [*Cy gist demoiselle Isabelle ...... Priez Dieu pour l'âme.*] This desecration of a sepulchral monument would excite a feeling stronger than mere regret under any circumstances, but it becomes especially reprehensible when one is told with apparent probability that this is no other than the tombstone of Isabelle d'Eu, Countess of Longueville, wife of Geoffry Marcel, governor of Pontoise, and castellan of Longueville, the great benefactress of the neighbouring abbey, within whose cloisters she was buried in the year 1339! " Pauvre châtelaine," observes M. Cochet, " elle croyait peut-être qu'une vie toute de bienfaits suffisait pour lui assurer du moins la jouissance de son tombeau. Hélas! elle ne savait pas que le temps dévore jusqu'à la pierre de la tombe : la vertu seule survit à la mort." [1]

The truth is, that most of the houses of this little

---

[1] Les Eglises de l'Arrondissement de Dieppe (1846), p. 254. To this excellent work I am indebted for several of the historical facts noticed in this little sketch.

town have been constructed out of the materials of
the old Cluniac Abbey, the site, and some of the
walls, of which are now occupied as a cotton-mill.
Founded about the year 1084, by the famous Walter
Giffard, Count of Longueville and Earl of Bucking-
ham, one of the companions in arms of the Conqueror, this establishment subsisted more than seven
centuries, but at length fell to destruction during the
furor of the Revolution.   The Castle of Longueville,
to which we paid a visit, is now a picturesque ruin,
and bears few traces of the period of its original foundation.   It must have been partially or wholly rebuilt
at a much later date.   The notion so prevalent
in this country, that when a castle and a religious
house stand in moderate proximity to each other, a
subterraneous passage once connected the two edifices, also prevails with respect to this castle and the
neighbouring abbey.   The parish church contains
several features of considerable interest to the eccle-
siologist, among which may be reckoned a number of
encaustic tiles of the sixteenth century, similar in
form and design to many I have seen in England, but
of a blue and sea-green colour.

Longueville stands on the little river Scie, along
whose beautiful valley winds the Dieppe and Rouen
railway.   Here accordingly we took our seats in the
train for St. Victor, the nearest available station
for Bellencombre.   The most striking object between
the two points is the Church of Auffay, which, as
viewed from the railway, presents a very striking and
majestic aspect.

St. Victor l'Abbaye has several points of interest
for the English archæologist.   It belonged in what
we call " Norman " times to the De Mortimers,
famous alike on both sides of the English Channel,

and descended from a common stock with the De
Warennes. They had a castle here, built upon an
artificial mound, after the fashion prevalent in England for Norman keeps. On the decay of the fortress,
this mound became inclosed within the circuit of the
walls of the Abbey of St. Victor. The abbey itself
had its origin in the relic-loving days of the eleventh
century—shortly anterior to the Norman Conquest.
Tormord, a priest of the country, having obtained
from Marseilles some relics of Saint Victor, enshrined
them in a precious casket, and made them the grand
attraction of a monastic foundation which speedily
sprang into existence on the spot. The abbey experienced many vicissitudes during its lengthened existence, which was nominally sustained until the
Revolution. During the eighteenth century its
functions were discharged by one solitary monk.
Among the forty-one abbots who ruled it through
a period of seven centuries and a half, were several
who distinguished themselves in letters and monastic
discipline, particularly l'Abbé François de Circassis'
and l'Abbé Terrisse. Circassis was a native of Cy-
prus, and a member of one of the principal families of
that island. At the capture of Nicosia he was taken
prisoner by the Turks, and conveyed on board the
vessel of Ali Pacha, the admiral of their fleet. At the
battle of Lepanto he was recaptured by the Venetians,
and of course immediately restored to liberty. Shel-
tered afterwards by Cardinal Bourbon, he completed
his academical studies, and became tutor to one of the
princes of the blood. In 1599 he was rewarded with
the abbacy of Saint Victor, which he held twenty
years, a period entirely devoted to the interests of
his monastery and the cultivation of sacred literature.
The Abbé Terrisse, well known to antiquaries as a

commentator on the 'Antonine Itinerary' and the
'Peutinger Tables,' on his promotion to the oversight
of Saint Victor in 1739, found the establishment in a
greatly neglected condition, and its buildings fast
hastening to decay. These abuses he reformed; and
in order to excite the inhabitants of the district to a
greater zeal for religion he established an annual
procession, which was sustained by the neighbouring
priests and gentry, and by sixty stout labourers. On
a certain day in July the procession wended its way
from the church in great pomp. First marched the
serving brethren, wearing red hoods embroidered with
the figure of the holy sacrament, and bearing the
banners, flags, and standards of the society. Next
followed the acolytes, the bearers of flowers strewing
the path as they went, and the incense-bearers ba-
lancing their censers. Then followed two gilt lan-
terns preceding the *soleil*, or pyx, containing the host,
which was suspended to a scarf worn round the neck
by a priest. The canopy over the head of this personage was supported by gentlemen wearing scarfs
of precious stuffs. In this order the procession advanced for the distance of about two leagues, and then
returned in the same order to the abbey. This
religious show seems to have been enacted for many
years—with what results as to the advancement of
religion in the neighbourhood we are not informed.
We Protestants smile at such a mode of stirring-up
the lukewarm to the fervour of piety, and moralists
may perhaps puzzle themselves a little to account for
such a procedure on the part of a man of the intellectual calibre of Terrisse, who enjoys the reputation of
being the founder of the Academy of Rouen, and
whose erudition seems to have been almost unlimited
in its copiousness and variety. He died in 1785.

There are at present few remains of the Abbey of St. Victor. On the outside of the church is a statue of William the Conqueror, with his crown, sword, and sceptre. It appears to be a work of the four-teenth or fifteenth century, and is accompanied by this inscription :—

> " Villelmus conquestor,
> Anglorum rex, Normannorum dux,
> Abbatiæ Sancti Victoris fundationem confirmavit
> Anno Salutis 1074,"

to which a poet of the place has added these pithy distichs :—

> " Anglia victorem, dominum quem Neustria sensit,
> Limina Victoris servat amica sui.
>
> Sit procul hinc inimica manus : vigil excubat heros ;
> Est Deus ipse intus : Crede, pavesce, cole ! " [2]

It is a tradition among the inhabitants of Saint Victor that the Conqueror caused to be erected upon their church-tower a beacon, which being lighted every night served as a guide to his army in their marches across the country. William is said to have entertained great veneration for St. Victor, who was accounted the patron of Christian warriors.

The shrine which contains the relics of the Mar-sellaise saint is still preserved here, though I did not obtain a sight of it. It is a little wooden chest, adorned with figures of the saint and of the twelve apostles. It is still resorted to as an object of popular devotion, and still, according to the belief of the peasantry, performs great miracles. One seems a little unprepared for such a statement as that which follows :—

" On the 21st of July, 1841," writes my friend, the Abbé Cochet, " I saw the church of St. Victor filled

[2] Cochet's Churches, i, 238.

with pilgrims. There were the sick, the infirm, the
wounded—people who rather dragged themselves
along than walked. Fathers brought their children,
and brothers their brothers upon their shoulders!
For here charity commences the solace of misery, and
the parable of St. Christopher renews itself every day
in the popular devotion. The afflicted first cast themselves at the altar beneath the stole of the priest to
recite portions of the gospels; then rising, they went
to prostrate themselves before the shrine of the holy
Confessor, kissed the earth beneath his feet, and
passed on their knees under the altar which supported
his relics, as if perchance from that sacred dust some
healing virtue might descend upon them." [3]

But our pilgrimage was of a different order, and I
must proceed. Accompanied by my friend P., I went
into an *hôtélerie* in the village for a slight refection.
It was about mid-day, and we found the common room
of the inn full of people, seated at several tables,
discussing some (to me) unintelligible viands. They
were mostly *en blouse*, and appeared to be haymakers
and other field-labourers who had come to take their
noontide meal. Here we inquired for a *voiture*, and
after some delay procured such a one as I never had
the honour of being seated in before. It may be
described as an oblong platform on two wheels, and
surrounded with a kind of fence or balustrade of
unpainted sticks. A board thrown across this served
as a seat for the three tourists, our coachman, a lad of
fourteen (dressed much like an English butcher-boy),
having a special seat for himself in front. The
harness was of cordage and sheepskin, and our horse
had once been grey: his name, as the *garçon* informed
us, was *Jean Baptiste!* the queerest appellation in the

[3] Les Eglises, i, 238.

whole circle of horse-nomenclature. With Doctor
Syntax for an outrider, we should have formed as
pretty a sketch for a humorous pencil as could
reasonably be desired.

Thus equipped, we departed from a spot once
favoured with the patronage of the Conquerer, in
search of another which had been the birth-place of
his puissant son-in-law, William de Warenne! The
country between St. Victor and Bellencombre is very
agreeable, and a ride of a few miles (probably four or
five) brought us, in the rear of St John the Baptist,
to the desiderated spot.

Bellencombre is a picturesque town-village or *bourg*
of one broad street, consisting of irregular antique
houses chiefly constructed of wood in the style known
in England as " post and panel" building, and flanking
the humble *mairie* of the district—for the bourg is
the chef-lieu of a canton and therefore possesses some
official consequence. It is seated on the western
side of the little river Varenne. This river, which
rises in, and gives name to, the neighbouring com-
mune of Omonville-sur-Varenne, is now more generally known as the rivière d'Arques, because it
passes the castle and town of Arques on its way to
join the Bethune, which debouches a few miles north-
ward at the haven of Dieppe. The town itself
originally bore the same name as the river, and from
it the De Warennes assumed their surname. It was
not until the graceful mound upon which the castle
stands had been cast up, that the spot assumed another
appellation and was called Bellencombre, which may
be literally translated " Bellus Cumulus"—" the fair
mound or pile."[4] This then was the object of our

4 Archæological Journal, vol. iii, p. 6.

pilgrimage, and we lost no time in directing our steps upwards towards its summit.

But alas! my anticipations of a *castle* were doomed to disappointment. A few massive walls of stone and brick, once a portion of the donjon or keep, constituted the whole of the existing remains of one of the chief fortresses of ancient Normandy. A few unintelligible fragments of rough masonry stood as the representative of that once redoubtable edifice, which, founded in the earliest days of feudalism, was one of the last strongholds which defended the rights of the last of the dukes of Normandy—our own John *sans Terre*—against the aggressions of Philip Augustus, the French monarch. Besides the fact of its having belonged to the powerful Anglo-Norman Earls of Warenne and Surrey, it had had other claims upon the notice of the English historical antiquary. In the fifteenth century the sounds of war again reechoed amongst its majestic towers. In 1418 it was taken by our army, and a memorial of its conquest by English swords is still retained in the name *le camp Arundel,* borne by a spot near at hand. In 1449, however, the *leopard Anglais* yielded again to the fleur-de-lis, and the standard of the French monarchy once more waved upon its time-honoured summit. After the disruption of Normandy from England, it of course passed away from the De Warennes, and its subsequent history is associated with the names of its distinguished castellans, de la Heuze, de Moy, and Fontaine-Martel. When it ceased to exist as a garrison is unknown, but from certain relics which I noticed on the spot it appears pretty certain that it was occupied as a private residence during the seventeenth century. Long subsequently it bore ample traces of its former strength and importance, in the

existence of two large and lofty towers flanking the
grand entrance of the keep.   From sketches taken in
1832, it would seem that these towers must have been
about fifty feet in height, with machicolations. Above
the principal archway there then remained the grooves
by which the drawbridge had anciently been lifted.
A picturesque growth of ivy which entwined these
remains added considerably to their beauty, while the
beech woods on the opposite side of the Varenne—a
part of the great continuous forest of Arques—formed
a lovely back-ground to the picture. See what remained of these stately towers at the time of our visit !

It will naturally be asked, what caused the dis-
appearance of such considerable architectural remains
in the short interval between the year 1832 and the
period referred to.—Listen !

In 1835 the ruins of this castle and the "fair
mound" upon which they stood were sold by the family
Godard de Belbeuf to a small proprietor—one Dillard.

Now this Dillard was (or *is*—for I have not heard of his death) one of those execrable pieces of existence —humanity I will not say—who have no feeling beyond personal aggrandisement—no reverence for anything venerable or ancient. Such a man I found the living territorial representative in Normandy of the mighty and high-souled De Warennes — the owner of the cradle of that chivalrous race !

He had not long paid down his purchase-money of ten thousand francs ere the deep silence which had settled upon these baronial walls was broken—not indeed, as of old, by the clashing of swords and the clangour of the trumpet, but by the echoes of the hammer and pickaxe of the destroyer. This carcase of the old Norman chivalry offered a tempting bait for the mercenary grub who had got it into his power. Old Dillard demolished what Old Time had left, bit by bit, stone by stone, and sold it by retail ! Tiles eight hundred years old he turned into cement, while the mortar of walls which might have survived as long as the neighbouring hills he counted as so much common sand. Donjon-keep and entrance-towers fell beneath his cruel strokes, and the arches of the bridge crumbled into the ditch under his withering touch. With a chuckle of heart-felt satisfaction he told us that he had sold eighteen thousand feet of freestone procured from the demolition of the entrance-towers only ! The chapel within the donjon had shared the common fate. Walls built for the defence of man and for the service of God had been alike overturned; for every stone brought its *sou* to the old man's coffer, and that was sufficient to outweigh with him every consideration of respect for antiquity and every sentiment of reverence for religion.

While I was mentally ejaculating three times three groans against Le Père Dillard for his sordid spoliation, my friend the Abbé was employed in philosophizing upon the loss which Normandy had sustained at his hands. His thoughts, as subsequently given to the world in his elegant work on the Churches of the Arrondissement of Dieppe, ran in this wise : " Few ruins once interested us more than those of Bellencombre. Those ramparts breached by time— those curtain walls covered with ivy—those fosses overgrown with brambles—those trenches continued down beyond the church—that old *enceinte*, which stretches itself into the town which it formerly enclosed—all these carried us backward to the middle ages, and made us for a moment believe ourselves transported to the reign of William or St. Louis, and to the bosom of feudal France. What a misfortune that this physiognomy of an old *bourg fermé*, like those on the banks of the Rhine, should have disappeared from our midst ! As it would be a curious spectacle amid the elegance and comfort of our modern civilization to encounter a rude warrior, with his weapons, his warlike gait, his coat of mail, and his iron helmet— so one would be able to frame a philosophical speculation upon those gloomy vaults, narrow loop-holes, deep dungeons, and long and silent subterraneous passages [which once existed here], as contrasted with our factories so bright and elegant, our workshops so brilliant and animated, our palaces of industry so lively, so spacious, so aerial, so transparent !"[5]

The church of Bellencombre stands within the enfossed enclosure of the ancient fortification. Its tower was, as M. Cochet remarks, at once an auxiliary and a rival to those of the castle donjon.

[5] Eglises, ii, 396.

"The banks of the Rhine constantly afford us an
analogous spectacle. There, as at Bellencombre, the
church-tower is a pyramid, pierced with semicircular
openings, rising above the transepts, and commanding
the neighbouring town in a fashion at once mysterious
and austere. The church of Bellencombre has suffered much from its vicinity to the castle. The two
transepts have been destroyed. The choir and the

nave, which have escaped, are of sandstone, with
piercings of the eleventh century. The construction
is rough and rude, as though produced by the hands
of armed men" during some short interval of peace.
As it must have been erected during the period
of De Warenne proprietorship, I made a sketch of it
from the castle mound as a slight *souvenir* of my
visit. The interior contains nothing beyond what is
seen in the generality of Norman country churches,
except an incised slab, covering, as the inscription

informs us, the "viscera and intestines of the noble and puissant Lord James de Moy, hereditary castellan of Bellencombre," who died in 1519.

As pilgrims never leave the shrines they visit without some tangible token of their having duly performed their "mission," I was careful to inquire of old Dillard for something of the sort, and was most unexpectedly gratified by his producing a bronze object, which proved to be nothing more nor less than an heraldric *wyvern* of about the thirteenth century. Now, recognizing in this misshapen work of medieval art the *badge* of the De Warennes, I was of course anxious to secure it, which I am happy to say I succeeded in doing, at the price of two francs. If possible, Le Père Dillard was more gratified than myself with this little business transaction. He had never heard of the De Warennes.

Before we left, the old man took us into his cottage, which is situated upon the apex of the "bellus cumulus," and showed us some medieval tiles, which he had taken from one of the corridors of the castle and laid down as a pavement for his kitchen. He also exhibited a slab of black marble, which he had found no great while before in his garden. It bore these lines :—

> "Mon . honneur . et . ma . vie .
> Sont . deux . lots . de . mon . bien .
> Quand . l'une . m'est . ravie .
> L'autre . ne . m'est . plus . rien . "

The old man little dreamed of my estimate of *his* honour as we bade him a no very hearty *bon soir !*

I learn from M. Cochet, that since this modern baron of Bellencombre's cupidity has been exposed in "Les Eglises," he refuses my friend access to the few walls which survive to mark the ancient abode of the De Warennes. This is of little consequence, since any visit to them only awakens emotions that are far from pleasurable. It is at least some consolation that his infamy as a destroyer is put upon record in two languages!

MISCELLANEA.

Brief Essays and Adversaria.

MISCELLANEA.

THE following story was told me by a clerical friend some years since. The narrator was chosen by his parishioners to represent them at the board of guardians in the "union" to which the parish was attached,—the other guardians, twelve in number, being farmers, whose educational attainments may be inferred from what follows. A document of some importance was to emanate from the board, and the chairman—a person little better qualified than his colleagues—was desired to draw it up, which he did accordingly. It was *ad rem* as it regarded the sense intended to be conveyed, but the grammar was of a sort that would have caused Lindley Murray a spasm. My friend, in a kind and delicate way, pointed out the errors, and suggested their correction; but one of the other guardians immediately rose, declared the paper to be perfectly grammatical, and begged the chairman to "put it to a show of hands" whether it was good English or not. This the latter immediately did, when it was decided by twelve farmers against one parson that the grammar was sound. Thus was the offence of maiming the Queen's English brought for the first time to trial by jury, the culprit himself presiding as judge !

This anecdote is no unapt illustration of the falsity of the proverb *Vox populi vox Dei*. No doubt the honest farmers imagined they had achieved a great victory over my friend. Twelve men against one, must, they thought, of course be right, though that one was in fact the only person who understood the merits of the case. Thus it is in matters of much greater moment: the voice of multitudes is deemed the utterance of Truth. I take it, however, that the many are usually as much in the wrong now as they were in the days of old, when the cry of "Crucify him! Crucify him!" reverberated through the Hall of Judgment, and drowned the feeble voice of the Roman governor helplessly demanding "What *is* Truth?"

I never heard whether the incidents embodied in the old-fashioned drama of the 'Maid and the Magpie' had a foundation in any real occurrence; but the following anecdote, for the particulars of which many living persons can vouch, offers a curious analogous instance of a domestic having suffered disgrace in consequence of an undeserved imputation of dishonesty.

About the commencement of the present century, a maid-servant, in the employ of a tradesman's family at Lewes, who had previously borne an unblemished character, was suspected of having stolen a favourite old silver spoon, the property of her mistress. It had been last seen in her hands, and there were strong circumstantial proofs of her having appropriated it to her own use. She lost her situation in consequence; and, in spite of her protestations of innocence, was turned abroad, characterless, upon the world. What effect the unjust suspicion had upon her subsequent conduct is not known, but she died some time afterwards without an opportunity of vin-

dicating herself from the charge. Many years later
the house in which she had served was partially
pulled down, when the missing spoon was brought to
light. Among the broken stones which had formed
the foundation of the kitchen, a rat's hole was discovered. In this cranny were found the skinny remains
of a rat still holding in its jaws an old-fashioned
silver spoon, which was at once identified as the object so long ago lost and now almost forgotten. It is
conjectured that some sweet or unctuous matter that
it might have contained, had served as a bait for the
four-legged felon, and that the rat in dragging the
prize into his narrow lair had so completely cut off
the means of egress that he paid the penalty of a
lingering death by starvation for his dishonest deed.
The shrivelled body of the thief now lies side by side
with the stolen property beneath a glass case in the
possession of one of my neighbours.

One of the best epistles I ever saw was that of
Politian to his Friend. There is not one redundant
word, nor one that could be spared : " I was very sorry,
and am very glad, that thou hast been sick, and that
thou art whole. Farewell."

One is sometimes astonished at the profound ignorance of common things which is manifested by people
whose social position and means of acquiring knowledge would lead us to give them credit for a fair stock

of information. It is not uncommon to meet in
ordinary intercourse men who would accept in good
faith a story of a war between William the Conqueror
and Charlemagne, or the statement that King John
signed Magna Charta in order to enable Henry the
Eighth to marry Mary Queen of Scots. Poor Mr.
——, of W—shire, was a gentleman in at least some
of the qualities which are essential to that title. He
was of ancient family, very rich, hospitable, and of
polished address, and had a fine taste in gardens,
architecture, and pictures,—but of his reading and
information the following anecdote will convey the
best idea.

He was once acting the part of *cicerone* in his
picture gallery to a numerous party of guests. On
arriving in front of a large painting representing a
man in old costume conversing with a lady, "That,"
said he, "is a picture of the Pope and his Wife. You
will observe that he is addressing her with great
earnestness, and she is listening to him with affec-
tionate interest." His friends might have passed the
matter by with a well-concealed "titter" among the
ladies, and an adroit turning of the conversation on
the part of the gentlemen, had not the old squire been
bent upon displaying the full extent of his ignorance.
Addressing one of the ladies, he said—"By-the-bye,
Mrs. G——, you have lately returned from Rome.
Pray are you acquainted with the present pope?"—
"I have seen him at St. Peter's," was her reply,
"but I cannot boast of a personal acquaintance with
his holiness." "Is he," inquired the old gentleman,
"a family man?" Mrs. G. evading the spirit of the
interrogatory replied, "that she really could not tell
—some popes had been members of good families, but
she had never heard whether the reigning pontiff

was of distinguished origin or not." "Madam," pursued the questioner, "you misunderstand me. Is he a family man—that is to say, has he any offspring?" "Oh, no!" responded Mrs. G. with as grave a face as she could command, "are you not aware that the Roman Catholic clergy are not allowed to marry?" "No, indeed, madam," was the rejoinder, "I was not aware of the fact!"

————

My friend, Mr. Simon Eldershaw, among some other strong dislikes, hated the science of mathematics. He did not go so far as to say, with a late distinguished head of an Oxford College, that it was "a very good science for carpenters." He even admitted its inestimable value to a particular class of minds; nor did he shut his eyes to its sublime results to mankind. But while he acknowledged the services it had rendered to astronomy, to navigation, and the various departments of mechanics and engineering, he denied its alleged utility as directed merely to the expansion of the intellect, without any view to its practical application to those sciences. "What can be more absurd (he would say) than the making of it so prominent a feature in the education of a large portion of our clergy? The young student who has embraced Cambridge as his Alma Mater is made to imbibe so much of what may be to him an unpalatable draught as will enable him to take his first degree, and he rarely perhaps cares to taste it again. This is worse than folly, for the time has been devoted to a useless pursuit when many other studies of the highest importance have had to be neglected. At length the young clergyman enters upon parochial duties; but what are his qualifications for the highest of all trusts, the gravest of all responsibilities? He should be critically acquainted with that volume which is to be his text-book in the instruction of the humble folk among whom he has come to dwell; but he can only read one fourth part of it in the original tongue; for alas! while he should have been studying Hebrew grammar, he has been poring over differential calculus. He is not a good theologian, for his opportunities of cultivating what is to be his main object in practical life have been few. He cannot say much upon the doctrine of the Trinity, for his energies have been too much devoted to trigonometry. He makes but a poor hand at a sermon on eternity, though he could tell you something considerable of the "infinite series." He knows his way through Euclid, but he knows little of the path by which he is to lead his flock to heaven. His angles help him but little in rubbing off the angularities of prejudice, and his tangents have no point of junction with the unsophisticated circle of which he should be the centre. He is acquainted with the sines of geometry, but dull at discerning the signs of the times. At length some humble inhabitant of the parish, a man of plain good sense and solid piety, who has made theology his leading study, and who can enter into the moral necessities of his neighbours— who, in short, is qualified in the very things that the young priest is deficient of—opens a meeting-house in the village street, and thus empties the parish church; while he who deems himself the only authorized teacher looks helplessly on, and deplores, too late, the misspending of his time upon inappropriate objects."

And, *me judice*, my friend was to a great extent

right, although it is not so much to a mathematical education as to a grand and general defect of the existing university system that such a failure as that indicated by Mr. Eldershaw is attributable. There are, it is confessed, many branches of education that are never designed to be applied to practical life, which are yet conceived to be very useful in the formation and culture of the mind; as the scaffolding of a house is essential to its construction, though it is to be removed on the completion of the building. So also many learn the sword exercise without any intention of becoming soldiers.

To such reasoning Mr. Eldershaw would reply, "Well, well; there may be *something* in that; but I am bold to say that the result is very inadequate to the labour bestowed. It is, as the sailors say, making 'three voyages for a biscuit,'—an Olympic struggle for a crown of parsley. Much is said of mathematics as to the effects produced upon the reasoning powers. Too much! It is said by those who, having spent years in the pursuit, compensate themselves for their lost time by asserting a lofty superiority over other men—their betters in everything else. I have known Cambridge men (my friend would continue) 'very middling scholars,' impudent enough to question the ability of men of real genius, sound classical scholarship, and great literary taste, because forsooth they had never studied mathematics. 'Nothing like leather' should be their motto! There are of course many exceptions; and a man may be truly great in mathematics as well as in philosophy, language, music, or any other science, and at the same time exercise due liberality towards other pursuits. In fact I never knew a *great* mathematician who was not also great in something else,—but, mark you!

12

(Mr. Eldershaw would add with great emphasis) not as a *consequence,* but merely as a concomitant."

" If I do not altogether object to mathematical science as a sharpener of the wits, I should still say that its moral tendency is rather bad. Did you ever know an exclusively mathematical man who had much *heart?* A cool, prudent, worldly-wise, calculating man, he is sure to be; but as to poetry, taste, generosity, *soul,*—a cipher would represent the exact quantity of each that he possesses. There's not a jolly feature about him. He wants you to establish everything you say by line and rule. He is like the Scotchman, who objected to ' Paradise Lost' because it " proved naething.' He makes everything so clear to his own apprehension that he loses the power of making others understand it. He is a bore—dry, stale, and unprofitable (said my impetuous friend), and I don't like him at all ! "

I recollect having met with two rather curious instances of the *tulit alter honores.* In the thirteenth century Peter le Marshal held lands by the service of keeping a palfrey in the king's stable at the king's expense,—" per serjantiam custodiendi unum palefridum in stabulo domini regis, sumptibus ipsius domini regis,"—a very pleasant way of keeping a horse ! In a church window in France there were formerly figures of an ecclesiastic and a young noble, with an inscription, stating that the window was the gift of the tutor of a certain lord, for which however *the said pupil found the money !* " Hanc fenestram fieri fecit M. V. tutor Domini N. N. expensis nihilominus dicti Pupilli."

There are many things in existence of which our philosophy does not dream, and many effects which seem to have a very obscure relation to their causes. Many notions once held to be superstitious are found to be real truths when that relation is by some chance discovered. Why does the natural philosopher deny the influence of the moon upon changes of weather, while he is compelled to acknowledge that the tides are governed by the phases of that luminary? The unsophisticated shepherd or waggoner is as certain of his weather creed as the astronomer is of the truth of his tidal doctrines, but he wants the mathematical proof which the other possesses. He relies alone upon his own observation and experience, and is satisfied with the fact without striving after any theory. There are many other instances of relations between one thing and another which cannot be accounted for upon the principles of a due and intelligible sequence of cause and effect; and your philosopher would deem such apparent relations as mere whims of the imagination, deserving no more credit than the ancient belief that the Goodwin Sands were caused by Tenterden steeple; but the relation would seem to exist nevertheless. Why is it that we are often forewarned by some indescribable impression of the approach of a friend to our door, when we had no *reason* whatever for anticipating his arrival? Why do our dreams so often exactly foreshadow coming occurrences? Why again should the want of an ear for music be so frequently associated, as it is known to be, with an incapacity to spell correctly? It cannot result from a mere want of delicacy in the organs of hearing, since the orthography of all languages differs more or less widely from phonetic forms. Once more, why should the child who receives the baptismal appellation of one of its parents more strongly resemble that parent, in personal and moral characteristics, than his or her brothers and sisters do? I have never heard this phenomenon mentioned by others; but I have established the fact to my own satisfaction by long observation, and the exceptions to the rule are marvellously few.

————

It has been much the fashion for some years past —more especially since the appearance of Sharon Turner's work—to ascribe all the excellences of the English character to an Anglo-Saxon source, but I have presumption enough to question the justice of this ascription. The Anglo-Saxons, it is true, bequeathed to us a noble language and an excellent code of laws, both of which however were originally shared by other nations of Teutonic blood, who have not greatly distinguished themselves in the annals of the world. It would be much more just to attribute the peculiar energy, enterprise, and power which seem to distinguish us from other nations, to the great *mixture of races* that has taken place in our island. The sturdiness of the Celt—the civilizing influence of the Roman—the sound civil polity of the Saxon—the maritime enterprise of the Dane—the military ardour and strength of character of the Norman, have all doubtless contributed their quota to the formation of the modern Englishman. Let us therefore thank the good Providence which thus successively, in the lapse of ages, recruited our strength by the infusion of foreign blood; and let us strive to ascertain, and imitate, and uphold, whatever was good and excellent in every people whose blood circulates in our veins, and avoid the peculiar vices of each.

It is a popular fallacy of the age to attribute everything old-fashioned and well-established to the Saxons. Thus, we sometimes hear such things as parliament and trial by jury described by public speakers as "good old Saxon institutions," though neither the one nor the other existed at all in its present form until after the incoming of the Normans. Some people also seem to think every plain old word in our language, Saxon. A certain M.P., not long since, told an audience that he preferred the word " schoolmaster " to " preceptor," on account of its being " good Saxon-English." Poor man! He little knew the etymology of the word he was advocating—that it was a compound of the two old French nouns, *escole* and *mestre*, while these are again derivatives of the Latin " schola" and " magister."

It may seem a somewhat startling assertion, but it is nevertheless true, of at least the south-eastern parts of England, that a *majority* of the names of places are so mispronounced by the peasantry as to render it a matter of difficulty for a stranger to identify the place with the rustic appellation. For instance, in Surrey, Bletchingly is called Birchen-lie—Dorking, Darkin —Reigate, Raggot — Newdigate, Nudgit—Horne, Hoordun—and Carshalton, Case-horton. People are now beginning to forget that the great fashionable " Brighton " is only an alias for " Brighthelmstone," the ancient name of the town. By the bye, there is an erroneous notion entertained by some guide-writers and others, that this *crasis* was adopted at the instance of the Prince Regent (George the Fourth)—Bright-helmstone being a word too long for his utterance ! The prince's aversion to "hard words" may have given rise to the misapprehension. When a youth he is said to have incurred the ire of one of his tutors by saying he should be *obleeged* to him for the explanation of some difficulty. " Can't you," sharply demanded the irascible old pedant, " open your royal jaws wide enough to say *oblige ?* " The truth is that the curt pronunciation " Brighton " was in use long before George the Fourth was born : I have seen it so written in a document of the time of James the Second. Sussex abounds with these corruptions in names. Selmeston is called Simpson—Folkington, Fowington —Alciston, Ahson—and Alfriston, Ahson-town. Rotherfield is Redderful—Mayfield, Mayavul—Lindfield, Linvul—Cuckfield, Cookful—Heathfield, Hefful—Henfield, Envul—Hartfield, Hartful,—and Wivels-field, Wilsful. Again, Wanningore is Warnmoore—Falmer, Farmer—Herstmonceux, Horsemowncez—Burwash, Burrish — Ticehurst, Tysus — Wadhurst, Waddus — Crowborough, Crowbór — Chalvington, Chanton—Frant, Fant—Hayward's Heath, Hewards Hawth — Werpesburn, Wapses-Boorn — Pevensey, Pemsey—St. Olave's Well, Tulley's Wells. The numerous terminations in *-ing* in West Sussex are all changed by the peasantry into *un*. Thus, instead of Worthing, Goring, Tarring, Didling, they say Worthun, Gorun, Tarrun, and Didlun. Further, Framfield is Frantful—Uckfield, Uckful—Hellingly, Herrin-lie—Hailsham, Helsome—Dallington, Dollinton —Ashburnham, Ashbrum—Stanmer, Stammer—Roeheath, Rowho-ad — Midhurst, Meddus — Petworth, Pettuth — Avisford, Hare's-Foot—and Chichester, Chiddister.

I have often been struck with the true wit that one meets with among the uneducated classes. People who cannot read seem to possess as keen an apprehension of unexpected analogies or contrasts as those who have had the best means of brightening their perceptive faculties by education. I once heard a remark made by a railway excavator upon the personal appearance of a gentleman who possessed an unfortunately light red or sandy complexion, and who was on this occasion attired in a light summer costume, consisting of a salmon-coloured cap and slippers, with a paletot and trowsers of kindred hues. " Bill," said he, " do you see that chap over yonder? *You could reckon him up all at once !*" Riding one day through one of the wretchedly crooked roads of the weald of Surrey, I remarked to the driver of my vehicle, that the man who originally made it could not have had a very good eye for straight lines. " Why, no, Sir," replied the man, " it seems to me that he thought as how *one good turn desarved another.*" Finding him a wag, I alluded to the old proverb that the miles of that part of the country were very " long and narrow." " Very true, Sir," was his prompt reply, at the very instant that our vehicle sank up to the axletrees in the mud,—" and not only that, but they goes *a good ways under ground !*"

The natural enmity subsisting between the wolf and the sheep, so often alluded to by scriptural, classical, and oriental writers, has given rise to a curious vulgar error, which seems to prevail in all quarters of the world. Sir John Ferne tells us, after Cornelius Agrippa, that " Nature hath im-

planted so inveterate an hatred atweene the wolfe and
the sheepe, that being dead, yet, in the secret operation of Nature, appeareth there a sufficient trial of
their discording natures, so that the enmity betweene
them seemeth not to dye with their bodies : for if
there be put upon a harpe, or any such like instrument, strings made of the intralles of a wolfe, be the
musitian never so cunning in his skil, yet can he not
reconcile them to an unity and concord of sounds : so
discording alwayes is that string of the wolfe." A
rather curious parallel to this strange fancy is found
in the East at the present day. A friend recently
returned from India informs me that a year or two
ago, his brother, a young gentleman in the Ninth
Lancers, having shot a wolf, took off its skin and
stretched it upon the door of an outhouse to dry.
One night, shortly afterwards, the skin disappeared,
and, on inquiry, it was discovered that a Hindoo had
stolen it for the purpose of converting it into the
head of a tom-tom, or native drum. The generality
of those instruments are covered, as is usual with us,
with sheepskin parchment, and the rascal was firmly
persuaded, that the sound of his drum thus prepared
would have the effect of breaking the heads of all the
tom-toms in the neighbourhood ! [1]

Among social *bores* (to use a slang phrase) there
are two that I especially dislike. The one lifts his
hands and turns up his eyes at the narration of every
commonplace matter ; the other is never surprised at
even the most extraordinary event. During a remark-

[1] This anecdote was communicated by me to a periodical publication about twelve months since.

able annular eclipse that happened some years ago,
while everybody else was fully occupied in gazing
at the unusual phænomenon, a pert young lady's-
maid, just arrived from London, expressed her dis-
gust for such vulgar curiosity by remarking in the
genteelest accents—" Deah me ; how singulah that
country people should take so much notice of an
eclipse—why we *frequently* have them *in town !* "

———

Some people do not believe in dreams : many do.
A septuagenarian friend of mine was once the means
of saving the life of a fellow-creature under very
extraordinary circumstances.　She dreamed more
than once in one night that a girl was lying in a state
of great illness and exhaustion in a certain remote
wood.　She told her husband her dream, and he, not
being skilled like Joseph or Daniel in the gift of
interpretation, advised her, after the manner of Eli to
Samuel, to go to sleep again.　In the morning, the
impression of the night's uneasiness was so strong
that she could not be dissuaded from her purpose of
sending a servant to the indicated spot.　There the
person seen in the unquiet invasion of her slumbers
was found, in a wretched state of squalor and destitu-
tion.　The girl was brought home and deposited in an
outhouse in the last stage of exhaustion.　By kind and
careful treatment, however, she was eventually restored to convalescence, when she told her benefactress, that she had for more than a fortnight previously
to her discovery in the wood subsisted entirely upon
blackberries.　As the poor creature gradually improved in physical health, it was discovered that her
reason was disordered, and she at last relapsed into
insanity.　A clue to her place of abode was however

12 §

obtained, and she was sent back to the workhouse, some five-and-twenty miles distant, from which she had so hazardously wandered.

A rather singular incident, showing the remarkable attachment which sometimes exists between the inferior animals and man, as well as the mysterious sympathy which may occasionally be noticed between beings gifted with reason and those whose highest endowment is instinct, occurred in the last days of the husband of the person mentioned in the last anecdote. He suffered from that "slow living death," consumption,—and, when he became too unwell to leave his chamber, his favourite mare, which was depastured in a meadow near his house, neglectful of her own well-being, would stand for hours, with her head over the garden-gate, as if in expectation of the coming of her master, to resume his old accustomed rides over the farm. The sight being painful to the patient, the poor animal was removed to a distant field. Not long after this he grew worse, and became subject to delirium. During one of his fits he appeared to be much distressed, repeatedly pointing to some piece of wearing apparel which accidentally hung near his bed, and ejaculating, "See, my poor mare is hung up!" No importance was attached to such a remark, made under so unhappy a deprivation of reason; but in order to soothe the sufferer the article was removed, when he observed, "It is all right now," and became more calm. Strangely enough, at the very moment of this occurrence, a labourer on the farm, passing through the field where the mare had been placed, found her fixed between the rails of a little foot-bridge—which she had been attempting to cross in order to make her way towards the house—in such a manner that she must have died had she not been speedily extricated! The master died a day or two subsequently, while the poor steed gradually pined away, and in a very brief space of time she also bade adieu to the light. The rationale of all this I leave to the psychologists : I merely record the facts as I have received them from living and unimpeachable witnesses.

————

The desirableness of a Dictionary of the English language which should serve as a standard of what really are, and what are not, legitimate words has long been acknowledged. What a pity that some means had not long ago been used for the determination of this point! Is it not a matter of importance, almost involving our patriotism, that we should come to a speedy determination as to what is English, and what is only mere " slang? " In writing, it is so much easier to adopt current expressions, right or wrong, than to study orthodox and authorized standards, that there appears to be little hope that our popular authors will ever reform the evil complained of. That an " Academy" for such a purpose would be inefficient is proved by the case of France, where new words are almost daily introduced. But surely it is the imperative duty of every one who hopes that his writings may descend to posterity to attempt some limit. As optimists in Latin style reject every word that is not Ciceronian, surely English writers might easily make a " magnus Apollo" of some standard author, whose works are sufficiently copious to embrace all necessary expressions. Should it be replied to this suggestion, that it involves a servility incompatible with a bold and vigorous diction, and that the very task of mastering the *copia verborum* of a prolific writer would be the labour of a life, I would say—Then let some patriotic admirer of "English undefiled" undertake the labour of expurgating our existing dictionaries of all words not occurring in the best writers with sufficient frequency to establish their title as genuine constituents of our ancient and copious tongue. The mere use of a word once or twice by Shakspeare, Milton, Johnson, or any other eminent writer, ought not to entitle it to retention, unless it can be shown to exist in contemporary and subsequent authors also. The man who should judiciously perform this task would deserve a noble monument—and his Dictionary would be that monument.

It will probably be further urged, that as English is a *living* language, it must and will *grow*. But is it not worth while to remember that languages, like trees, arrive sooner or later at maturity, then remain for awhile unimpaired, afterwards manifest symptoms of gradual decay, until lastly their stock dies in the ground? My fear is, that we have got past the first stages—those of healthy growth and maturity, and that without careful trimming and pruning, our tree will soon hasten onwards to utter decay. The multitudinous new sprigs and leaves daily budding forth among its sturdy branches will, on examination, prove to be not so much the true products of its own vital energy, as *parasites* which are drawing their nourishment from it and hastening its destruction. One thing is certain : if some of the men who of old delighted in and advanced its growth, could look up from their bed of dust, they would be both astonished and indignant at the large increase of ivy, moss, and lichen, in the shape of classical and continental words and idioms which now cluster around it, to say nothing of the filthy *fungi* known as "slang," which corrupt and defile its every branch.

There appear to me to be three distinct causes of corruption now in active operation upon our language. The first and least objectionable of these, is the constant formation of new and unnecessary derivatives, adverbs from adjectives, verbs from nouns, and such like, which tends greatly to the weakening of the vigour of the old mother tongue: Secondly, the pedantic introduction of foreign words by scholars, men of science, and others. This is an old fault—at least as old as the first half of the seventeenth century, as a slight glance at many of the writers of that period will sufficiently prove. What we call Johnsonianism is much older than Johnson's days. It was both practised and decried (and no wonder) in the time of James the First. Old Verstegan loudly complains of it in his 'Restitution of Decayed Intelligence.' Thus he tells us of some one who expressed himself in terms like these:—"As I itinerated, I obviated a rural person, and interrogating him concerning the transitation of the time and the demonstration of the passage, found him a mere simplician!"—whereas, adds our honest antiquary, had he only asked what's o'clock, and which is the way, he might of the said "simplician" have been in both matters well informed. But without any intentional pedantry, we very often find the technical terms of science and art brought first into ordinary language, by brilliant writers in Reviews, &c., and apologized for by *Italics*, but afterwards retained in all good faith and Roman simplicity by their imitators.

What a mass of terms from astronomy, geology, chemistry, painting, and the like, have thus become what old ladies call "Dictionary words," within the last twenty years, to the great inconvenience of ordinary readers. The third source of corruption is the frightful increase of "slang" or "cant" expressions of various kinds which are constantly being added to our colloquial language, and which slip one after another, to its great disfigurement, into the written tongue. The universities, to which we ought to look for a better example, are inexcusable for the use of many such words as "freshmen," "gyps," "to pluck," "little goes," "spoons," "rustication," and a host of other vulgar conventionalisms. Law, physic, art, and even divinity too, as well as the illiterate mob, have each their by-words, that are becoming candidates for admission into our dictionaries, and that will, doubtless, at last achieve that undeserved position.

These loose observations are the result of a train of thought suggested by a word, which, having sprung up (I think) within the last ten years, is now found in nearly every Review and Newspaper—I mean the word "*reliable*." Reliable evidence, reliable information, and similar phrases, abound everywhere; but the absurdity of the expression, by whomsoever invented —to say nothing of our having already the nervous old word "trustworthy," and its synonym "credible" —is a sufficient reason for its immediate rejection. To rely is a verb neuter, and cannot precede an accusative without the intervention of the preposition "on," or "upon" to make it equivalent to "trust" this preposition is indispensable, and therefore if the new word be anything at all, it is not "reliable," but *relionable !*

Why is the strongest part of a castle called a *Keep?* This question has often suggested itself to my mind when viewing old baronial fortresses. The common notion seems to be that the name originated in the fact that prisoners were *kept* there. The French equivalent is *Donjon,* whence may come our word "dungeon," and this may have suggested the etymology. I do not doubt that the baron who had a prisoner of mark would place him within the strongest walls which his feudal abode could supply. But for obvious reasons he would locate himself and his family there also. Now in our eastern, and several other provincial, dialects, the more usual sitting-room of a family is still called the "keeping-room." I think, therefore, the keep or principal part of a castle was so called because its lord and his domestic circle *kept*, abode, or lived there. Shakspeare uses the word "keep" in the sense of to dwell or reside :—

> "And sometime where earth-delving conies *keep*."
> *Venus and Adonis.*

And again :—

> "And held in idle price to haunt assemblies
> Where youth, and cost, and witless bravery *keeps*."
> *Measure for Measure*, i, 4.

Among the eccentric characters of the Weald of Sussex, in the latter half of the last century, was a worthy but very ignorant man, who, influenced by the religious zeal consequent upon the exertions of Whitefield and Wesley, undertook the office of a teacher, and became quite popular amongst his rustic neighbours in that capacity. Several of Master S ——'s quaint remarks have become current traditions. One of these is, that—"The apostle Paul, though a very good man, was a *shocking bad grammarian*. Why he calls himself 'less than the least;' and how could that be, my friends? It's very bad grammar indeed!"

One day Master S. explained the passage of scripture, "Darkness shall cover the earth, and gross darkness the people," in the following way: "The airth, you know, my friends, is natterally black and dark, but our hearts be a vast deal darker still—a *gross* darkness kivvers them. A gross—why that's *twelve dozen* you'll say. Very true, my friends, so it is; and the heart o' man is twelve dozen times darker than the airth itself!"

———

Our language appears to me to suffer almost as much from the introduction of new and "refined" pronunciations as from the importation of new words. Great changes in this respect have taken place within the last half century. Our grandfathers did not pronounce p-u-t as *poot*, but as *pút*, which would now be accounted as shocking vulgarity; neither did they call beans and peas, *beens* and *pees*, but something much more approaching the Irish—*banes* and *pays*. I have frequently noticed that the late Mr. Davies Gilbert, who was remarkable for an adherence to old modes, pronounced the word k-e-y, not as *kee*, but as *ké*. The true orthoepy of the English language must be sought rather among ploughmen and grooms than in drawing-rooms and fashionable pulpits.

Sometimes, even in words derived from the classical languages, the vulgar put the accent upon the right syllable, while the usage of educated society sanctions a mispronunciation. Now this must result from modern corruption. An example will best illustrate my meaning. The Londoner talks of going to the *theātre*, or to St. *Sepúlchre's* Church, and in both cases he is right; for in the Latin from which they are derived the accent is placed upon the penultimate syllable—*theātrum* and *sepúlchrum.*

The rapidly-increasing popularity of the study of antiquities suggests considerations not undeserving of the attention of the thoughtful. "Aspice" and "Prospice" have always more or less engrossed the minds of men busied with what concerns present and prospective self-interests. They have been their watchwords, and have become the topics of innumerable prudent wise saws and proverbs. But "Respice" is almost a new word in the world's vocabulary. History has indeed always engaged the interest of some, but the views of the past have generally been much distorted by the prejudices of party, or obscured for want of such light as the careful and accurate study of antiquities is alone calculated to throw upon it. We read Assyrian history with new eyes since the spade and pickaxe of Layard have been at work; and we know more of the primeval races of Europe from the explorations of modern barrow-diggers than from all written records whatsoever.

A few years ago—less than twenty, certainly—the word antiquary was deemed by general society as the synonym of something very eccentric, crabbed, and "queer." The greatest genius of his time, Sir Walter Scott, though full of love for old times and manners, could only depict one of his favourite characters who indulged this taste in such a way as to throw indirect censure and ridicule upon it. But what a change has since come over us! Owing chiefly to the zeal and practical intelligence of three or four living men, whose efforts have never been sufficiently acknowledged, archæology has been raised to the true dignity of a science. A few kindred minds in various parts of the kingdom emulated the example set in the metropolis, and now counties, which formerly owned but two or three men versed in the pursuit, boast of Archæological Societies which reckon their numbers by hundreds, are sanctioned by mitred and coroneted brows, and occupy a place amongst the most popular institutions of the day. There is doubtless much of the caprice of fashion in this—a zeal that will wax cold; but nevertheless, the results to our literature, and to the feelings of society, will remain, and prove eminently beneficial.

———————

In the middle ages, and even down to a much later period, every considerable eminence near our coasts was surmounted by a large pile of brushwood, which was attended by a light-armed horseman, called a Hobiler, who, in case of any sudden incursion of the enemy, set it on fire for the purpose of alarming the surrounding country. Sometimes a mischievous person would contrive to ignite one of these beacons, and thus arouse the inhabitants of a whole district to the apprehension of an imminent danger. Several royal proclamations were issued for the suppression of this reprehensible species of practical joking. The following is a metrical version of a story told to the disadvantage of a certain southern town, whose chief officers had formerly the character of being rather illiterate and foolish :

Our Mayor once received a proclamation
  From the Queen's majesty,[2] which threatened those,
Throughout the length of this her English nation,
  Who should her subjects' feelings discompose,
By *firing beacons,* and exciting fear
(In vain) that some invading foe was drawing near.

His worship having spelt the document,
  Stalk'd most majestically down the street,
When lo, a hissing, and a grateful scent
  At once his tympanum and nostril meet
From out a cottage door: he straightway cross'd
The threshold. "Nay," says he, "I'm not mistaken:
  'Tis so indeed! This wretched sinner,
  In order to provide her worthless husband's dinner,
Doth boldly break the law—by *frying bacon!*"

A court forthwith was call'd, the case unfolded,
  And the vile criminal at length assoiled,
On the condition—she being first well scolded—
  That henceforth all her pig-meat should be *boiled!*

––––––––

The gigantic effigy on Wilmington Hill, referred
to at page 178, is locally known as the "Long Man."
It is a rude outline of the human figure, 240 feet
long, holding in each hand a staff of the same length.
It appears that the outline was originally incised
through the turf, leaving the chalk bare, but as it has
not been kept *scoured,* like the famous White Horse
in Berkshire, the depression has become so slight as
to be invisible upon the spot; and it is only when the
light falls upon it, at a particular angle, that it can be
seen from a distance. At Cerne Abbas, in Dorsetshire,

[2] Queen Elizabeth.

there is a similar figure, 180 feet long.   This, Mr.
Sydenham, in his ' Baal Durotriges,' considers to be
an early British monument.   Both these figures
occupy a slope on a chalky down, and both lie immediately opposite to a religious house.   I am inclined
to consider them rather the works of medieval monks
than of our Celtic ancestors, though it is difficult to
guess at the motive which could have prompted them
to the execution of such quaint portraitures.   See a
notice of this relic of other times, by the Rev. G. M.
Cooper, in the ' Sussex Archæological Collections,'
vol. iv, p. 63.

THE WILMINGTON GIANT.